Mainstream of America Series ★

EDITED BY LEWIS GANNETT

THE FRENCH AND INDIAN WARS

THE FRENCH AND INDIAN WARS

The Story of Battles
and Forts in the Wilderness

EDWARD P. HAMILTON

Doubleday & Company, Inc., Garden City, New York, 1962

For SALLIE

AUTHOR'S NOTE

The question of the use of footnotes gave me a great deal of thought. The scholar will never be happy unless they are used most copiously, and the general reader is then quickly scared away. If footnotes are used but scantily, nothing really is achieved, and if none are used at all, only the scholar is displeased. Since this is not intended as a scholarly dissertation, but is a book designed primarily for the general reader, I decided after much thought and discussion with my friends among the professional historians to dispense with footnotes entirely and instead to deposit a completely annotated copy of this book in the library of the Massachusetts Historical Society, where doubters will be able to examine my authorities to their heart's content.

I have drawn heavily on primary sources, manuscripts, transcripts, and printed works. One of the most rewarding of all these was the great collection of material assembled by Francis Parkman and now owned by the Massachusetts Historical Society. The colonial documents published by the State of New York have of course been invaluable, as also have been the Lévis Papers published by the Province of Quebec. Bougainville's journal, part of it in the Parkman Papers, and all of it printed by the Archivist of Quebec, is of the greatest value. Pargellis' *Military Affairs in North America* is a mine of information concerning the last of the colonial wars. Many other similar sources have been drawn on, but they are too numerous to mention here. Parkman's and Gipson's great works have been invaluable in keeping the broader picture clear to me at all times, and many other secondary works have allowed me to examine and to consider the conclusions others have arrived at in their studies.

PREFACE

It was with very considerable doubt that I was persuaded to undertake this book. The French and Indian Wars have been so wonderfully covered by Francis Parkman and their later period by Lawrence Gipson that any further work seemed quite redundant. My publishers, however, felt that there was need for a single volume which would tell the history of the great struggle in somewhat briefer form, and they asked me to undertake the work.

Much of the necessary research had, I thought, already been done in connection with my studies of the colonial wars as they had affected Fort Ticonderoga, the restoration which I have the privilege of serving as director. I soon learned otherwise when it came to putting my story on paper. I have had the rare good fortune to be able to spend each half year when the fort was closed working at the Massachusetts Historical Society, where there exists one of the great mines of primary material concerning this period, as well as a mass of secondary works. It would be entirely possible to write a most excellent book on the French and Indian Wars merely by drawing upon the works of Parkman and Gipson, and I of course have drawn upon them, both intentionally and unconsciously, the latter something no one can avoid entirely, so completely have they covered the subject. I have, however, used many other sources, and have myself retraced their earlier explorations through much original material.

My thanks are due first of all to my friend and college classmate, Bruce Lancaster, who put me in touch with my publisher, and then was most persuasive that I should undertake the task. Much appreciation I also owe to Lewis Gannett for his encouragement and the guidance he gave to an inexperienced author. Other friends have been most helpful, such as Dr. Henry F. Howe, who managed to straighten out my thoughts on the Indian of the colonial days, although he may not quite approve of the picture I have drawn. Dr. William N. Fenton most kindly clarified some points on the Iroquois culture that had confused me. Three other friends, all highly qualified colonial historians, have shown me the great kindness of reading the manuscript of the book in search of errors and omissions and have offered suggestions for improvement. Perhaps I have not accepted all of their advice upon some subjects where there is room for argument, for after all I am writing the book, but their suggestions have been of very material help. So I owe a great debt of gratitude to Father Joseph R. Frese, S.J., of Fordham University, Stephen T. Riley, director of the Massachusetts Historical Society, and Clifford K. Shipton, director of the American Antiquarian Society. I also greatly appreciate the most helpful hand that my friend Walter Muir Whitehill gave me in connection with the final revision of the book. I wish to thank Jane M. Lape, who, in the slight intervals between her duties as librarian at Fort Ticonderoga and her extra-curricular activities of raising race horses for the Saratoga track, has been able to translate my crabbed scratchings into legible typescript. Lastly, I must record my particular obligation to the man who during my college years first interested me in the history of our frontiers, the late Frederick Jackson Turner.

EDWARD P. HAMILTON

Fort Ticonderoga, N.Y.
June 22, 1961

CONTENTS

LIST OF ILLUSTRATIONS

Black and White

Color

IT IS a crisp December day in 1682 at Deerfield on the Massachusetts frontier, over one hundred miles west of the salt waters of Boston Bay. Nehemiah Alden is hauling in a sledgeload of firewood, but he pauses a moment to admire the new house he has just finished. It is a fine one, he thinks, even better than the one the Indians burned during the massacre seven years ago. His children's children will still find it good.

Johannes Peltz sits this same day in his little trading house at Schenectady, a dozen miles west of the Hudson River, and wonders how many skins the Mohawks will bring in today. He has almost enough now for a shipment. Should he sell it at Albany or send it by sloop down the river to New York?

Gustav Peterson lives on the shore of the Delaware River at the place we now call Chester. Today he is going to ride a few miles upriver and try to have a word with William Penn, who, they say, is busy this week laying out the streets of the new town he is going to call Philadelphia. Peterson hopes that Penn will lease him some land farther west, perhaps even as far as a score of miles from the Delaware.

Beverley Brown this bright December morning is sitting in the little office of his plantation on the James, deep in conference with his trusted overseer. Is it time to think of planting those lands he owns just above the falls? Some people are starting to call the place Richmond. It seems quite a way from the settled security of tidewater Virginia, but now that Bacon's Rebellion is over and done with, the frontier is certain to move westward.

Huger Smith is riding along the banks of the Ashley River near Charleston on the way to look over his rice plantation and to discuss with his overseer the matter of buying that land his friend Cooper offered him last night. Probably he should not take the risk, it is so far from the ocean, all of fifty miles.

It is still a fine day but a rather chilly one out in La Baye des Puants, which today we call Green Bay, Wisconsin, and Père Jean Dumoulin of the Society of Jesus smiles to himself as he puts the finishing touches to the crucifix he is carving for the altar of his little chapel. It is much more handsome than the old one that Père Allouez hurriedly made when he founded the mission a dozen years ago. Père Jean stops for a moment and gazes out over the still unfrozen waters of the great bay. How goes it with the others of his order back in Quebec, almost a thousand miles to the eastward?

Still farther to the west, at Starved Rock in the Illinois country, Jacques La Framboise for a moment stops his work on the stockade of Tonty's new fort and straightens up his aching back. It is still stiff from poling La Salle's boat all those weary miles back up the great river that flowed into salt water in the country that his leader had named Louisiana. La Framboise leans on his spade and looks out over the wide plains across the river, where a herd of wandering buffalo show black against the light carpet of snow that fell during the night. He too is thinking of far-away Quebec, but his thoughts lie in far different channels from those of Père Dumoulin, the Jesuit.

What a contrast between the colonies of the two great nations! Those of Britain hug the seacoast and the tidal rivers, nowhere more than two score miles from where a seagoing vessel can sail, while the outposts of New France have crossed almost half the continent. Why this great difference? Two major factors were the cause, the civilization that nurtured the colony and the geography of North America. In this book I shall try to tell of the clash between the colonies of these two European powers, and how their endeavors to colonize and to fight were largely determined and regulated by the mountains and rivers of our continent.

Chapter I

THEY WENT BY WATER

THE waterways of North America were the paths of trade and of war. Stand on the top of the Mohawk Trail in Massachusetts, on the Laurel Hill in Pennsylvania, or on the crest of the Blue Ridge in Virginia and look to the east. Forget the roads and the motor cars of today and try to imagine yourself down on the plain at your feet just starting to climb up the slope on your travels to the west. Remember that there is no road at all, and that you must carry on your back all that you will need, blankets, powder, lead, ax, food, and perhaps some trade goods you hope to turn into furs. Or possibly you are so fortunate as to have a pack horse or two, but remember that grass grows in but few places in the primeval forest, and that your horses cannot live on leaves or the bark of trees. A very considerable portion of the contents of their two-hundred-pound packs must be devoted to forage.

Now stand on the shores of Lake Champlain, on the banks of the Mohawk, the Hudson, or the lower James. Load your bateau, your dugout canoe, or your barge as deeply as you wish, but it still will glide easily through the water and carry you and your cargo over many a long mile with little effort. Sometimes a storm will delay you, and at places you must carry your craft and its load by rapids or over divides, but these are minor hardships compared to those that you would meet on land. On your back you can carry perhaps seventy-five pounds, but your canoe can take over five hundred pounds and your bateau thrice that. Is it any wonder that the waterways of colonial

North America were the routes which man chose for his travels?
⸱ Indian trade goods and packs of furs were easily moved by canoe,
but warfare's supplies and munitions demanded stouter means, such
as the bateau, the whaleboat, and the barge. The first of these, the
bateau, was the work horse of the northern regions. Built much like
today's Gloucester dory, it might have a length of from eighteen to
as much as forty-five feet, this latter length used primarily under sail.
The origin of the bateau is obscure, but this type of craft became
the standard lake and river boat of both the French and the northern
British colonies, probably as early as the start of the eighteenth century and certainly so by its middle years.

The average bateau such as the British built for military use appears to have had a length of perhaps twenty-five to thirty feet, while
the French made them materially larger, particularly when for use on
the Great Lakes. In 1737, for instance, the Quebec government ordered the construction at Kaskaskia in the Illinois country of fifty
bateaux, forty feet long by nine feet breadth, and capable of carrying
up to twelve tons. The water route to some of the western posts of
New France, such as that leading to Fort Duquesne at the Forks of
the Ohio, required the use of smaller bateaux than the large lake craft
and the French made these as well. Lewis Evans, a keen student and
reporter of conditions in the British Colonies in the mid-1700s, recorded that the Mohawk River bateaux such as were used in the trade
to Oswego were twenty-five feet long, three feet three inches wide
by two feet deep, and could carry a load of fifteen hundred pounds.
In 1758 General James Abercromby's bateaux on Lake George each
held twenty-two soldiers and their provisions for thirty days. The latter would have consisted of about two barrels of salt pork, four of
hard bread or flour, and a couple of bags of dried peas, rice or cornmeal, with a total weight placed by Evans at over sixteen hundred
pounds.

The bateau was the most common watercraft of the rivers and lakes
of North America for generations, from the Ohio to the St. Lawrence,
and from the Mohawk to the Kennebec, yet no example is known to

survive, and there exist but few descriptions, and those rather scanty. Peter Kalm, a Swedish naturalist and a diligent observer and recorder, in writing of his North American travels in 1749, tells of this type of craft as it was made in the vicinity of Albany, where dugout canoes, hewed out of a single log, were also commonly used. The National Maritime Museum at Greenwich, England, has two or three dimensioned drawings of what evidently are colonial bateaux although they bear neither identification nor date. In the summer of 1960 the remains of a number of these boats were found on the bottom of Lake George close to Fort William Henry. Unfortunately only the bottoms remained, the side planking and most of the ribs having rotted away.

If we add together all the bits of information, we can define a bateau as a double-ended, flat-bottomed boat of lapstreak construction, very much like a modern dory, but without the latter's stern transom. Bow and stern were long and slanting although not as much so as in the later lumbering bateaux of the rivers of Maine. The sides of some flared outward like those of the modern dory, while others had the sides amidship built almost vertical in order to make it easier to push them along with poles, less arduous work when in shallow water than rowing. In deep water they were rowed and sometimes sails were extemporized out of blankets if the wind was right. They could be poled up relatively swift water, and, when this was not feasible, they often were hauled up against the current by men harnessed to long ropes.

Bateaux often were hurriedly and roughly built. Six men could put one together in two days, including sawing out the boards, but the work would be much expedited when a sawmill was at hand. The examples recently found in Lake George show evidence of hurried construction, the ribs having been roughly hacked out with the bark left on in places. The average British bateau was too lightly built to be of any use for carrying heavy cannon unless great care was exercised, and barges or flatboats were more suited to this purpose. The latter probably were little different from those on the Delaware which

Lewis Evans described as "made like troughs, square above, the heads and sterns sloping a little fore and aft; generally 40 or 50 feet long, 6 or 7 feet wide, and 2 feet 9 inches or 3 feet deep, and draw 20 or 22 inches water when loaden."

Whaleboats were in common use during the last French war for scouting and similar purposes. Many of them were bought on Cape Cod and Nantucket and brought up the Hudson, while others were built on inland waters. So far as can be learned they must have been much like the later Nantucket whaleboat, except that the center-board was unknown at that time and it is doubtful that they were put under sail. They were light, fast, easily rowed boats, each of which could hold a maximum of ten men without provisions.

A good-sized bateau sometimes had its bow altered and a cannon of medium size mounted to shoot directly forward, aim being taken by shifting the boat. The British also built catamarans composed of two bateaux carrying a platform upon which a cannon was placed, but usually cannon fire was not attempted from these small craft. Both countries built little armed sloops, schooners, and brigs on the lakes, and these were essentially for military purposes, not that of freight carrying.

Trade goods, provisions, and military supplies usually moved by bateau, although a part of the Canadian trade to the west still went in the great birch master canoes, some as much as thirty feet long and able to carry a score of men. In an Indian-made, birchbark canoe, the bark is used not as a structural member but primarily as a waterproof envelope, which is supported internally by longitudinal slats and ribs exactly like the later canvas canoe of the white man. The much inferior elm bark canoe of the Iroquois, however, lacked these lengthwise members and to a considerable extent depended upon the strength of the bark. Its life was materially shorter than that of the birch canoe, but it was more quickly made.

Except for great rivers like the St. Lawrence and the Mississippi, waterways seldom ran where one wanted to go without some interruption of one sort or another, and it was at times necessary to carry

RIVERS and MOUNTAINS

boats and goods around rapids and waterfalls, or to make a portage from one river system into another. In many cases these carries were fairly short and did not present serious difficulties, since sufficient men could move and re-imbark boats and cargoes without undue hardship. When the portage was of considerable extent and on a much-used route, ox teams might be stationed at the place, the goods transported across and loaded on to a new set of bateaux. The French at one time did this at Niagara. On the other hand at the portage from the Hudson to Lake George in 1758 the British hauled their empty bateaux across the divide on ox teams, and their whaleboats on low, man-drawn wheeled trucks. At the falls of the Oswego where the carry was quite short the bateaux were often dragged over while still loaded, and someone eventually contrived an installation of log rollers which greatly eased the operation. Many portages had great strategic importance, such as those at Niagara and "The Great Carrying Place," now Rome, New York, where the carry from the Mohawk to the Oswego began, and forts were built to guard them.

Now look at the map of eastern North America and note those formations of lakes, rivers, and mountains which have to so large an extent determined the growth and the history of our country. On page 7 is a simplified map of a large part of eastern North America. Only the most important geographical features have been shown and all else left out for the sake of clarity. At the top, toward the north, the mighty St. Lawrence forms a water highway from the open Atlantic deep into the heart of Canada, and it reaches on through rapids and a thousand little islands into the easternmost of the Great Lakes. It is the only natural waterway which allows direct access to the west. Now look at the great mountain chain that follows the Atlantic seacoast from the south bank of the St. Lawrence south and westerly through the Green Mountains, the Adirondacks, the Alleghenies and on into the Great Smokies, until at last, not many miles north of the Gulf of Mexico, it subsides into the coastal plain. Here is a great barrier over a thousand miles long that divides the seaboard from the central plains. The St. Lawrence bypassed it to the north, while the flat lands

of Georgia and Alabama allowed access to the west around the southern extremity, but throughout its length this great mountain chain
presented an almost impenetrable barrier to any movement to the
west.

⌐   This line of mountains lay between the colonies of the two nations,
but the geography of North America greatly favored the French who,
by means of the St. Lawrence and the Great Lakes, could easily pass
around the northern end of the mountains and reach the heart of the
continent. A bateau put into the river at Quebec could pass all the
way to the western end of Lake Superior, one thousand miles to the
westward, or could make its way to the present site of Chicago, where
under certain favorable conditions it could even be floated over the
divide to descend the Mississippi to its mouth in the Gulf of Mexico.
Nature had given a tremendous advantage to New France. Once the
British colonist had left tidewater and turned his face to the west,
he saw the great mountain barrier ahead of him wherever he looked.
To be sure there were rivers, but they had their sources in the mountains and formed no passes through which man might move to the
western lands.

The Appalachian Mountains throughout their entire length were
broken in only two places by corridors which gave access into the
fertile lands beyond, and these two corridors were to become the great
strategic routes of North America, the easy routes for trade and,
practically speaking, the only ones for military effort. The most important by far at this period extended from the center of the British
colonies directly to that of New France; this was the north-south
thoroughfare of the Hudson and Champlain valleys. Nowhere reaching an elevation of more than a couple of hundred feet, it extended
from tidewater on the Atlantic to tidewater on the St. Lawrence.
There were, to be sure, a few barriers to travel, but they were minor
in view of the immense strategic importance of this vital waterway. In
the Richelieu River, the outlet of Lake Champlain, there were some
rapids to overcome, but then the waters of the narrow lake lay open
to the south for a hundred miles with nothing to obstruct passage

except possible high winds and lofty waves. A little to the west of Champlain and its tributary, Lake George, there rises the Hudson River, flowing south and eastward, until, passing within a score of miles of the southern end of the lake, it turns southward and, stretching almost like a tightened string, pours its waters into the Atlantic Ocean. For untold years before the coming of the white man the Champlain-Hudson Valleys had been the hunting ground and the warpath of the Indian, and throughout the colonial period it was to be a vital factor in the making of our history.

The other corridor went from east to west, from the Hudson to the Great Lakes. During the earlier wars this route was little used, but it gained rapidly in value as the years went by, and eventually was to be of epic importance in the history of New York and the west. This was the Mohawk River, extending from the Hudson westward, almost to Lake Oneida and the Oswego River, which flows into Lake Ontario. Early in the nineteenth century it would furnish the bed of half of the Erie Canal. In the earlier period its great value lay in the fact that it gave the British a possible access to the Great Lakes and the Ohio country, with the opportunity of diverting more of the fur trade of the west away from New France.

As we look farther south along the Atlantic coast we note other rivers, great ones some of them, the Delaware, the Susquehanna, the Potomac, the James, the Roanoke, the Pee Dee, the Savannah, names famous in our history, but all are coastal streams and none gave the British access through the Appalachian barrier. The men of New France, on the other hand, could go almost where they would. Theirs were the Great Lakes, whence short portages put them on the upper waters of the Ohio with direct access to the Gulf of Mexico. The great central plains were theirs to subdue, exploit, and occupy, while the mountain barrier guarded their eastern flank and served as a safe shelter from which their Indian war parties issued to wreak havoc on the frontiers of the colonies. Unless the British could breach the high and rugged Appalachians, they would be condemned forever to the narrow coastal plain of the Atlantic seaboard, another Chile, and

France would hold the greatest part of North America. How this great barrier was first infiltrated by far-ranging fur traders, followed soon in time, but many miles behind in space, by the settlers, and how British military expeditions tried, failed and then at last succeeded in penetrating through the two strategic corridors of the Appalachian chain is the story which this book has to tell.

From Albany to Montreal, from one civilization to another of a vastly different kind, was less than two hundred miles as the wild goose flew, yet those miles lay through a trackless wilderness, most of it uninhabited save by the occasional Indian hunter. But straight through this empty land of forests and mountains, almost as straight as if drawn by a chalk line, ran the shining waters of the Richelieu River, Lake Champlain, and the Upper Hudson, which stretched south to Albany, where anchored ships from the seven seas. Save for a short land carry of a dozen miles near where the Hudson suddenly swings to the east at a point some forty miles north of the Mohawk's mouth, a canoeman could paddle his way from tidewater in the Hudson well into Canada, with only a few land miles to cover to reach the St. Lawrence at Montreal. In winter the way lay clear for snowshoes and sometimes skates, while only the occasional gale could hold up the summer traveler in times of peace.

These two hundred miles could be covered quickly, if we will make ourselves think in terms of the days, really not yet too far behind us, when the horse determined our standards of speed. In 1690 Captain John Schuyler led a raiding party from the south end of Lake Champlain nearly to Montreal and, after a fight, was back in Albany in eighteen days. Eight years later, this time on a peaceful mission, he took nine days for the trip from Albany to Montreal. In 1754 Nathaniel Wheelwright, traveling in November to Montreal as the agent of Governor William Shirley of Massachusetts, took seventeen days for the same trip, including two wasted at Fort St. Frederic while he was persuading the French commandant to let him pass, and he was forced to wait out another three days of high winds and boisterous waves. An army, with its barrels of hard bread and salt pork and its

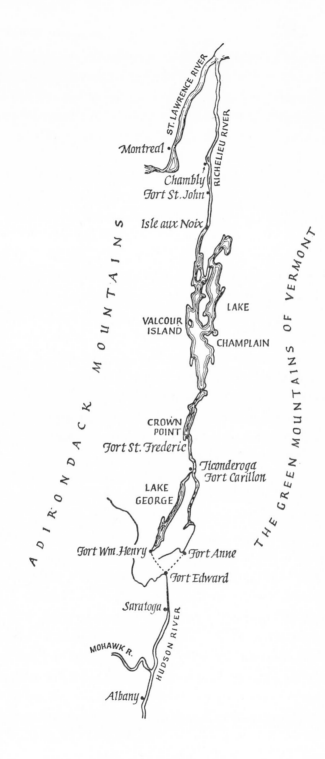

ST. LAWRENCE RIVER

RICHELIEU RIVER

Montreal

Chambly
Fort St. John

Isle aux Noix

A D I R O N D A C K   M O U N T A I N S

LAKE

VALCOUR
ISLAND

CHAMPLAIN

T H E   G R E E N   M O U N T A I N S   O F   V E R M O N T

CROWN
POINT

Fort St. Frederic

Ticonderoga
Fort Carillon

LAKE
GEORGE

Fort Wm. Henry

Fort Anne

Fort Edward

Saratoga

MOHAWK R.

HUDSON RIVER

Albany

great guns and mortars, might take longer, but the lightly equipped raiding party, the fur trader, and the smuggler could easily slip from one civilization deep into the other in the course of a single week.

From Albany to the bend of the Hudson where Lydius built his trading post, and where Fort Edward was later to rise, there were by the early 1700s crude roads and trails, and a man could travel on horseback if he did not care for a canoe. His horse could carry him on beyond Lydius' station for another dozen miles to Wood Creek in the vicinity of today's Fort Anne, where he was forced to a canoe or a bateau. There was, however, another choice open to him and he could instead go overland, by what soon became a good road, from Lydius' to the head of Lake George. At the northern end of this lake there was a steep portage of a couple of miles before one reached the waters of Lake Champlain. Most travelers seem to have preferred the Wood Creek portage and the drowned lands of the southern end of Champlain, where, as Nathaniel Wheelwright reported in his journal, the wild duck lay in such vast quantities that their noise made it difficult to talk, and muskrats built their houses by the hundreds.

The great highway traversing this wilderness was perhaps not too good a one by the standards of today, but for the man of the eighteenth century it left little to be desired. Back and forth over this great throughway were to struggle first the French and the Iroquois, aroused to anger by Champlain's musket shot of 1609, then New France and the British colonies, and finally Britain and the new United States. Whoever controlled this waterway held a threat to the other that was far-reaching in its consequences, and men were to struggle and die for well over a century in the conflicts that flared up and faded away along its length.

Between Albany and the upper forts, William Henry and Edward, there were a few places where rifts obstructed the Hudson and made the passage difficult and at times impossible for loaded bateaux. By 1755 or soon thereafter a good road extended all the way to Fort Edward. The cheapness of water transport, however, gave this method a decided advantage, and the normal routine of forwarding supplies to the lakes, when river conditions permitted, was this: at Albany the barrels were loaded on bateaux which carried them the dozen miles to Half Moon, today's Waterford, just above the mouth of the Mohawk. They were then transferred to wagons or ox teams and hauled overland to Stillwater, some twelve miles farther north. Scows then took over for the dozen miles of river travel to Saratoga, now Schuylerville, and finally wagons and ox teams carried them the last thirteen miles to Fort Edward, with the head of Lake George another dozen miles beyond.

The operation of moving provisions to an army on the frontier was a vast one, demanding much muscle power of both man and beast. An estimate made early in 1758 by the British supply officer at Albany for the operation of supplying twenty thousand soldiers at the head of Lake George with food for one month called for three weeks of good weather to move the required 5760 barrels of pork, beef, and bread. A thousand bateaux, eight hundred wagons, and a thousand ox carts were needed, and each barrel would have to be handled five separate times before it reached its destination. This took no account of the additional labor of moving up the purely military supplies, cannon, shot, powder, and the hundreds of other items required for a campaign which would certainly last longer than the single month for which this estimate provided.

The other corridor, the valley of the Mohawk, for many years was of relatively little importance since it ran west into an empty country, then of value only for the furs it produced. Early in the eighteenth century the British established the great trading post of Oswego, and the Mohawk corridor then became the supply line of this British foothold on the Great Lakes. Oswego in turn guarded the western approaches to the fertile Mohawk Valley. Just upstream from its junction with the Hudson the Mohawk pours its waters over a high fall, and goods for transport to the west usually were teamed sixteen miles across the flat, sandy plain from Albany to Schenectady, and then put on board bateaux.

There were some reefs and falls along the river, but relatively little trouble was to be met over the ninety miles that took one to "The Great Carrying Place." Here one left the Mohawk and portaged four miles to Wood Creek, which flowed into Lake Oneida. The length of the portage was greater in times of low water, and one then had to carry his boat nearly twice as far. A few miles of Wood Creek, narrow and not easy to pass through, and then the open water of Lake Oneida, some twenty miles in length, must be crossed. The lake emptied into the Oswego River which had only one troublesome spot, the falls twelve miles up from its mouth. The portage there was a short one of a few hundred feet, but it was succeeded by about a mile of quite wicked rapids, which, however, were usually negotiated safely by loaded boats. Stephen Cross, whom we shall meet again later in the story, in 1758 watched a whaleboat manned by four venturesome volunteers, try to prove their boast that they could run the falls, where the water dropped about a dozen feet in the course of thirty yards. The boat turned turtle and two of the crew were drowned. In all it was some 170 miles from the Hudson to Oswego on Lake Ontario, and on the average it took a military convoy a little over two weeks to make the trip. Lewis Evans, the early colonial map maker and geographer, held that it could be made in a week, and perhaps it could have been by a small party in canoes.

The time required for travel in North America during the colonial period was always significant. Boston's sprightly schoolmarm, Sarah Knight, made a trip from that city to New York along the coastal road in 1704. Allowing for a visit along the way, it took her eight days. Her journal is a lively one, well worth reading for some of the amusing adventures she enjoyed, such as crossing a river in a dugout canoe so narrow that she hardly dared to breathe for fear of overturning. One night she was given a bed in a miserable little room separated by only a board partition from the tavern's tap room, which was full of roistering rustics. Sleep did not come to the good lady, and at length in desperation she got up, lighted her candle and composed a poem which began:

I ask thy aid, O potent rum!
To charm these wrangling topers dum.

Who says that the Puritans had no humor and never got any fun out
of life? Her petition was answered shortly, the topers went home,
quiet reigned and the lady got her sleep.

Some fifty years later General Jeffrey Amherst's brother also took
eight days for the trip; it would appear that roads and bridges had
shown little if any improvement since Mistress Knight's day. The
fastest trip between the two cities was usually made by land from
Boston to Providence, requiring nearly two days, then by water
through Long Island Sound to New York, a trip which in one case in
1757 required five days, including almost two lost by bad weather. At
this same time there existed only a single east-west road of any length
or importance, always excepting Braddock's road, now abandoned to
the encroaching forest. This was the road between Boston and Albany.
As far as Springfield it ran through settled country with little towns
and taverns every few miles, but, once the traveler had crossed the
Connecticut on a ferry, he entered a stretch of near wilderness and
faced the steep hillsides of the Berkshires. The Reverend Samuel
Chandler, who set his face to the westward in September 1755 to
join General William Johnson's army, said that after he left Westfield
he went "over the mountains that rise like going upstairs." Many a
colonial soldier went off to war by this road, and Amherst marched
his British regulars over it when they returned from the capture of
Louisbourg. Later it became the stage road to Albany, meeting the
New York post road at Claverack. Today it is Route 23 and surprisingly little changed, for there are only a few towns along it and much
of the countryside remains near wilderness. When Nathaniel Wheelwright, the wealthy Boston merchant who apparently acted as a spy
for the French during two wars and died a defaulting bankrupt, made
the trip over this road on horseback in 1753, it took him seven days.

An interesting comparison between land and water travel is shown
in two trips made to Fort Duquesne, the Pittsburgh of today. Each

took the same time to complete, one month. The water trip from Montreal was some six hundred miles long, and portages at Niagara and today's Erie, Pennsylvania, had to be passed. From Carlisle, Pennsylvania, a wagon had to overcome two hundred miles of dubious roads in 1759 to reach the fort, renamed Fort Pitt by the British, and then had to rest ten days before returning empty, a trip of twenty days.

A boat trip from New York to Albany would last anywhere from as little as three days up to almost two weeks if weather conditions failed to favor, and from the latter city northward to Lake George an ox team, hauling a load of seven barrels of bread or pork, needed some five days.

The trip from Philadelphia to New York in the 1750s could be made either by road all the way or by sailing packet as far as Trenton, then by land to New Brunswick, and by water the rest of the journey. Peter Kalm traveled both routes, and each took him the same time, about three days, but the water trip must have been more pleasant, although subject to delay by storms or calms.

Water routes of course had one great fault; they froze in our northern regions, and all shipping ceased until the spring thaw. In most cases the ice-covered surfaces made excellent roads for sleds and sledges, and man could travel on skates or snowshoes. There is little if any mention of the use of skates by the military beyond that of their employment by Rogers' Rangers upon occasion, but they had been well known all over northern Europe for centuries. It probably was seldom that the lakes and rivers were sufficiently free from snow to allow them to be much utilized, and the Indian snowshoe was much more generally used, particularly by the French. There are records of British regulars being ordered to learn to use snowshoes, a few pairs being issued to each regiment. There seems to have been no British use of snowshoes for an expedition, although Lord Loudoun planned, but was unable to carry out, a winter snowshoe raid on Fort Carillon at Ticonderoga. Military operations, except for nuisance raids, normally ceased as winter came on, and then had to wait until spring had dried into early summer. The British had an advantage over the French in

their climate. Spring came to their northern colonies at least two
weeks earlier than to New France, and hence their campaigns could,
at least in theory, be off to an earlier start. Another material asset
was the possession of ice-free ports, allowing communication with the
home country and the shipping of supplies to continue throughout
the year, whereas the last ships of the season had to leave the St.
Lawrence by November, not to return until early spring.

Occupation of the land of the American continent to a great extent
was determined by geography. Not only did the coastal plain and the
valleys of the great rivers furnish the best land, but the sea and the
rivers allowed access and circulation. Once the more desirable regions
along salt water had been occupied, the advancing frontiers thrust
their way up the valleys of the rivers, compressed often into long
fingers of settlement bordered on both sides by the confining mountains. The series of maps of the settled regions, inserted following
page 154, endeavor to outline these areas as they existed in North
America at four different periods in our history. The colored portions,
red for the British (and Dutch) and blue for the French, are intended
to represent the regions occupied by an essentially resident population.
Their forward limits mark the frontier of settlement, not the more
advanced frontier of the wandering trapper and fur trader, and they
of course are far from precisely determinable. In the case of New
France, where the truly settled areas were restricted, advanced posts
and forts have in some cases been shown, while those of the English
have not. The result, I think, gives a relatively true picture of the
areas of the northeastern portion of the continent effectively occupied
by the two contending nations.

Chapter II

FLEURS-DE-LIS ON THE ST. LAWRENCE

T HE settling of the first British colonies in the New World, and of those of the Dutch and the Swedes do not concern us here. Nor can we enter into the problems they met in dealing with the Indians. It was only after the colonies had put down their roots and made the new land their own that they could give thought to any contest with the French. For many decades the frontiers of New France and those of the British and Dutch colonies in America seemed far apart, and rivalry for the fur trade had not yet produced the intensive competition that was to come.

The Indian problem of the first settlers of Massachusetts Bay had been solved for them by the great plague of 1616 which practically eliminated the red man from the area of the first settlements, and the Pequot War of 1637 curbed the Indians who remained in the Narragansett region. The two races then lived in peace for a generation until King Philip's War broke out in 1675. This was almost a knock-out blow to New England, although the Iroquois to the west refused to join the eastern Indian federation and so the Hudson River settlements were spared the tomahawk. The war, at last brought to a successful conclusion by the victorious white man, set New England back many a year. The cost in lives, in burned settlements, and in money for the war chest was staggering. For years to come New England was more concerned with repairing the ravages of that war than with rivalry with the distant French.

The French had settled Acadia, the Nova Scotia of today, in 1605, after a year's occupancy of an island in Passamaquoddy Bay, but it was not to be a permanent outpost of France. Temporarily abandoned, then resettled, Acadia was to remain a most sparsely occupied region for years to come, fought over and held by one side or another until its fate was finally decided by the last of the colonial wars.

Samuel de Champlain in 1608 had raised the fleurs-de-lis at Quebec. In the summer of the following year he had been persuaded to accompany a war party of Algonkian Indians against their ancient enemy, the Iroquois, and at Ticonderoga on Lake Champlain his arquebus had hurled death at the Indians from the south. This fateful little skirmish brought the enmity of the Iroquois upon the French, and over the years other causes, some of them economic in nature, were to intensify it. The French were soon to feel the wrath of the Iroquois.

The early years of Canada make a fascinating tale. Champlain's problems as acting governor, his explorations to the westward and his taking the warpath with the Hurons against the Iroquois to the south of Lake Oneida, the push of the early missionary priests toward the region of the Great Lakes, Champlain's 1629 surrender of Quebec to Sir David Kirke, the English privateersman, its return to the French four years later, the Jesuit missions out in the Huron country of Georgian Bay and the sad fate of that unhappy nation at the hands of the mighty Iroquois, the founding of the mission post of Montreal by Sieur de Maisonneuve and his little band of dedicated men and women in 1642 and its difficult early years, all these are beyond the scope of this book. Nor can we follow the ascetic Bishop François Laval as he strove to make the Roman Catholic Church master of the state in Canada, succeeded for a moment, yet failed at last as King Louis XIV finally took over control of the colony.

We must pass by the heroic struggles of puny New France as it resisted the mad incursions of the Iroquois, armed with guns by the Dutch traders of Albany, and the never-ending struggle for survival against the painted hordes, until at last in 1665 the King sent soldiers to help the little colony. We cannot linger to learn of the moves and countermoves of France and England in Acadia, and the intrusion of Puritan trading posts into the fringes of that region, nor of Governor John Winthrop's involvement of Massachusetts in the squabbles of the rival French claimants for Acadia and his betting on the losing horse. All this can be read in the glorious pages of Francis Parkman's great books, but we must leave the early days of New France behind, and move on into the time of the colonial wars.

Montreal in 1660 was the outpost of New France, the head of navigation on the St. Lawrence and the jumping-off place for those few daring souls who ventured farther west. There were about forty houses there, a fort and a palisaded stone windmill, with perhaps a hundred and a half Frenchmen, about a third of whom had families there, a weak and puny little settlement, threatened continually by the Iroquois but still managing to survive.

It was at this time that a large force of Iroquois planned an attack down the Ottawa River against Montreal. A young French officer named Dollard in some way learned of this impending inroad and determined to stop it. He gathered together a group of sixteen companions, and they all swore to fight to the death against the Iroquois. Accompanied by friendly Huron and Algonkians they advanced up the Ottawa until they found at the Long Sault a small abandoned stockade. There they took their stand and awaited the savage onslaught. Seven hundred Iroquois attacked the little band of martyrs— all were to die save two or three loyal Indians—and for more than a week the Iroquois were held at bay. Soon all but five of the friendly Indians deserted, but the Frenchmen fought on. At last the defense collapsed as, one after another, the Frenchmen laid down their lives for their country. But they had succeeded in their purpose, for the Iroquois had had enough and gave up all thought of an attack on Montreal that year. Indian troubles, however, continued to plague the little colony and repeated pleas were made to the home country for help. At last in 1665 the King took heed and sent the famous Carignan-Salières regiment of hard-bitten regulars across the seas to New France.

When the soldiers of that veteran regiment at last reached the waters of the wide St. Lawrence, they sailed for many a mile without seeing a single habitation of a white man. Then they reached the mouth of the Saguenay and there before them was the first slight sign of civilization, the little trading station of Tadoussac where the Company of the West traded for the furs from the regions south of Hudson's Bay. Then followed many miles of empty forest and rugged cliffs until the settlements of Beaupré, the populous seigniory of Bishop Laval, were reached. Here the land was open and prosperous, covered with little farms. Next the Isle d'Orléans, and then Quebec itself came in view, towering high above the river, but still a puny town of about seventy houses, its château built only of wood. As the soldiers went on up the river along the northern shore they saw an occasional little settlement and then Three Rivers was reached, a fur trading station huddled within its little stockade. Farther seigniories and occasional cabins with their cleared fields carried the frontier of New France on to Montreal, the seigniory of the priests of St. Sulpice, with its fortified stone windmill, its little wooden huts and the seminary of its overlords.

Upstream from Montreal timid little settlements were starting to appear here and there until at La Chine civilization ceased. Here was the last outpost, the point of departure for those who dared the far west, for China as the early explorers believed, and the land, save for an occasional mission post, belonged to the aborigines. Had some of the soldiers of Carignan followed the south shore of the St. Lawrence, they would have seen much the same picture but even fewer signs of civilization. Soon these same soldiers would build forts at Sorel and Chambly on the Richelieu, the pathway of the raiding Mohawk, and before many years settlers would be pushing south up that fertile valley. This, however, was still in the future, and almost every house in New France could still be seen from a canoe on the St. Lawrence. Such was the Canada of 1665, a long line of scattered settlements along a great waterway, a mere fringe of civilization bordering a vast wilderness, three little villages, and a population of less than 3500 souls. Until but a few years before all Canada had in effect been a mission, ruled by the Church with the object of Christianizing the Indians. Only recently had the King taken over control and established civilian government.

The soldiers of Carignan built forts in the valley of the Richelieu and advanced the frontiers of New France southward well toward the northern end of Lake Champlain. In January of 1666 an expedition of regulars and Canadians braved the rigors of a northern winter and marched south over the frozen lake to chastise the Mohawks. Nearly two hundred miles of wilderness lay between the last French outposts and their objective, the Mohawk villages on the river of that name. Each man must carry in addition to his arms and ammunition, bearskin and blanket for the frigid nights and food for the entire trip. The expedition went astray and failed to reach the Mohawk towns. Instead it met Dutchmen from Albany who asked why they invaded the lands of the British, for the Dutch colony had recently been ceded to Britain. Thus for the first time an army from New France stood on the threshold of the British colonies. In later years raiding parties of Frenchmen and Indians would carry the torch and the hatchet into these regions, but never again would a hostile army penetrate so far south, save for that of General Burgoyne and it marched in defeat, its arms surrendered at Saratoga. The French were short of food in 1666; they secured some supplies from the Dutch, then struggled back to Canada with nothing but suffering as their reward.

In October of the same year the French tried again. The Marquis de Tracy, sent by the King to Canada as viceroy, led a new expedition south by water up Lake Champlain and on by Lake George, called Lac St. Sacrement by the French. Three hundred boats and canoes carried the first waterborne army of white men, forerunner of many that were to follow that great waterway, some from the north and some from the south, until nearly 150 years later the last of them all was defeated by Thomas Macdonough at the Battle of Plattsburgh in 1814, and our northern gateway was closed, we hope for all time. A hundred miles of wilderness lay beyond the head of Lake George, but this time the French found their way and the five great palisaded towns of the Mohawks went up in flames. The news of this expedition gave anxiety to the British, but it thoroughly cowed the Mohawks, who begged for peace and also for Jesuit missionaries to live among them. Peace lasted for almost twenty years.

Louis XIV's new interest in Canada resulted not only in the sending of soldiers to curb the Iroquois, but settlers were induced to migrate across the ocean, as were young women destined to be the wives of Canadian bachelors. A governor, Sieur de Courcelle, was sent, in addition to Tracy, the viceroy, but the real gift to New France was Jean Baptiste Talon, the intendant, the officer charged with the civil and economic control of the colony. He was a most able man, conscientious and well intentioned, and he did much to better Canada during his seven years of labor, years which saw the population double itself through births and immigration.

There now followed a few years of peace and quiet, and the colony prospered. Talon had nurtured local industry, encouraged the fisheries, started shipbuilding, set up a brewery, and opened iron mines. He served New France well. In 1672 a new governor came, the fifty-two-year-old Comte Louis de Frontenac, a great soldier, but vain, arrogant, fiery, headstrong, and possessed of a most terrible temper. Moreover he was almost bankrupt and he intended to recoup his fortunes in the new country. He would stand no opposition to his wishes, and he clashed with almost every official with whom he came in contact. Talon, the intendant, almost at once retired to France and so avoided an open break. His successor, Duchesneau, who came in 1675 after an interregnum during which Frontenac served as intendant himself, thus enjoying full power for a space, was for years to feud and squabble with the governor, usually over petty matters such as precedence at church and who sat where at the meetings of the council. Frontenac also managed to antagonize Bishop Laval, no mean adversary by any standard, as well as the Jesuits, and this did not help his cause. He made an attempt to introduce a measure of democracy into the government of New France, but the King at once vetoed it. The country was fated to remain a tightly regulated despotism so long as the lilies floated over the land.

Frontenac was skilled and successful in his dealings with the Indians. His establishment of Fort Frontenac at the outlet of Lake Ontario was proof of his belief in the great importance of the west, as was his encouragement of La Salle's explorations and the penetration by the *coureurs de bois* into the headwaters of the Mississippi. Despite his achievements the feuding and the contention between Frontenac on one side and the intendant and the Catholic Church on the other ultimately led to the recall of both officials. The fiery governor had served New France well, and a few years later was to save it from probable destruction, but meanwhile he was to gnaw his knuckles in idleness and genteel poverty until at last he returned to fulfill his destiny.

In 1682 La Barre, the new governor, reached Quebec to find the ashes of half the city still smoldering. All the lower town save for one house had just gone up in flames, dwellings and warehouses full of goods, fifty-five buildings in all. An inauspicious start for a governor who was to prove unequal to his task. But this was not the only problem that awaited him, for the Iroquois, forgetful of Tracy's punitive expedition against the Mohawk towns in 1666, were again ready to make trouble. They had recently conquered their southern neighbors, the Andastes, were free to seek victims elsewhere, and had started to move west against the Illinois nation, allies of the French. Frontenac had done his best to keep the peace among the Indians until his recall, and it was La Barre who inherited the crisis. In the next chapter we shall see how he handled it.

Chapter III

FIRST CLASHES

T HE New Netherlands had been surrendered to England by the Dutch in 1664, recaptured nine years later, and then finally ceded by the peace signed in 1674. The region then became the proprietary colony of the Duke of York, later King James II, and in 1684 he sent Colonel Thomas Dongan across the Atlantic as his governor. Dongan, a Catholic and a younger son of an Irish baronet, was eventually to become the Earl of Limerick. He knew France well and was partial to the French, but he was a loyal and capable servant of Great Britain. At the same time he was well fitted to deal pleasantly and sympathetically with the Canadian authorities. He entered into a lengthy and courteous correspondence with La Barre, the Canadian governor, in which he claimed the region south of the Great Lakes for his country, a rather unreasonable claim in view of the early French explorations to the west. It seemed, however, worth trying in the hope of securing at least some of the fur trade of that vast area.

Dongan was a farsighted man and one of the very first to realize that the future of North America lay in the west. Thence came the beaver fur, vital to Canada, and also much desired by the Dutch traders of Albany. From the more southern regions came the buckskins from which were made the work clothes of the laboring men of Europe. The French through their missions and trading posts were getting the fur down the Ottawa and the St. Lawrence to Montreal, but the hungry traders of Albany got only the dregs, despite the fact that their trade goods were equal to or better than those of the French, and were sold considerably cheaper. At this period, for instance, Albany gave a gun for two beaver, while the Montreal traders asked five. A British red blanket, of better quality than a French one, cost one beaver, while Montreal demanded two.

The British governor in 1685 tried the experiment of sending the Albany trader Rooseboom with eleven canoes of trade goods to Michilimackinac on the northern side of the Straits of Mackinac, opposite the Mackinaw City, Michigan, of today. The plan may have been initiated by the Albany fur traders, but Dongan heartily approved and encouraged it. The trip was most successful, and the Indians asked the British to come again the following year. This was the first real penetration of the heartland of Canada's fur trade and it could not be countenanced by the French.

It would be wise at this point to look for a moment at the Indian nations and their various allegiances. South of Lake Ontario along the Mohawk Valley from the Hudson, on west to Niagara and down into part of Pennsylvania lived the mighty Iroquois, the Five Nations, that group of warlike tribes that had overrun many another race and were the military masters of eastern North America. They were an agricultural people dwelling in compact villages of bark long houses, shaped like today's Quonset huts, and surrounded by stout stockades. Ever since Champlain's unfortunate musket shot in 1609 they had preserved their enmity against the French, yet they refused to acknowledge the King of England as their master, despite all the efforts of Dongan. They tended to favor the English on the whole, particularly so the Mohawks, the most eastern of the tribes, but throughout the entire period of the colonial wars the Iroquois exercised a dubious neutrality, cleverly playing one side off against the other, as it seemed to them to be to their advantage. At this period we can consider them to be definitely anti-French, but that did not necessarily mean pro-British. For the moment we have no concern with the Indian tribes to the south of the Iroquois.

North of the St. Lawrence and to the eastward dwelt the Algonkian tribes, the Micmacs of Nova Scotia, the Montagnais of Quebec, and the Abnaki and Penobscots of Maine, while farther west and to the north of Lake Ontario were the Hurons, akin to the Iroquois but their deadly enemies. The more northern Algonkians were essentially hunters and not agriculturists, since the climate of their lands could not be depended upon for crops of Indian corn, the staple cereal of the more southern Indians. The Hurons of the Georgian Bay country, north and a little west of Lake Ontario, were essentially agricultural, growing corn, beans, and pumpkins. In 1649 they were utterly defeated and driven from their lands by the Iroquois. The survivors fled in many directions, some eventually taking possession of today's Green Bay, Wisconsin, where they were joined by Ottawas who had fled the banks of that river in fear of the Five Nations. Finally they moved to the vicinity of Detroit and Sandusky, and throughout the colonial wars adhered to the French cause.

Thus we find the French holding the Great Lakes region firmly, both through ease of access by the St. Lawrence and the Ottawa and through the Indian tribes whose allegiance they retained. During all these years of strife the French could depend upon the help of these tribes of the region they called the *"pays d'en haut,"* words that almost sing as you read them—the high country, the far west. They also had various relatively small groups of mission Indians, theoretically Christian, in practice savages little different from their western kin. Their priests, however, could control them to a considerable extent, and their aid could always be depended upon for a raid against unfortified English settlements.

In 1684 the Canadian governor, La Barre, a man of sixty, an administrator rather than a soldier, and one inclined to boastful talk and rash action, had set out with a little army of about one thousand men to chastise the Senecas, the most westerly of the Five Nations. Eventually he reached Fort Frontenac, where he delayed until much of his army became sick, and then proceeded with the remainder to a place called La Famine, near the present Pulaski, New York. It was well named, for provisions became short and the expedition went hungry. Instead of fighting Senecas, La Barre held a council with some of their leaders, made a shameful peace with them, and set off for Montreal, his tail between his legs. Miserable as the whole performance was, it nevertheless was an overt invasion of territory claimed by the British, with whom the French were then at peace. No blood was shed, and the British were not directly involved, yet this futile march can perhaps be said to have initiated the colonial wars.

When the news of La Barre's deflation by the Senecas reached the French Court, he was at once recalled. His successor was the Marquis de Denonville, an experienced and pious officer, of the highest personal character, but somewhat irresolute. Dongan and Denonville exchanged a number of pleasant letters, while each at the same time engaged in violent intrigue with the Indians.

The relations between the two governors soon became tense, particularly so when Dongan again sent English traders to Michilimackinac and heard rumors that Denonville planned to build a fort at Niagara. The diplomatic duel continued without material result until the summer of 1687, at which time Denonville started out to punish the Senecas. Reinforced by *coureurs de bois* and wild Indians from the western Great Lakes, the army amounted to some three thousand men in all. They landed near what is now Rochester, New York, and marched south a score of miles to the Seneca capital. A party of the Iroquois tried to ambush the French but was quickly defeated and driven off. The French ravaged the countryside, destroying all crops and villages, while their barbarous allies cut up the Seneca dead and put them in their pots to boil.

Denonville's blow landed in thin air. The Senecas fled to the eastward, largely unhurt but burning with rage and desire for the bloody revenge they were soon to achieve. Not only had Denonville invaded lands claimed by the British, but he had made the Iroquois fighting mad without doing them any very serious harm. He assembled his forces, went to Niagara, vital gateway to the far west, and built a stockaded fort on the site where La Salle had constructed one in 1678. Denonville then returned to Quebec. He had sown the seeds of trouble, and New France was soon to reap the hurricane.

When Governor Dongan heard of these actions of the French he naturally was aroused to wrath and at once took action, attempting to stir up the Indians against Canada, and demanding from Denonville the return of the second party of Michilimackinac traders, who had had the bad luck of encountering part of the French expedition and being stripped of their goods and clapped into jail. Denonville of course refused, and there ensued a furious interchange of letters that accomplished nothing. Matters finally quieted down and the peace between the two colonies was not outwardly broken. Nevertheless the Iroquois continued to harry the Canadian settlements with small war parties, and no man could think himself safe outside a stockade if he lived west of Three Rivers. Sir Edmund Andros now came from England to replace the able Dongan, who returned home to the honors he deserved. The policy which he had established regarding the Iroquois and the west continued unchanged under the new governor.

A short season of relative peace followed, but at last on a stormy August night in 1689 the lightning struck New France. Fifteen hundred Iroquois warriors erased from the map the settlement of La Chine, a few miles above Montreal. Men, women, and children were butchered without mercy, burned, tortured, and even spitted on sharpened poles and roasted like Christmas geese. When it was over the Indians camped in a nearby wood and celebrated their success with captured brandy. They were so sodden with drink that they could easily have been annihilated, but French troops, coming up mad with desire for revenge after viewing the victims, were restrained by order of the cautious Denonville. They obeyed, but with anger in their hearts. For weeks the Iroquois remained in the neighborhood, killing everyone who had the bad luck to be caught outside a stockade, ravaging the countryside but never attacking any fort or strong point. Houses and crops were destroyed over a large area around Montreal. Thus did the great Iroquois nation take its revenge for Denonville's hapless raid into the Seneca country.

Now there arrived news of formal war between France and Britain and of the recall of the Canadian governor. Denonville was a good man and he meant well, but his accomplishments were negative. Louis XIV sent as the new governor the redoubtable Count de Frontenac, now seventy years old but full of fire and fight. When governor of Canada some years before he had quarreled so with the other officials, and had been so touchy, high handed and irascible that the King had at last found it necessary to remove him, despite his accomplishments as governor. Now in the days of Canada's direst need he returned, the one man ideally suited to the task at hand.

Denonville had firmly believed that all of Canada's Indian troubles were caused by English intrigue. He decided that the only solution was to conquer New York, and in the last days of his governorship he sent an agent to France to propose such a plan. After much delay the idea was approved, but it was Frontenac, the new governor, who was ordered to execute it. Once the city of New York was seized, all non-Catholics were to be exiled, except such skilled artisans as might be temporarily retained as slave labor, and their possessions given to new settlers brought from Canada and France. It was believed that nine hundred Canadian troops and six hundred militia, assisted by two warships, would be sufficient to conquer a province of some eighteen thousand people. The expedition would then move on and take over all the New England colonies, a somewhat overambitious project.

Frontenac arrived in Canada close on the heels of the tragedy of La Chine to find everything in confusion and the western Indians wavering in their allegiance. On the one hand he undertook to repair the relations with the Indians of the Great Lakes region and to attempt to pacify the Iroquois, while on the other he plotted trouble for the English. Instead of a military expedition against a legitimate objective Frontenac planned to let loose Frenchmen and painted Indians upon unsuspecting settlers. Hitherto Indians had carried on such savage warfare, but no white man in America had yet engaged in planned massacre of white men. It was a nasty business, and one which once started would of necessity be followed by both sides. The great military expedition against New York degenerated into petty raids against unsuspecting farmers and tradesmen. Savage *coureurs*

de bois and bloodthirsty mission Indians were hurled against the
frontiers of New York and New England and a new form of warfare
was introduced into North America, one in which the French ex-
celled.

Three war parties were formed. The largest, composed of 114
Frenchmen, mostly *coureurs de bois* rather than soldiers, and 96 Christian Indians, assembled at Montreal in January 1690. Led by sons
of the Canadian noblesse, they plodded their way south through the
deep snow up the Richelieu River and on up Lake Champlain. It is
almost impossible for us today to visualize the fearful hardships of
such a trip in the depth of winter. Encumbered with snowshoes, each
man had to carry or to drag behind him everything that he would
need for perhaps a month, blankets, arms and ammunition, and, most
important of all, his food. Much of this would be lashed on top of
a special form of sledge, a long board perhaps a foot wide, its front
end turned up so that it looked like a great ski. In later expeditions
dogs were sometimes taken to drag these sledges, but in this expedition it would appear that each man had to haul his entire load himself.

One cannot but wonder today what impelled these men to undergo
such terrific toil and discomfort. As to the Indians the answer is simple, the underlying desire to kill, the hope of loot, and certainly to
some extent the encouragement and the inspiration, to our minds evil,
given them by their missionary priests. The white men probably
responded to other motives, and religion must have had an important
part, for the religious wars when Catholic fought Protestant to the
death were not many years behind. Another urge was probably the
chance of a thrill and of relief from the monotony of daily life. Whatever the motives, they were to continue to impel the Canadian to
raid and massacre the Dutch and English settlers for many a bloody
year to come.

The objective of the Montreal raiders had been Albany, but the
Indians sulked and forced a change to the smaller village of Schenectady. Seventeen days of toil took the party from Ste. Thérèse, the

last French outpost on the Richelieu and brought them to the un-guarded gates of the little Dutch settlement. They arrived in the middle of a frigid February night. Half frozen but not daring to light fires, they could not postpone their attack until daylight. They slipped through the open gate in the stockade, surrounded the cluster of cabins and uttered the war whoop. Thirty-eight men, ten women, and a dozen children were put to the hatchet, while some fourscore more were taken prisoner. All houses but two were burned, many of the oldest prisoners released, and the French headed back on their long trip north, loaded with plunder and twenty-seven prisoners. After some delay they were pursued, almost as far as Montreal, and a few stragglers were killed or captured.

Another and smaller party of raiders struggled through the wilderness toward the New England frontier, and late in March burst into the little settlement of Salmon Falls on the New Hampshire-Maine border. The hamlet was destroyed and nearly half its inhabitants massacred. Some of the prisoners were turned over to the Indians for torture, and the band retreated northward, but soon met Frontenac's third war party and joined with it. Late in May the combined forces, now totaling four or five hundred men attempted to surprise the fort at Casco Bay, where Portland stands today. The sudden assault failed, but an English sortie was annihilated and the fort invested and besieged in the conventional European manner. The trenches were soon carried to the walls of the fort and the English cause became hopeless. Promised quarter, the garrison surrendered, marched out, laid down its arms, and was at once overwhelmed by the Indians, with many a life lost and almost all the rest carried away as prisoners of the savages.

Thus did Frontenac initiate King William's War by murderous raids on undefended settlers and the massacre of those who were promised safety. In fairness, however, it must be said that once the Indian was unleashed he could not be controlled, and much of the cruelty, torture, and massacre indulged in by the Indians could hardly have been prevented, particularly in expeditions where they formed

a large percent. The French must be blamed first for initiating the
use of the Indian in raids upon the English and then for condoning
his cruelties. The English, however, at once took the hint and re-
ciprocated to the best of their ability, but they were never so effective
in their use of the red man.

These were not the first raids along the Maine and New Hampshire
coasts in these years, for the Abnaki Indians of the region, some of
whom had moved to Canada, egged on by the French and encouraged
by their missionaries, had anticipated the declaration of war and had
carried the tomahawk and the torch to the settlements of Maine and
New Hampshire. These, however, were Indian raids pure and simple
and not military expeditions led and partly manned by white men.

It was but natural for New York and New England to react violently when goaded by Frontenac's raids, and retaliation was immediately initiated. A joint expedition of 750 men and as many
Iroquois as could be persuaded to join was to be led by Fitz-John
Winthrop of Connecticut, grandson of Massachusetts' first governor,
John Winthrop, down the Champlain Valley against Montreal. At
the same time Sir William Phips, the Maine shepherd lad, youngest
of twenty-six children of one mother, who had dredged Spanish gold,
fame and a knighthood from the warm waters of the Caribbean, was
to sail up the St. Lawrence and attack Quebec by sea.

Hitherto almost nothing has been said of Acadia, Nova Scotia as
it is called today. Save for the little colony of 1604 on the St. Croix
River, which lasted but a year, Port Royal in Acadia was the earliest
French settlement in Canada. First occupied in 1605, it was soon
abandoned but re-established five years later. Raided by the English
and undergoing great privations, the French had still managed to
keep a weak hold on Acadia throughout the years. In 1654 it was
occupied by the English but was restored to France by the Treaty
of Breda thirteen years later. There were scattered fishing stations
and a few little farms, but during the seventeenth century it was of
little importance except perhaps as a base for French privateers. When
King William's War started, Massachusetts sent Phips on an ex-

pedition against Acadia. He captured Port Royal without difficulty and returned in triumph to Boston in time to take command of the fleet which was to assail Quebec.

The land army of untrained militia levies marched to the head of Lake Champlain and that was that, for there were no boats or canoes to carry them down the lake. Anthropologists tell us that there is an imaginary geographical line, the birch line, which is important in their art. North of it grow the big birches from which canoes can be made, while those unfortunate people who live south of it must content themselves with canoes of elm bark, canoes much inferior in quality. This birch line passes through Ticonderoga, and where Winthrop's army lay there was nothing but elm for the canoes. Moreover it was late in the season and the elm bark could no longer be peeled from the trees and so canoes could not be made. Thus it was that the little army was forced to turn around and march back to Albany.

There was, however, one little gleam of light, and the British struck a blow, petty indeed, but nevertheless the first successful attempt at retaliation against the bloody warfare initiated by Frontenac. Captain John Schuyler, grandfather of General Philip Schuyler of the Revolution, led a small band of Dutch and their Indian allies north down Lake Champlain and on down the Richelieu. Nine days after he left Winthrop at the head of Lake Champlain his party attacked Canadians at La Prairie, on the St. Lawrence a little upstream from Montreal. His Indians got out of hand, attacked too soon and killed six French settlers, four of them women, and took nineteen prisoners. The Indians refused to attack the stockaded fort, and the raiders returned home after destroying about one hundred and fifty cattle. Not a raid to be very proud of, but it showed Canada that the British could strike back. From now on savage warfare was to ravage the frontiers of both colonies for years to come. Next year Frontenac set a price of ten crowns for the scalp of an Englishman or -woman, or Indian for that matter. This was soon lowered and a higher price paid for prisoners, but it was often simpler to bring back a scalp tied to the belt than to escort a live prisoner back to Canada. A precedent had been set which both colonies would long follow.

Now that the matter of scalps has come up it might be of interest to mention that Indians soon learned that a good scalp could often, after a little judicious cutting and trimming, be made to pass as two or even three. The Indians of the Illinois country found that part of the hide on the head of a buffalo, if carefully plucked and scraped, could sometimes be passed off on an unsuspecting French officer as the real thing. Scalping, of course, was normally done on the dead or badly wounded, but in itself it did not necessarily cause a mortal wound, and the victim survived upon occasion.

The other prong of the attack on Canada got off to a late start. Phips's naval attempt was ushered in by bluster. After getting his fleet up the St. Lawrence to the great basin before Quebec, no mean feat by itself as the navigation of parts of the St. Lawrence was very tricky, he sent an officer to Frontenac to demand the surrender of the city within one hour. The written summons and a watch were insolently handed to the fiery governor in front of his staff. Instead of the expected explosion Frontenac for a wonder restrained his temper and returned a courteous but peremptory refusal. There is little need to detail the fumbling attacks that Phips made—they amounted to nothing. His ammunition soon became well nigh exhausted, and both his men and his ships suffered considerably from the fire of the French. The staff on the flagship was cut by a French ball, and the admiral's flag fell into the river, to be recovered by the French, an inauspicious omen. The land forces were re-embarked and the fleet sailed sadly back to a disillusioned and dismayed Boston. There was much straggling and some ships were lost. One was wrecked on Anticosti Island, and five of the crew cobbled up a makeshift cabin and sail on a skiff and sailed it back to Boston in about forty days, a voyage of nearly a thousand miles.

Thus the year 1690 saw two great British expeditions, great that is by the standards of the little colonies that manned them, collapse in utter failure. They were both led by amateurs, capable and well-meaning men but utterly unskilled at warfare, and they were composed of untrained farmers and tradesmen, commanded by inexperienced officers. The French on their side had a great leader, skilled officers and some trained regular troops. It is small wonder that the English were repulsed.

The spring of 1691 saw the Iroquois resume their raids on the Canadian settlements, but the Indians felt that they alone should not fight what was largely the battle of the English colonies, and they demanded that white men should also do something. New York decided to strike a blow against Canada, and one of the great men of colonial New York came forward to be the leader. Peter Schuyler was one of the leading men of Albany, a prosperous trader, a man of complete integrity, and the first mayor of his little city, in which capacity he was also the chief in Albany's dealings with the Iroquois. He achieved a remarkable influence over the Indians of the valley of the Mohawk. They called him "Quider," the nearest that their tongues could come to Peter. He held their devotion in war and in peace, and under successive governors he was the colony's right hand in all Indian affairs for many years. His portrait has come down to our times, that of a big, stern-faced man, but back of that tight-lipped mouth one can see just a hint of a smile. Later in life he was to become judge, member of the council, and, for a year, acting governor of New York, but at this time he was an active man of thirty-four and major of militia. He attempted to repeat his brother John's feat of the previous year, but with a force somewhat larger, half English and Dutch, half Indian.

His party paddled north down Lake Champlain in June of 1691, stopping at Ticonderoga to build another canoe or two, and at the mouth of Otter Creek, where they threw up a small breast-high fort of stone. They made a leisurely trip and it was not until early August that they left their canoes, with guards in a stockaded strong point, a little south of the French fort of Chambly, and started over the flat plain toward La Prairie and its fort. The French, warned by scouts, had sent one force to La Prairie and another of some three hundred men to Chambly with orders to get behind the English and prevent their retreat. Schuyler's band reached La Prairie during or just after a violent storm had driven the French to seek shelter and, it is said, the warming comfort of brandy. Be that as it may the French were taken by surprise and suffered considerably from the first volleys of the English. Once the initial surprise was over, however, Schuyler realized that he was greatly outnumbered, moved to a defensive position, and after a few more shots withdrew unpursued toward his canoes. He had, up to this time, suffered few losses and done considerable damage. Soon, however, he came in contact with the force sent to cut off his retreat, which had sheltered itself behind two great fallen trees and effectively blocked his advance. A brisk fire fight developed. The English finally broke through and scattered the French, but suffered heavy losses. It was a lucky escape for, if the French had played the hand right, almost no Englishman should have gotten away. Schuyler's force regained its canoes without further trouble and returned to Albany. Little was achieved by this raid when its cost was considered, but it did show the French that the English could produce some quite competent bush fighters.

The Iroquois continued to raid and harry Canada but they caused more nuisance than real damage, although occasionally some little settlement was overrun.

During this period appeared one of the heroines of Canadian history, Madeleine de Verchères, a girl of fourteen. Her father and mother were both away, and, unsuspecting of trouble, the inhabitants were working in the fields. Suddenly twoscore Iroquois appeared. Madeleine ran to the stockade and closed the gate just in time, for a savage snatched off her neckerchief as she darted in, so close was the race. With a garrison consisting of an old man, two militiamen and her ten- and twelve-year-old brothers, she organized the defense. The militiamen were craven, first running to hide, and then attempting to blow up the stockade in despair. She drove them out to the firing platform and instilled a little courage into them. The puny and ill-assorted band of defenders held the post for a week until relief at last arrived.

Frontenac believed in carrying the war to the Iroquois. Early in 1692 he sent a party of three hundred men to surprise the Indians on their hunting grounds. The attempt was successful despite the terrible hardships of a campaign made in the depth of a Canadian winter. The expedition finally cornered a party of Iroquois, killed most of them, and took the rest to Quebec, where the pitiless Frontenac had two of them burned at the stake as an example to the world of how New France treated her enemies.

In January 1693, Frontenac sent six hundred Canadians and Indians on the long and arduous snowshoe march up the Champlain Valley to assail the Iroquois again. Sixteen days of toil brought them to the Mohawk country, where they destroyed three of the Indian towns and captured nearly three hundred, mostly women and children. Then they leisurely started back toward Canada, shortly to be pursued by Peter Schuyler and a hurriedly assembled posse of citizens and Indians. The pursuit caught up, and an inconclusive fight resulted, from which the French broke away and continued their retreat. Schuyler had to wait for provisions to catch up with him before he could follow. When he again made contact with the fugitives, they swore that they would kill all the prisoners if not allowed to withdraw unmolested, and Schuyler was forced to call his men off.

In the course of the last contact several Frenchmen had been killed. The pursuers had exhausted their provisions, so the Iroquois warriors of the party filled their stomachs with boiled Canadians. Schuyler was as hungry as anyone and gratefully accepted some soup offered him, but when he found a hand floating in his bowl, he lost all appetite.

There were now to be two or three years of quiet on the New York frontier, while the action shifted eastward. Phips had captured Port Royal in Acadia in 1690, but he had left no garrison, and the following year the French reoccupied the town. Acadia in those days included not only Nova Scotia, but today's New Brunswick and an undetermined part of Maine. The area was thinly settled, but a considerable number of Abnaki Indians lived there, and they became useful tools to the French. The Baron de St. Castin's post at today's Castine on Penobscot Bay was the farthest advanced French post. The British station at Pemaquid, which had been destroyed in 1689, was rebuilt in stone three years later, and became the colonists' stronghold on the Maine coast.

In January of 1692 a group of French and Abnaki Indians surprised the unguarded hamlet of York on the Maine coast, killing at least half a hundred settlers, and capturing many more, but a few months later another raid on Wells met with failure. A period of comparative quiet now intervened, but two years later Oyster River, now Durham, New Hampshire, was overwhelmed and many women and children massacred in cold blood. Part of the murderous crew split off a few days later and killed some twoscore in the Groton, Massachusetts, region.

The fort at Pemaquid was too much for the French to endure, and its destruction was decreed in 1696. It furnished a most undesirable point of contact between the British and the Abnaki, too many of whom were now somewhat inclined to peace, and it was also a trading post that diverted furs from New France. Two French warships, a few soldiers, and a horde of painted Indians descended upon the fort and brought artillery into action, something no frontier post was well able to resist. The fort, inadequately garrisoned and with an incompetent commander, at once surrendered, and was razed to the ground before the French departed. For once the prisoners, and a few women were included, were protected from the Indians, and there was no massacre. The whole long New England frontier was now exposed to French and Indians, who usually avoided attacking defended garrison houses and preferred the lesser risks of slaughtering unsuspicious farmers and their wives and children. For years to come New England's frontier settlers were to live and work with their muskets always at hand.

In the spring of 1697 Indians fell upon the outskirts of the Massachusetts village of Haverhill. Hannah Dustin, only a week out of child bed, and a neighbor who had been nursing her, were carried away, and the baby smashed against a tree. Weeks later she amazed her sorrowing family by returning, accompanied by the nurse and a small boy, and bearing ten fresh Indian scalps. She had been allotted to a small Indian family that separated from the main party. One dark night each of the women filched a tomahawk and applied it to the sleeping Indians. Only two escaped.

The attacks on the Maine frontier were made to a very large extent by Indians alone, urged on by their mission priests and sometimes led by a Frenchman or two. The raids on the Albany frontier, on the other hand, were by combined forces of Canadians and Indians, under command of French officers. The raid on Oyster River, for instance, was made by some 230 Indians, led by two Frenchmen and Father Thury, the priest from the mission on the Penobscot.

Unfortunately there can be no doubt that some, at least, of the Canadian missionary priests urged their flocks on to massacre the English. A French report of this period states that Father Jacques Bigot, the Jesuit missionary at St. Francis, had gone to persuade the relatives of the Indians of the Sillery mission to join the French in the war. Father Vincent Bigot of the Kennebec mission was equally energetic in the cause, and Father Thury, the priest at today's Old Town on the Penobscot, was congratulated by the King for his efforts to encourage his Indians to go on raiding expeditions and rewarded for his warlike endeavors. A Canadian priest a century ago, in writing a history of the Indians of eastern Canada, said that the Abnaki tribe considered the New Englanders to be enemies of their faith, and that they were taught by their missionary priests, who usually accompanied them on their raids, that they really were crusaders marching against the infidel.

The missionary priests of Canada were of many kinds, ranging from the saintly martyr Isaac Jogues of the Jesuits to the Bigots and the Thurys, and the militant Father Piquet, whom we shall meet in another two generations, and on to his contemporary Father

Tournois of the Caughnawaga mission, who was deeply involved in the smuggling trade between Albany and Canada. Today we are convinced that much of what some of these priests did was utterly wrong, and it was when measured by our present standards, but by their standards it was not. Their concern was with the soul and not with the flesh. We must remember, moreover, that these were all devoted and high-minded men, actuated by what they sincerely believed to be right, and it is not for us, with all our advantage of hindsight, to attempt to judge them by the morals of today.

By 1696 Fort Frontenac had been repaired and garrisoned and Frontenac again moved against the Iroquois. The Count was now an old man of seventy-six yet he took the field himself, accompanied by an army of 2200 men. They poled, hauled, and paddled up against the current and rapids of the St. Lawrence, and then along Lake Ontario, whose waters with little warning could churn up waves like those of the open ocean, to the mouth of the Oswego River, and up it to Lake Onondaga. At the falls of the Oswego, fifty war-painted Indians, howling and singing at the top of their voices, took Frontenac and his great bark canoe up on their shoulders and bore him over the portage. What a spectacle that must have been! When the expedition landed and marched through the woods, the governor was carried forward sitting in an armchair lashed to two carrying poles. Thus did Frontenac take the field. He was to live for another two years, but this was his last campaign. Sixty-one years before he had gone on his first in Holland.

The Frenchmen found only an empty countryside, for the Onondaga capital, near the Syracuse of today, had been burned and abandoned. Desolation ruled. The Indian allies, thirsting for blood, were most unhappy that their enemies had escaped. Only one very old man was captured. They tortured him at length, but he endured all that they could inflict on him with great courage. Toward the end he cried, "Learn, French dogs, how to suffer, and you Indian allies of theirs, who are even lower than dogs, remember what you must do when at last you suffer my fate." Then they put him out of his misery.

The French lingered to destroy the growing corn and the harvest of the previous year and then started the long trip back to Montreal. This raid failed in its objective, just as had that of Denonville on the Seneca country nine years before. Frontenac believed that the famine resulting from his destruction of their crops and food stores would essentially destroy the Onondaga nation, but the British, who had been unable to assemble a force in time to march to the assistance of their Indian allies, sent provisions to tide them over to the following year. Thus Frontenac's last campaign brought forth only the proverbial mouse.

A year or so later the Peace of Ryswick ended King William's War, and in the fall of 1698 Frontenac lay on his deathbed, a great governor, although a difficult one, and a true servant of his King. He, first of all the governors of Canada, appreciated the vital importance of the west, not merely as a source of beaver skins, but as a land that must be occupied and held. Contrary to orders from the King, he re-established Fort Frontenac, knowing it to be the key to the colony's west, and the years were to prove him right. Two generations after his death the fort fell, and with it fell Canada's west.

Chapter IV

FRONTIERS RED WITH BLOOD

T HE War of the Spanish Succession began in Europe in 1701, and it was a mighty one, made famous by the Duke of Marlborough's campaigns and the great victories of Blenheim, Ramillies, and Malplaquet. It resulted in a greater England and an exhausted France. On this side of the Atlantic it was known as Queen Anne's War and here it was a futile war which, with one single but important exception, produced nothing. Armies which got nowhere were raised and then disbanded, and there was one great catastrophe, as well as long years of suffering along the bloody frontiers of New England. The French, for fear of arousing the Five Nations, left New York in peace. There was in effect a truce between Canada and that province, and the Marquis de Vaudreuil, the governor of Canada, promised the Iroquois he would make no attack in that direction provided the English did not initiate one. Instead he concentrated his efforts in egging the Abnakis of Maine and the Iroquois of the Caughnawaga mission on the St. Lawrence against the weak and defenseless seaboard frontiers of Maine and New Hampshire and the backwoods settlements of the Bay Colony.

It was not until the summer of 1703 that the war was felt in America. In August of that year the little village of Wells, the frontier settlement along the Maine seacoast, was overwhelmed by a pack of howling Abnaki, and twoscore, mostly women and children, were slaughtered or led away as captives. Other little hamlets and isolated garrison houses were assailed at the same time, and many a scalp was taken. About five hundred savages in all, led by a few French-men, were involved in these shameful attacks on simple farmers and fishermen. The total English losses this summer, both in slain and captured, were probably in the nature of one hundred and fifty, mostly women, children, and old men. The attacks were usually made on lonely houses while the menfolk were absent.

One of the Wells captives was Esther Wheelwright, a little girl of seven. She, a simple unlettered Puritan maiden, was to have a most unusual future. Esther was taken to Quebec and given by her Indian captor to the Canadian governor, in whose household she lived for some time, with the promise of being returned to her people when the occasion should arise. But her fate was to be far different. Some wealthy lady in France had sent a Canadian priest a sum of money with which, as Esther told a relative years later, "to make a nun." The priest accordingly bought her from the Marquis for 1400 livres, a very material sum, and she was put in the convent of the Ursulines, where she lived a long and apparently not unhappy life. In her later years she achieved about the most unusual position for a Puritan girl that one could imagine when she became Mother Superior of the convent.

The purpose of the French was to make certain that the Abnaki were deeply involved in warfare with the English to the eastward, and that they should keep the New England frontiers constantly harassed with raids and incursions, while at the same time peace was to be maintained in the Champlain and Hudson valleys. Only too well did the French remember La Chine and the Iroquois ravages that had followed the destruction of that unhappy village, and at all costs the Five Nations must be kept quiet in their long houses. More-over there was a lively and very profitable smuggling trade along the Champlain Valley which neither the Dutch traders of Albany, the Caughnawaga Iroquois, nor some of the French wished to see inter-rupted. The result was that the New York frontier was spared the hatchet, and, although colonial levies twice started north to war down the Champlain Valley, they never got far enough to draw blood.

The little village of Deerfield lies on the edge of the Connecticut Valley, and in 1704 it formed part of the western frontier of Massachusetts. It was fairly large and had forty-one houses, fifteen of which were inside a large stockade, too large for effective defense. There were about three hundred people in the village one night late in February of that year, and the snow was deep over the surrounding fields. It had drifted up against the stockade in places, almost to its top, but no one worried for no enemy would be foolish enough to think of campaigning in the depth of winter. Fifty Canadians and two hundred mission Indians nevertheless had braved the northern winter and had painfully made their way south on snowshoes. There was a firm crust on the snow and they left their packs and snowshoes some little distance away, and quietly approached the stockade just before dawn. They climbed it without difficulty, thanks to the drifted snow, shouted the war whoop and set to their horrid work. There is no need to detail the massacre, it was like many another. Some were lucky, got their doors and shutters battened down and held off the Indians, but others were not so fortunate and fell victims to the painted savages. The Canadians and Indians at last drew back, for the countryside began to threaten as angry Englishmen saw the light of the burning houses and turned out like buzzing hornets. Relief headed toward the stricken town, too late to punish the raiders seriously but in time to speed their departure and to cause them to leave behind a few more of their dead. When the count was finally taken, it was found that some half a hundred English had been killed, and more than twice as many dragged away as prisoners. Almost half the houses had been burned. The raiders did not escape unscathed, about forty of their bodies were found in the village and its vicinity. When the Canadian governor reported the success of this expedition to the French Court, he called the little village a fort and magnified its simple settlers into a garrison of soldiers.

The raiders and their unhappy captives plodded up the Connecticut River as far as the White River, where they swung northwest across the Green Mountains to the headwaters of the Winooski, eventually coming out on Lake Champlain near today's Burlington. Some score of the prisoners who could not stand the pace were knocked on the head or died from utter exhaustion, the remainder reached Canada safely, and in most cases were kindly treated. Eventually some sixty of them returned to their homes, while others remained and were absorbed into the Canadian civilization. Eunice Williams, daughter of the Deerfield minister, became an Indian squaw and more than a generation later she came back to Deerfield on a visit to her people, accompanied by her Indian husband. One of her grand-children became a student at Dartmouth in the early days of that college, and later in life he tried to pass himself off as the lost dauphin, son of Louis XVI.

Up to this time the raids of Queen Anne's War had been made on isolated houses or puny settlements. Deerfield was a considerable village, had existed for well over a generation, and had survived a previous massacre and burning during King Philip's War. The news of its near destruction caused much excitement in the Bay Colony and demand was heard for speedy retaliation. Benjamin Church of King Philip's War fame was now a very fat but still bullheaded man of sixty-five. The news of Deerfield nearly gave him apoplexy and he at once headed for Boston to beg the Massachusetts governor to strike back against the French. Church was commissioned to raise a force and see what he could do, but he was ordered not to attack Port Royal in Acadia, possibly because some of Boston's elect may have been engaged in a little illegal but profitable trade with that town. On the other hand plans for an attack on this place were already under way in England, and it would not have been wise to anticipate them. Church raised a force of some seven hundred colo-nists and Massachusetts Indians and set off to eastward. On the way he cleaned up St. Castin's settlement at today's Castine in Maine and then went on to Grand Pré, the principal village of the fertile Minas Basin in Acadia. He burned all the houses, but took care to harm no inhabitant. Then he broke down the dikes and let the sea flood back into their reclaimed pastureland. Despite his orders, he could not resist having a look at Port Royal, but decided that it was too strongly held and so sailed back to Boston.

In 1705 both Canada and the British Colonies came to the conclusion that it would be sensible to forget the war in Europe and to maintain a neutral peace in America. A proposed treaty was prepared but since the Canadian governor insisted on the exclusion of the English from the Canadian fishing grounds, the New Englanders refused to sign. The matter dragged on for another year or two and then was dropped. In the case of New York peace was, practically speaking, maintained throughout the war, although no written treaty was ever signed. The Marquis de Vaudreuil disregarded orders from France to attack the New York frontiers, and gave as his reason unwillingness to risk disturbing the Five Nations. He had solemnly promised the Iroquois not to attack Schenectady, Albany, or New York.

Port Royal may have been a fine port for carrying on an illegal trade with the French, but it also was a harbor for privateers and out-and-out pirates who preyed on the New England fishing fleet and the coastal trade. And so, even if it meant stepping on the toes of some of Boston's best, its capture was decreed. In 1707 Massachusetts sent an expedition against Port Royal, but the commander was quite incompetent and the expedition was an utter failure.

A dynamic and interesting character now enters our story. Samuel Vetch, Scottish soldier of fortune and adventurer, was the son and grandson of Covenanter clergymen, but he did not follow in their footsteps. Instead he took to the sword and then abandoned it for trade after marrying into the prominent Livingston family of New York. He became active in the Albany Indian trade and its accompanying smuggling down the Champlain Valley to Montreal. Then in 1702 he moved to Boston and engaged in the illegal trade with Acadia. He was said to have sold guns and ammunition to the French and the Indians of that region. He made several visits to Canada, one of them on official business in connection with the exchange of prisoners. Vetch was caught at least twice in illegal trade, once in conjunction with a group of Massachusetts' leading citizens, but he escaped any penalty through technicalities. He believed that the Canadian question must be settled once and for all, and he vehemently urged the complete reduction of Canada and the total expulsion of the French from North America as the only lasting solution to New England's troubles. Vetch sailed to England in 1708 to plead his case. He must have been a forceful and effective speaker for he convinced Queen Anne, and she promised to send warships and troops in the coming summer to supplement the forces to be raised by the colonies. The plan called for a two-pronged attack, by land down the Champlain thoroughfare, and by sea up the St. Lawrence. In the spring of 1709 a colonial force of some fifteen hundred men was raised, but the Five Nations were quite unenthusiastic and did little to help. The French effort to hold them neutral had been largely successful. Nevertheless all the Iroquois except the Seneca sent some warriors. Further colonial levies were to be assembled in Boston to go with the fleet.

Colonel Francis Nicholson commanded the Lake Champlain army. At one time or another he was either governor or lieutenant governor of five different American colonies, a most extraordinary record. He was also a fellow of the Royal Society, and active in the Society for the Propagation of the Gospel in Foreign Parts, an Indian missionary society which still exists today, although with altered objectives. He was a sound and practical man, but of little military experience. Nicholson's expedition advanced north from Albany as far as Wood Creek at the southern end of Lake Champlain, the old camping ground of Winthrop's 1690 expedition, and awaited the arrival of the British fleet. Meanwhile sawyers and carpenters were set to work making bateaux.

The French soon learned of the little army and sent a large party of Canadians and Indians to drive it off. They went south to the vicinity of Crown Point, their ardor cooled a little, and they stopped to think it over. Then some of them mistook a party of their own men for English. Each fired at the other, then all panicked and the whole troop hurried back to Canada. Nicholson's force continued to while away the time and suffer various camp diseases, due mostly to lack of sanitation, while it waited for news of the fleet. The fleet never came. In October Governor Joseph Dudley of Massachusetts was notified by the London authorities that they had changed their plans and sent the promised warships elsewhere. Nicholson sadly burned his bateaux and remaining supplies, and the expedition marched south and broke up. Vetch's great plans collapsed into nothingness through Queen Anne's failure to keep her promise. He had, however, engineered the best co-operative effort by the several colonies that had been achieved up to that time.

That winter of 1709–10 Nicholson went to England to seek renewal of the expedition during the coming year, as did Peter Schuyler, the "Quider" of the Iroquois, an older man than when we last saw him but still an active one. Schuyler took with him to the British Court four Mohawk chieftains. They were made much of in London and thoroughly lionized. One cannot but wonder what those savages thought of the vast smoky city of London, the Thames teeming with watercraft, and of the pomp of the Royal Court. Portraits of the chiefs were painted, and engravings made from these are today among the great rarities of "Americana."

Ships and men were again promised for the following spring, but it was not until July that they at last reached Boston. This year the plan was less ambitious. Port Royal in Acadia was the target, not all Canada. Nicholson commanded with Vetch as his right-hand man. The expedition, which finally got off in the late summer, consisted of fifteen hundred colonial levies from the New England colonies and four hundred British Marines, the whole carried in six smallish warships and some twenty-four transports. The fleet reached Port Royal without incident, and the fort and its little town were captured easily and expeditiously. This was the third time the English had taken the place. On both previous occasions it had been returned to France when peace was made, but this time it was to remain British, and with it the French were eventually to lose all of Acadia.

In England court intrigue was busily at work. Queen Anne's favorite had long been the Duchess of Marlborough, but the royal sun ceased to shine on her and a Mrs. Abigail Masham took her place. A new expedition was planned against Quebec for 1711, and what was more natural than that Mrs. Masham's brother, Colonel Jack Hill, should lead it? As admiral of the fleet Sir Hovenden Walker, a relatively unknown sailor, was selected. Nicholson again was to take an army down the Champlain Valley, while over six thousand British regulars and marines, accompanied by fifteen hundred provincial troops, were to sail up the St. Lawrence against Quebec. In the early summer a great fleet of warships and transports crowded Nantasket Roads in Boston Harbor. For the first time that city saw British soldiers and sailors in real numbers, and neither citizen nor soldier was entirely sure that he cared much for the other. Hurried raising of colonial troops, requisitioning of supplies, voting of money, fixing of price ceilings on various goods, desertions of regulars and other complications together made life in Boston a hectic and lively one for a few summer weeks.

The fleet of some seventy vessels sailed at the end of July. Vetch, who had been made governor of Port Royal, now renamed Annapolis Royal, commanded the provincial troops. The expedition proceeded northeast to the mouth of the St. Lawrence without incident, then started up that great river. Beyond the island of Anticosti it ran into fog and a strong east wind. The river at this point is some seventy miles wide, and Admiral Walker believed that he was near the south shore, while in fact he was well to the north. As darkness came on he hove the fleet to under topsails, their bows pointing south. Soon one of his officers reported land. The admiral assumed he meant land ahead. Actually the land was astern, to the north. Walker ordered the fleet to wear ship on to the other tack, with bows pointed north, and the admiral went to bed. Shortly his sleep was disturbed by a young army officer intruding into his cabin and imploring him to come on deck. There were breakers all around them.

Walker at last aroused himself, put on dressing gown and slippers and came on deck, certainly a most unnautical-looking admiral. It was all too true. His fleet was on a lee shore with a stiff breeze blowing and the rocky shores of the St. Lawrence just ahead. Most of the ships managed to anchor, or to claw their way up wind and get clear, but eight transports and two supply ships piled up on the rocks and reefs of the north shore, even today a most inhospitable region. Nearly a thousand lives were lost that foggy night. Walker and Hill still had a mighty force at their command, but the disaster so shook their nerve that they turned tail and headed for home. Vetch tried to make them continue on up the great river, but panic ruled the high command, and the expedition collapsed. Nicholson meanwhile had again been waiting at the head of Lake Champlain with his land forces, and for a second time he was forced to march in disgust back down the Hudson with nothing to show for the summer's work.

Quebec may have suspected that an expedition was projected by the English, but the first news that one was actually on the way did not come until early August. An officer, François de la Valterie, made a perilous trip with three companions from the French fort in Labrador, bearing a letter, carried there from France by a little fishing smack, which warned of the imminent approach of Walker's great fleet. The messenger reached Quebec after many weeks of travel by canoe through dangerous waters and shortly was sent back to his post. Imagine the surprise of the Canadians when less than a month later he was back again with a startling report. At the Isle aux Oeufs, about 160 miles downstream from Quebec he had found signs of a great shipwreck, "about 1500 to 1600 dead bodies, of which about a score were women, part of whom had infants in arms; . . . also saw on the shore [dead] horses, sheep, dogs and poultry, . . . 300 to 400 great iron bound casks, many shovels, picks [and] mattocks . . ." Great was the rejoicing and loudly and happily were the Te Deums sung in Canada that fall.

Even in recent years simple fisher folk living near Isle aux Oeufs claim that sometimes on a foggy night the faint outlines of great ships can be seen looming up through the mist with scarlet-clad soldiers and women in white crowded behind their ghostly bulwarks.

This was practically the end of Queen Anne's War, although some of the unhappy settlers along the New England frontier would most certainly have had different ideas, as French-led Indians continued to harry them, regardless of a theoretical peace. This relatively short-lived war had left the New York frontier undisturbed, and, save for the futile expeditions to Wood Creek, nothing happened in the west. The New England frontier was to continue to suffer for years to come. One gain had been made for England and the colonies, for they held Port Royal, that breeding ground of privateers, and perhaps of the fortunes of some Boston merchants, and with it went the beginning of the acquisition of all of French Acadia.

Chapter V

INDIANS, RUM, AND BEAVER

T HE Indian and the part he played in the colonial wars is a difficult subject to cover with complete fairness. There is a great mass of material to show what the white man thought of the Indian and both French and British were essentially in agreement as to what they believed him to be. Unfortunately the Indian left no records telling his side of the story, and so cannot speak for himself. Thus one is forced, somewhat unfairly, to accept the evaluation made by his more or less prejudiced white contemporaries. The degree of bias will run the gamut from that shown by the devoted priest of an Indian mission to the violent hatred of the New Englander who had just seen his wife scalped before his eyes.

Some readers undoubtedly will be displeased and perhaps shocked by the Indian that appears in this book. He is, however, drawn from the writings of his contemporaries, French missionary priests, professional soldiers of both nations, Protestant chaplains, and plain civilians. This is the Indian of Canada and the northern frontier after his civilization had broken down under the incursion of the white man. What he was before, what he later became, and what he may have been elsewhere in America at this time do not concern the present story.

The Indian of our period was a savage of the age of stone who had suddenly been plunged into the age of firearms, of Voltaire, and even of the first glimmerings of the Industrial Revolution. He had evolved a way of life which suited his environment, and had developed a culture which, though crude by contemporary European standards, was well suited to his need before the coming of the white man. Then all was changed. During the earlier years of the colonization of North America some of the native tribes tried to resist the white man, as did the Pequots and the Narragansetts in New England and the Powhatan Confederation of Algonkians in Virginia, while the mighty Iroquois for many years struggled with the French along the St. Lawrence. Eventually resistance ceased, and the civilization of the red man started its decay.

The Indian had something the Europeans wanted, furs and deerskins, while the white man offered tantalizing articles in exchange, knives, kettles, guns, woven cloth, all things which made easier the life of the savage. And it was soon found that the Indian had an inordinate craving for liquor, the brandy of the French and the rum of the Englishman, and would do anything to get it. Moreover, while the white man drank in order to feel happy and to enjoy himself, the savage drank to get drunk, and there was no halfway business about it. When the Indian was drunk, as long as he could stand on his feet he was absolutely uncontrollable and capable of all evil, even against his own family.

A missionary to the Indians living a little south of the Mohawk Valley wrote in his journal in 1753: "Any time in the night if we awake [we] are obliged to hear the songs & halloes of drunken Indians. A barbarous doleful noise you know it is." At another time he wrote: "We soon saw the Indian women and their children skulking in the adjacent bushes, for fear of the intoxicated Indians, who were drinking deeper. The women were secreting guns, hatchets and every deadly or dangerous weapon, that murder or harm might not be the consequence." This constitutional weakness of the Indian for alcohol was soon to be exploited to the limit by the white fur traders, despite attempts by the authorities of both New France and the British colonies to keep liquor away from the Indians. Thus one great and thoroughly evil influence had begun to work its destruction on the red man's way of life.

During the earlier years of the North American colonies the settlers had concentrated their efforts on securing a sound footing in
the new land, defending themselves against attacks by Indians who,
fairly or unfairly deprived of their lands, at times tried to eject the
intruding white man. Later, when the colonies of the two nations had
attained a degree of security from savage inroads and looked toward
further expansion of settlement and of the fur trade, they came into
conflict, and warfare resulted. The Indians now were employed as
combatants, most effectively by the French, less so by the English. In
any case the cruelty and blood lust inherent in the red man was given
encouragement and opportunity and his old civilization was further
broken down.

The Indian of the mid-1700s was a vastly different man from his
ancestor of a few generations before, corrupted as he was by the
liquor of the white man and by those blandishments which encouraged him to raid and butcher the settlers of the opposing colony.
Devoted priests had performed miracles of missionary work among the
Canadian Indians over many years. There had been failures, and
great ones, as when all the long and productive endeavors in the
Huron country had gone for naught when the horde of conquering
Iroquois rolled over that nation like a tidal wave and drove the unhappy remnants to distant lands. There had also been success. Sizable
missions had sprung up at a number of places in Canada. At the best
of them, and Abbé Piquet's mission at La Presentation might well
be taken as an example, the Indians had been transformed into farmers and had, apparently, absorbed some of the white man's way of
life. These Christian Indians of the missions appeared at first sight
to be merging into a European form of civilization, but despite their
choral singing, their cultivated fields, and their pigs and chickens,
they remained Indians beneath a thin veneer of domestication. Super-
ficially they were Christians, but in their dealings with others there
is no evidence that they ever applied the principles of Christ's
teachings.

Whatever he may have been at home, at his Canadian mission or in his native forest, the Indian that the New Englander too often saw was a bloodthirsty savage, led on by French officers and sometimes by priests to the slaughter of helpless settlers. There the Indian was in his element. Put him up against an armed enemy of nearly his own size, and he had little enthusiasm for a fight. He was most happy when he could pounce on an unsuspecting farmer at his plow, or on a farmhouse full of women and children, or when he could scalp the corpse someone else had killed. Face to face with an armed enemy, he usually skulked in the woods and let his white companions win the fight, so that he later could take the scalps and the plunder. A French Jesuit missionary wrote of the Mohawks in 1660: "None [are] more courageous when no resistance is offered them, and none more cowardly when they encounter opposition." This was an extreme view by a somewhat biased observer, but the actions the Indians of colonial times actually showed in battle prove that there was considerable truth in the statement.

The Indian was vain and boastful, cruel and ruthless, flighty and undependable, brave when cornered, and expecting no mercy from his enemy. These characteristics were his by nature, but before the coming of the white intruders they had been not unfitted to his way of life, and they had been tempered by better qualities, such for instance as his hospitality, his exacting code of honor and his well-developed tribal organization. The white man, however, soon so debauched the Indian, that his old way of life broke down, and all his evil characteristics became exaggerated.

The French employed the Indian much more effectively than did the English, and by far the major part of the recorded cruelties and massacres were carried out by French Indians, some from the missions and others wild men from the Great Lakes region. It was mostly the Iroquois who assailed the French, initially on their own volition, but later, although in a relatively small way, as agents of the British. Their cruelty was proverbial, probably greater than that of any of the other tribes of the northeast.

Dr. Caleb Rhea was a surgeon in one of the regiments in the 1758 attack on Fort Carillon at Ticonderoga. In his journal he noted the arrival just before the battle of Sir William Johnson and his howling, whooping Mohawks, and then, just after the battle, he wrote: "I can't but take notice of the crual nature of our Indians, I look on 'm not a whitt better than the Canadians for when they took a prisoner their custom was to confine him and making a ring round him with their company, then scurging him with whips, or pricking with sharp pointed sticks, taring his nails out by the roots, sculping alive and such like torments, they wou'd shout & yell [as I may say] like so many fiends, these frolics they would sometimes hold all night long and perhaps be two or three nights murdering one prisoner and at such times they would generally have rum enough to get drunk."

Many Indians changed sides freely and sometimes even frequently. The Indian "Jerry," probably a Delaware or a Shawnee, was with Braddock in the 1755 expedition against Fort Duquesne. He deserted, joined the French and fought against the English at Braddock's defeat. He was captured but released by Dunbar for fear of offending the Pennsylvania Indians. Then he joined the Tuscaroras, the tribe that made the Five Nations Six, and came to Albany in the summer of 1756 in the train of Sir William Johnson. Retribution caught up with him. He had the poor judgment of publicly boasting of the English scalps he had taken the year before, and the next morning his head was found grinning on the top of a post set up in the camp of the 44th Regiment at Schenectady.

Such was the Indian of the colonial wars. Cruelty to enemies and torture of prisoners were inherent in his upbringing. Not only did he hope to deal both out to his captives, but he in turn expected to receive no mercy himself if taken prisoner. He treated his white enemies exactly as he did those of his own race, and his cruelty was not specially directed at the Europeans. Moreover the newcomers were encroaching on his hunting grounds, pushing him farther and farther west, although he perhaps did not yet fully realize it. The civilization of the European was not for him, and he absorbed the bad traits of the white man while learning little that was good. In the case of the mission Indians of Canada, some were led by their priests to war against the English heretics, while almost all were encouraged by these same agents to follow French leaders against the British frontiers. When both his native traditions and his spiritual guide combined to urge the slaughter of the British colonist, the butchery and the scalping carried out along the colonial frontiers became inevitable.

The Iroquois were the great warriors of eastern North America, Mohawk, Oneida, Onondaga, Cayuga, and Seneca, banded together into a great fighting federation, the Five Nations. Most of them lived in the present state of New York west of the Hudson in an area surrounded by Algonkian tribes, but they were of a different race. Over the years they had conquered and subjugated all their neighbors, the Hurons to the northwest, the Andastes and Delawares to the south and the Eries to the west. Early in the 1700s the Tuscaroras moved up from the south into the Iroquois country and were added to the confederacy, which the English now started to call the Six Nations, while the French held to the older designation. Their sway extended westward over tribes living south of Lake Erie and over much of the Ohio Valley, and southward beyond the Delawares and the Shawnees of Pennsylvania. Thus in effect the power of the Five Nations extended from modern Indiana to Massachusetts and from the Adirondacks south nearly to Virginia. The council of the league met at Onondaga near today's Syracuse, New York, and its power was something to be reckoned with by all, both red men and white.

In 1750 the Five Nations were somewhat over ten thousand in number, living in perhaps fifty villages, in which by this period separate cabins had largely replaced the earlier long houses that had held up to as many as twenty families apiece. Their warriors numbered in the neighborhood of fifteen hundred or perhaps a little more. The women held a position of unusual importance among the Iroquois, much more so than among other Indian nations. To a large extent property was vested in them and some of them acted as electors and as members of a woman's council. No real matriarchate, however, existed, although that condition was certainly approached.

After their unsuccessful attempts to unseat the French colonies in the later years of the seventeenth century, the Five Nations withdrew into a position of neutrality between France and Britain, and played one nation against the other to the best of their very considerable diplomatic skill. On the whole they tended, at least in the early 1700s, to favor the British somewhat despite all Canadian attempts to gain their loyalty. For years French priests and blacksmiths, the latter always much sought by the Indians to repair their tomahawks and guns, lived among the western tribes of the Iroquois and tried, but with scant success, to turn them to the French interest. The Iroquois had considerable business as middlemen, securing the furs from the western Indians, and bringing them to the British traders at Albany. Just how much of a factor this was in their leaning toward the British is still being argued by historians today, but it certainly had some weight. A considerable number of the Five Nations, mostly Mohawks, had been persuaded to move to the Jesuit mission of Caughnawaga at Sault St. Louis, just across the St. Lawrence from Montreal, and these Indians became most active in smuggling furs down to Albany and bringing illicit British trade goods back to Canada.

At the Caughnawaga mission there was a large and active trading establishment owned by the Desaulnier sisters, who by 1750 had operated at this place for nearly a quarter century, almost entirely in illegal trade with Albany. Working in conjunction with the priest of the Jesuit mission, Father Tournois, the sisters were attempting to detach the Indians of the mission from the French and to persuade them to set up what in effect would be a separate little neutral trading state. It would be the center of operations for the smuggling trade with the British colonies, the major share of the profits of course going into the pockets of the Demoiselles Desaulnier.

Disaffection grew alarmingly among these mission Indians, and the situation became so dangerous by 1751 that Governor de la Jonquiere felt it necessary to take action. He learned that Father Tournois was

not a Frenchman at all, but a Dutchman, who naturally felt drawn
to his fellow countrymen who were the traders at Albany. The governor closed the trading post, and eventually exiled both the sisters
and the priest back to France. This of course brought on a fine row,
as the Jesuits rushed to the aid of Father Tournois, and the sisters
started exercising their not inconsiderable influence in France. For a
while there was a pretty how-de-do, but the King eventually backed
up the governor, after suggesting that he be a little more diplomatic
next time that Jesuits were involved, and all quieted down. The
Caughnawagas, however, now complained that they could not exist
without the goods which formerly came from Albany, and the comedy
ended with the Canadian governor solemnly giving these Indians a
license to engage in the smuggling trade up to a certain specified
amount each year.

The Five Nations of the mid 1700s were far from what they had
been some two generations previously. Wars had depleted their manpower, and French intrigue had weakened the old solidarity of the
league. An English missionary who knew the Indians well wrote in
his diary in 1756: "The Six Nations have in former times made
themselves terrible by warlike achievements, but their name and
character begins to sink. They are divided between French and English—have lost numbers in needless wars—have been poisoned to death
by our spirituous liquors; hence it [is] that they have lost much of
that influence which they used to have over other nations."

In 1738 a young Irishman arrived in the Mohawk Valley. He was
only about twenty-three, and he was poor, but he had two most helpful
connections. His uncle was a captain in the British Navy, and soon
to be an admiral, who had married a De Lancey, a family long
prominent in New York politics. The captain's brother-in-law, James
De Lancey, was now chief justice of the colony, and later was to be
lieutenant governor. The young man, with such relatives as this, was
obviously off to an excellent start. William Johnson had come to the
Mohawk country to manage a grant of land which his uncle had secured in the region. He was an able youth, gay, likable, and pleasant,

friendly and adaptable. Johnson settled on his uncle's land, which lay along the Mohawk River just west of present day Amsterdam, New York, and proceeded to seat a few farmers on the grant. He opened a store and trading post on the Mohawk, and later a second one farther to the south at Oquaga, an Indian town on the headwaters of the Susquehanna River. His trade prospered from the very start, and soon he largely abandoned his uncle's interests and set up for himself. Johnson really liked Indians, came to understand them, learned their language and traded with them on an absolutely fair and honest basis, something no other Indian trader did in those days. Soon he secured a great influence over the Iroquois, one even greater than that wielded by Peter Schuyler a generation and more before. Shortly after reaching the Mohawk, Johnson had taken a German girl as a consort, and had married her on her deathbed. She was soon replaced by an Indian, niece of King Hendrick of the Mohawks, who disappeared after a few years and was succeeded by Molly Brant, sister of the famous Chief Joseph Brant. She kept his house for him until his death.

Johnson's power over the Five Nations became great, and the Indians trusted and esteemed him to a greater extent than they did any other white man. There are many references which show that the English fur traders generally were the very scum of the earth, full of trickery, violence, and immorality. Johnson, on the other hand, was the soul of honor in all his dealings with Indians, and they soon realized that they could trust in his integrity. As early as 1746 he had achieved a position of eminence among the Indians of the Mohawk Valley and the lands a little to the south. In this year he appeared in Albany, dressed as a sachem of the Mohawks, and Governor DeWitt Clinton appointed him military commander over the Five Nations. From then until his death just before the American Revolution he was Britain's most effective agent for dealing with the northern Indians.

The Albany Indian commissioners, whose duties and powers dated back to the closing years of the previous century, continued to function in theory. Most of them were themselves engaged in fur trade and thus were attempting to regulate an operation in which they were deeply involved, and hence far from disinterested officials. Johnson was really the colony's Indian agent under a somewhat dubious commission, and he resigned in 1751, feeling that the work he was doing required a commission from the King. Meanwhile as a member of the Governor's Council he continued to work for good relations between the British and the Iroquois, and incidentally to feather his own nest further through pushing his trading and other mercantile operations and by securing grants of additional land. In 1748 he had been made colonel of militia, and at last in 1755, General Edward Braddock gave him a royal commission as superintendent of all the northern Indians. Johnson was one of the great men of colonial North America, and for many years by far the most important man on the northern frontiers of the British colonies.

His manor house on the banks of the Mohawk some thirty miles west of Albany was open to all comers, and visitors of every sort, Indians, missionaries, soldiers, and travelers from abroad, all enjoyed his cordial hospitality. After the fall of Canada he moved a few miles westward to Johnstown, where he built a new mansion, flanked by twin blockhouses. Here he lived out a life most useful to the British Empire, surrounded by his Mohawks, his hosts of friends and visitors and his flock of half-breed children.

With the single exception of gunpowder, the Indian trade goods of the British were of considerably better quality than those offered by the French, and they were sold at a materially lower price. The French never were able to produce a scarlet cloth which would approach that made in England at anywhere near the same price, and the French copper kettles, an article of great value to the Indian, were cruder and heavier, the latter a factor of importance to a roving people. The higher price of French goods can be at least partly accounted for by the overload required to meet the graft and privilege which was always rampant in Canada, but the lack of quality is harder to explain.

The Stone Age Indian had become dependent upon many of the

products of the white man's civilization, and no longer was satisfied
with clothes of skin and implements of stone. His basic wish, after
guns, powder, lead, and rum, was for woven cloth, for blankets and
garments, but there were also many other articles he desired. A New
York law of 1720 forbidding the export to Canada of Indian trade
goods listed the most important staples: "cloaths, known by the name
of Stroudwaters, Duffales or trucking cloth, Indian blankets, Indian
coates, half thicks [a cloth], gunns, kettles, stokins, shirts, flints,
steeles, all [awl] blades, swords, pistoles, powder, lead or any other
goods—commonly called—Indian goods." Other important items not
listed were vermilion pigment, knives—the scalping knife was usually
only an ordinary wood-handled butcher's knife—needles, thread, beads,
ribbons, and silver ornaments such as brooches and bracelets.

Rum and the French equivalent, brandy, were of course a vital
article in the fur trade, particularly for the western Indians. The use
of liquor was forbidden at times but rules of this sort were meaningless
and never could be enforced. Many of the Indians realized the evil
that alcohol wrought on a people who drank only in order to get
drunk, and they protested violently against its sale. All fur traders
appear to have used liquor to some degree, and even William Johnson
carried it to his trading posts. He did, however, apparently use care
and restraint in its employment. At his post at Oquaga, near today's
Binghamton, New York, the local Indian chiefs in 1753 requested
that no more rum should be brought there, and that the supply then
on hand should not be used. Then at a formal council one said: "My
brother, Colonel Johnson, my dear brother, pity us; your battoe is
often here at our place & brings us rum and that has undone us.—I
would have you bring us powder & lead which we want—bring us
clothing what we want and other things what ye choose only don't
bring us any strong drink." At another time and place the Indians
protested: "We know it to be hurtful to us to drink it. We know it
but if people will sell it to us, we love it so that we cannot refuse.
But when we drink it, it makes us mad." The traders' answer to the
authorities trying to stop the sale of liquor was that they "were obliged

to carry some [rum] or the far Indians would not trade with them."

The British fur trade on the northern frontiers was carried on almost entirely through the two key points of Albany and Oswego. The western Indians, or their middlemen, the Iroquois, brought their furs to one or the other of these places, while the illicit trade with Canada came south up Lake Champlain to Albany and New York. This north-south trade was, as far as can be learned, almost entirely illegal, either because one or the other colony forbade it at the moment, or because, when not forbidden, the duties were so high that it was worth evading them. New York politics in the early to middle 1700s was deeply involved in the Indian trade. The retail operation at Albany and Oswego was favored by the Livingston faction, while the De Lancey group was back of the great wholesale trade north through the Champlain Valley. It was to a large extent through this latter trade that the French secured much of the trade goods needed to supply their own posts, and the volume was very considerable—in 1720 it was reported to amount to over £10,000 per year, several hundred thousand dollars in the values of today. In 1720 Governor William Burnet, son of the famous Bishop Gilbert Burnet and himself an able, active, and far-sighted servant of the British Crown, secured passage of a law forbidding export of Indian goods in the hope that it would cut off much of the French trade and force the furs to New York. For a while it worked, trade goods became extremely scarce in Canada, and French Indians from the far west came to Albany to trade. The law, however, was soon repealed and the smuggling trade persisted, essentially unchecked.

Whereas the British on the northern frontiers followed the policy of persuading the Indians to bring their furs east to market, the French by the early 1700s believed in taking the trade to the Indians through the establishment of many trading posts in the fur country. There were over forty such posts in all, the majority in the region of the Great Lakes, some regular forts like Duquesne or Frontenac, but many others only small stockaded establishments with garrisons of perhaps a mere half a dozen men. This great network, supplemented by independent traders, the *coureurs de bois,* some licensed by the French authorities to trade but many not, was effective in securing the fur of the west, but much of it failed to reach its only legal market, the monopolistic Compagnie des Indes, and instead went up the Champlain Valley to pay for the smuggled trade goods.

The British, through direct trade at Albany and Oswego and indirect dealings with the smugglers of Caughnawaga, secured a good share of the furs of the west, and had a sizable market for their excellent trade goods as well. Had the export of the latter to Canada been effectively stopped, the Indians would have been forced eastward with their furs to the British trading posts. In 1717 Indians of the Five Nations told New York's Governor Hunter: "Our people are furnished with . . . goods . . . at Irondequoit [near Rochester, New York] which stops a great deal of peltry coming hither [to Albany]; but the French are supplied with all these goods from people here at Albany which goes first to Canada . . . and so to Irondequoit . . . If you will stop that trade of goods being carried from hence to Canada the other trade will fall of course."

The British trade on the central and southern frontiers faced a difficult geography. There were no water routes such as New York possessed, and the great mountain masses must either be crossed or bypassed around their ends far to the south. Pack horses were used instead of bateaux, and the difficulties encountered were naturally much greater. Nevertheless the southern traders penetrated far into the west, farther even than did those of the northern British colonies. Late in 1750 John Patten, a trader from Philadelphia, was seized by the French at their Fort Miami—today's Fort Wayne, Indiana—and his goods and thirteen pack horses confiscated. He had believed that peace existed, and it did, but Patten should have realized that the French, war or no war, would not allow such an invasion of their territory. At about this same time traders from South Carolina were in the Ohio country, and were said to have even reached the Mississippi.

The post at Oswego was the greatest source of annoyance to the French, but the Miami Indian town of Pickawillany, a mile or two north of today's Piqua, Ohio, was almost as bad. Here English traders had established a fortified trading house flying the British flag, and carried on an extensive trade with the Indians of the region. As many as fifty traders might congregate there at one time. The local chieftain, who rejoiced in the incongruous name of "La Demoiselle," was most friendly to the English, who called him "Old Briton." Suddenly, early in the summer of 1752, a band of Chippewas, led by two Frenchmen, attacked the town. They had picked a time when most of the men were off hunting, and only a very few traders were present. The Chippewas cleaned up the place, killed "La Demoiselle" and some of the traders, while the rest were captured. Then they roasted "La Demoiselle" and the heart of one of the traders and feasted. That ended Pickawillany as a British trading post, and with it went the British sphere of influence in the Ohio country. An attempt to revive it two years later was to be made by the governor of Virginia but the attempt would fail.

The basic fur of the northern trade was beaver. By the middle 1600s fashion had started to decree that men should wear large hats of felt, and it was found that beaver fur was by far the best material from which to make them. The skin itself was not used. The fine short underfur, the so-called "beaver wool," was stripped from the skin and formed into a hat by the felting process. Felt hats are made today in exactly the same basic way, except that rabbit and other cheap furs are used, as well as wool. By the end of the 1600s New France was normally exporting about 150,000 skins each year, while New England and the middle colonies could produce an annual crop of only something over eight thousand beaver. Later, as Albany pushed its trade farther west and Canadian furs moved south up the Champlain Valley, the discrepancy became much less. By the first third of the eighteenth century it would appear that about half, and perhaps even more, of the furs originating in New France passed into the hands of the British. The fur trade, however, was the lifeblood of Canada, while to the British colonies it was only one of several productive activities. Beaver was always a monopoly with the French, assigned by the King to some favored group. After 1719 La Compagnie des Indes held the franchise and set the price, but much Canadian beaver went elsewhere, usually ending up in British hands.

Farther south the beaver disappeared and was replaced as the Indian's medium of barter by the deerskin. The southern colonies did a great export business in deerskins. During the mid years of the eighteenth century, for example, the export of skins from Charleston was never less than 150,000 pounds a year, while as early as 1730 Virginia was annually exporting about 200,000 skins. A few years later the trade working out of Augusta, Georgia, required two thousand pack horses and about six hundred men.

Britain had another great source of fur, the Hudson's Bay Company, but this region need hardly be thought of in connection with the colonial wars, it was so remote and so empty. "The Governor and Company of Adventurers of England Trading into Hudson's Bay," perhaps the most sonorous title in the English language, had established trading posts along the shores of the bay during the latter half of the seventeenth century and enjoyed a monopoly of the fur trade under its charter. At one time or another the French seized some of the posts and held them for a period, but the Treaty of Utrecht in 1713 confirmed Great Britain's possession of the region. The Hudson's Bay Company farmed the region solely for its furs, and on much the same basis as that which the French tried to apply in Canada, but it was much more successful in its operation, and quantities of most excellent beaver reached its posts from the surrounding country and the far northwest. Much of it was sold to French hatmakers.

The French believed Canada to be of value to them only for the furs she produced, the land itself was thought of no value beyond supporting a population sufficient to maintain the trade and to grow sufficient food to feed the country. At times an excess of grain was produced which allowed some export, but this never amounted to much. Thus the French followed a false economy, dependent upon a continuing market for beaver. The British, on the other hand, soon

came to know the value of the land and to consider the fur trade a
valuable by-product but not an end in itself. Thus their economy
spread over a wide base, including wheat, corn, swine, cattle, lumber,
tobacco, rice, potash, and naval stores, all products of the land.

Chapter VI

THE LAND OF EVANGELINE

Q<small>UEEN</small> A<small>NNE</small>'s War had left Port Royal in Acadia in the hands of the English, who renamed it Annapolis Royal. The Treaty of Utrecht in 1713 awarded all of Acadia to the British Crown, but its boundaries were not defined. Isle Royale, the Cape Breton of today, was not a part, and there the French were soon to build the great maritime base of Louisbourg. All of today's Nova Scotia was included, although the French later were to deny this, as well as an undetermined part of modern Maine, perhaps as far south and west as the Kennebec. This southern boundary had always been claimed by the French while they held Acadia, but, once that province was awarded to Great Britain, they blandly stated that Acadia stopped at the St. John River or thereabouts, and hence all of Maine from that river to the Kennebec, unaffected by the treaty, remained French. Only bitter war was to determine what the boundaries really were.

We will have a clearer picture if we think of Acadia as the modern Nova Scotia, for it was within this area that all the little wars and troubles of the next half century were to take place. What England took over in 1713 was an empty country of swamps, lakes, and forests, bordered in places by great tidal marshes and grasslands which were in time to prove most fertile. Except for wandering bands of Micmac Indians the land was almost entirely unsettled. The French population was only about 1800, descendants of the two or three hundred peasants from La Rochelle and Brittany who had settled there early in the previous century. There was never much further immigration, and these initial colonists were, practically speaking, the ancestors of all the French Acadians. These people had learned how to build dikes, and thus were able to convert the tidal marshes into fields of great fertility and to develop an agriculture which, with relatively little labor, produced a life of considerable abundance. They also built boats, and engaged in fishing. Most of their settlements were around the edges of the Bay of Fundy. They were a simple people, with few wants, prosperous by their standards, happy and contented. They lived in peace with the local Indians, with whom they had intermarried to some extent.

The peace treaty provided that the Acadians had a year during which they could leave the ceded lands and migrate to French soil, otherwise they would become British subjects. The Board of Trade was that London body which through direct as well as indirect methods in practice controlled colonial affairs. The Board soon realized that it would be most unwise to allow the Acadians to depart, as it would greatly weaken the new colony and at the same time strengthen Cape Breton Island, where the French authorities were endeavoring to attract them. Accordingly various obstacles were put in the way of their departure, and only a small number left.

It must be realized, however, that if they had really wished to leave, the petty little garrison at Annapolis Royal could have done little or nothing to stop the Acadians. For many years Britain's power in Acadia was limited to the range of the cannon in the fort at Annapolis Royal. The real answer is that the Acadians did not want to leave. They had sent agents to inspect the new lands offered them by the French, and the report was not favorable. When the year of delay provided in the treaty had run out, the Acadians technically became British subjects. The Board of Trade decided not to force matters but instead to require only that the Acadians should take an oath of allegiance, and trust that time would turn them into Englishmen.

For almost forty years the question of the oath was to plague Acadia. It really was the only thing that the British required of these former Frenchmen, and conversely it was the only thing they refused

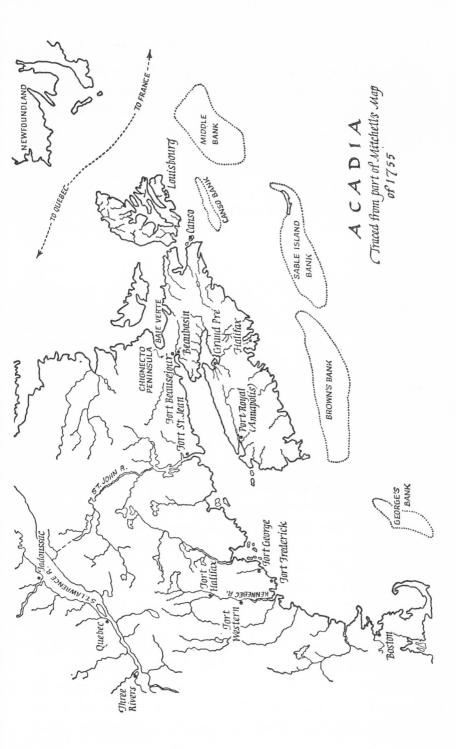

ACADIA

Traced from part of Mitchell's Map
of 1755

NEWFOUNDLAND

TO QUEBEC

TO FRANCE

MIDDLE BANK

Louisbourg

CANSO BANK

Canso

SABLE ISLAND BANK

BAIE VERTE

CHIGNECTO PENINSULA

Beaubasin

Grand Pré

Halifax

Fort Beauséjour

Fort St. Jean

Port Royal (Annapolis)

BROWN'S BANK

ST. JOHN R.

Tadoussac

ST. LAWRENCE R.

Fort George

Fort Frederick

GEORGE'S BANK

Fort Halifax

KENNEBEC R.

Quebec

Fort Western

Three Rivers

Boston

to give. From time to time halfhearted attempts were made to administer the oath, and many Acadians took a qualified oath under which they were exempted from bearing arms for Britain. This qualified oath was never approved by England, but was administered on occasions by British officials in Acadia in order to secure some apparent evidence of compliance. The Board of Trade always side-stepped a final showdown on the oath of allegiance. They dared not let the Acadians leave until there had been a sizable influx of British settlers, or at least until there were more military posts in the province. Their departure would leave an empty countryside and would materially strengthen the French, so, despite talk and threats, the British kept putting off final action, and the Acadians were strengthened in their belief that it was all a bluff, and that they could maintain their allegiance to the French King and yet continue to occupy their fruitful lands, free from annoyance or control by the British.

Soon they began to be known as the neutral French, and in effect the British authorities became quite indifferent to the Acadians, and paid little or no attention to them. So matters continued for a generation, and the French settlers had many children, increasing fivefold in population in less than forty years to a total of some ten thousand souls.

They were a simple and unlettered people, with little or no contact with the outside world, and wanting none save for their religion. Their priests were Frenchmen, appointed to them by Quebec. Only the barest handful of the Acadians could read or write, and they lacked natural leaders. Their priests, the only educated men among them, automatically took over the leadership and guided the simple people as they wished, and the way usually was that of France. Some of the priests served only God and believed it best to work in harmony with the British, but one or two served France as well and, perhaps, before all else. The Canadian priest was much more than just a clergyman, he was also the teacher, the civic leader, and the counselor of his flock. This was specially so in Acadia where there was practically no civil government, and the people were isolated,

callow, and illiterate. Francis Parkman's characterization of the Acadians is still perhaps as good as any. "They were all alike a simple
and ignorant peasantry, prosperous in their humble way, and happy
. . . Their mental horizon was of the narrowest, their wants were
few, . . ." Add that their basic love, except perhaps for their religion,
was for their land. Left alone by the agents of France, and guided by
priests who restricted their duties to religion, they eventually would
almost certainly have become good citizens of Britain.

In 1739 Paul Mascarene, a British engineer officer with long experience in the region, took over Acadia as the acting governor, and
for the next ten years he exercised a mild and just rule over its people.
He had a force of only a little more than one hundred soldiers, and so
could hardly have done otherwise had he wished. Mascarene was a
good man. He executed his orders and carried out his duties but he
also tried to rule the Acadians with a kind and understanding rein.
As an exiled French Huguenot he could appreciate their viewpoint
and attitude better than any Englishman. For ten years, part of which
were war years, his was a gentle but firm and correct rule over his
province.

There appeared on the stage in 1744 the man who might well be
called the evil genius of Acadia. With the best of intentions in the
world, he was probably the basic cause of the final expulsion of the
unhappy people. He was the Abbé Jean Louis le Loutre, missionary
to the Micmac Indians since 1740. He enjoyed a pension from the
French Crown and thus was independent and able to devote all his
energy—and active and effective it was—to molding his Indians to his
will. While there can be no doubt that his underlying motive was
religious, he actually practiced a secular and military profession, leading his Indians to battle against the British and attempting to drive
the heretics from the land. It is probably not stretching the point too
far to say that, had the Abbé restricted his activities to the clerical
and devoted his energy to teaching his Indian followers to practice a
Christian religion, the Acadians today would populate all of Nova
Scotia and never would have undergone their sad tribulations. Instead

Le Loutre worked his will upon this simple people, threatening them with his Indians, while the British authorities were weak or negligent when they should have been firm, and too firm when perhaps they should have been a little more forebearing.

In 1744 Le Loutre led a band of three hundred of his Micmacs against the British at Annapolis Royal, and he was able to get within the immediate vicinity of the fort without any of the nearby Acadians warning the British of his approach. This might be considered as carrying neutrality a little too far. The Acadians may have been neutral, but very little was required to tip the scales and make them anti-British. To be fair to them, however, it must be said that the great majority appear to have maintained a proper neutrality throughout Nova Scotia's days of trial. The attack on Annapolis achieved nothing material, but it showed the English that Le Loutre and his Indians were far from neutral and that they and the Acadians must be watched and prevented from further mischief.

This is the story of Acadia from its cession to Britain in 1713 through the subsequent years of peace, years when the Acadian people were increasing vastly in number, were living under the British flag and yet maintaining an inner allegiance to France. England had neglected them shamefully and had allowed them to build up a belief in the safety and permanence of their most equivocal position. A fanatical mission priest had forged his Indian converts into a sword answerable only to his hand, and through the threat of his Micmacs had achieved great influence over the simple Acadian people. All too soon a great storm was to burst over the land, and, the innocent, for to a great extent the Acadians were the innocent bystanders in an impossible situation, were to suffer for the wrongs of others.

Chapter VII

THEY FOUGHT WITH FLINTLOCKS

To understand the battles and sieges of the colonial wars, one must know the weapons with which they were fought, very different from those of our day. There was little change throughout the entire period, but these remarks apply perhaps a little more to the later years than to the earlier ones. During the seventeenth century the 16-foot-long pike, merely a great spear, was still a favored weapon for infantry, used in conjunction with musketeers. As late as the end of the century some European authorities still believed in a ratio of one man with a pike to each who bore a musket. The pike was of great value in resisting a charge by mounted men. By 1700, however, it had practically disappeared from all armies, and the flintlock musket had become the standard weapon of the infantry. Earlier forms of muskets with matchlocks or wheel locks had been used during America's earlier years, but throughout the colonial wars the flintlock was universal.

Such a weapon had a barrel some three and a half feet long and a bore of a little less than three quarters of an inch for the standard musket. Civilian guns of course varied considerably, and Indians preferred a somewhat smaller caliber. The French musket carried a ball noticeably but not materially smaller than that used by the English. The average regulation musket weighed about ten pounds, was smooth-bored, and had no rear sight on the barrel. It fired a round lead ball which fitted the barrel quite loosely in order to allow for powder fouling the bore and thus reducing its effective diameter. Sometimes buckshot were used in addition to or in place of the single ball. The powder was the old smoke-making black powder, and the smoke it produced was very considerable, often clouding the battlefield in a fog of gray obscurity when no breeze blew to clear the air.

The musket was solidly and somewhat crudely made, suited to rough usage by heavy-handed peasants. It was fired by a flintlock, a mechanism which caused a piece of flint, a natural stone, to strike sparks from a piece of steel. The priming was contained in a hollow spoon-shaped pan which abutted against the side of the breech of the barrel at a point where a small touchhole or vent was drilled through the wall of the barrel. The flash of the priming passed through this hole and ignited the main charge in the barrel. Although it takes time to describe it, the operation itself was almost instantaneous. The delay between pulling the trigger and the discharge might be between a tenth and a fifth of a second.

The accuracy of the weapon was poor when judged by modern standards, a good musket was capable of hitting a man-sized target quite consistently at fifty or even sixty yards, but beyond that distance it would largely depend on luck. The extreme range was perhaps a quarter of a mile, but only against large concentrated targets was it worth shooting when the distance was one hundred yards or more. The flint wore out in use. A good piece, shaped into a standardized form and size by a skilled flint worker, was good on the average for twenty or thirty shots, and then, if a fresh piece was at hand, the old one was discarded. Sometimes one could reshape a worn flint after a fashion, but it would be a makeshift job at best. Flints were cheap and were provided in vast quantities for military expeditions. Braddock's expedition of about 2100 men took along with it 142,000 flints, as well as 1800 more of smaller size for pistols. The best British flint was almost black in color and cleanly shaped into a rectangle, while the French used an amber-colored stone, less well made on the whole and with a rounded back.

Today flints for muzzle-loading firelocks are still being made in the village of Brandon in Suffolk, England, exactly as they were made

THE MUZZLE LOADING FLINTLOCK MUSKET
1700-1830

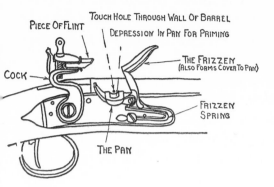

PIECE OF FLINT

TOUCH HOLE THROUGH WALL OF BARREL

DEPRESSION IN PAN FOR PRIMING

COCK

THE FRIZZEN
(ALSO FORMS COVER TO PAN)

FRIZZEN SPRING

THE PAN

PIECE AT HALF COCK, FRIZZEN OPEN. YOU POUR A LITTLE POWDER INTO HOLLOW IN PAN AND SNAP FRIZZEN SHUT. THEN YOU POUR POWDER CHARGE IN TO MUZZLE, DROP IN THE BULLET AND RAM DOWN A LIGHT PAPER WAD WITH THE RAM ROD. A PREPARED PAPER CARTRIDGE IS A PAPER TUBE HOLDING BALL AND POWDER FOR PRIMING AND LOAD, ITS PAPER IS USED FOR THE WAD. THE MILITARY NORMALLY USED CARTRIDGES; CIVILIANS LOOSE POWDER FROM A POWDER HORN AND A BULLET POUCH.

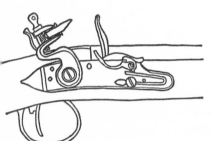

BRING COCK BACK TO FULL COCK AND YOU ARE READY TO FIRE.

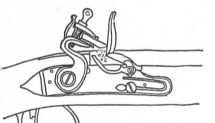

YOU PULL THE TRIGGER, THE FLINT IS KNOCKED SMARTLY AGAINST THE FRIZZEN, MAKING SPARKS AND KICKING BACK THE FRIZZEN THUS OPENING PAN AND EXPOSING PRIMING TO SPARKS. A FLINT IS GOOD FOR SOME 20-30 SHOTS BEFORE IT WEARS OUT.

THE COCK IS STOPPED BY A SHOULDER, THE FRIZZEN SNAPS ALL THE WAY OPEN. THE PRIMING IGNITES AND FLASHES THROUGH THE TOUCH HOLE SETTING OFF POWDER CHARGE IN THE BARREL. THERE IS ALMOST NO TIME LAG BETWEEN PULLING TRIGGER AND GUN GOING OFF IF GUN IS PROPERLY MADE AND IN GOOD CONDITION, PERHAPS $\frac{1}{10}$ TO $\frac{1}{5}$ SECOND. YOU NOW PULL COCK BACK TO HALF COCK, AND YOU ARE BACK WHERE WE STARTED IN TOP SKETCH.

WITH THIS MILITARY MUSKET YOU SHOULD HIT A MAN ALMOST CERTAINLY AT 50 YARDS. MUCH BEYOND THAT IT WOULD BE A MATTER OF LUCK, ALTHOUGH BULLET IS EFFECTIVE MUCH FARTHER. YOU COULD LOAD AND FIRE 3 TO 4 TIMES A MINUTE. THE FLINTLOCK RIFLE WAS MUCH MORE ACCURATE BUT NOT SO WELL SUITED TO GENERAL ARMY USE.
~ FORT TICONDEROGA MUSEUM ~

over three hundred years ago. They formerly came in various sizes, from about half an inch square, suitable for small pistols, up to about an inch wide and half again as long and perhaps three-eighths of an inch thick, the size suitable for the large muskets or wild fowling guns of two centuries ago. Today only two or three of the middle sizes are still made. They are exported to Africa and to this country for sale to antique gun enthusiasts. Knapping is the technical term for shaping the flint, and the pub in Brandon rejoices in the name of The Flintknapper's Arms.

A musket of this period, if well made and properly maintained, was a sound and practical weapon. Under normal conditions it might be expected to miss fire once in perhaps twenty or more shots, usually on account of a poor or worn-out flint. In the rain it was practically useless, and in damp weather its priming required constant watching and renewing. Sometimes the touchhole through the barrel wall became plugged up with powder fouling and the priming flashed but failed to ignite the charge. This was called "a flash in the pan" and is the source of the term still used today. When we realize that all the wars of Europe and America were fought with this weapon from well before the time of the Duke of Marlborough until almost a generation after the Napoleonic era, and that the flint firelock as it was usually called, was used by some of our troops in the war with Mexico in 1848, we will appreciate that it must have been a practical weapon well suited to its purpose.

In the early days of the colonial period the soldier loaded his piece from a powder flask or horn and a bullet pouch, and the civilian and the militiaman continued to follow this method. By the early years of the eighteenth century, however, the paper cartridge had come into general use in all armies. It was merely a paper tube containing the lead ball and the proper amount of powder, usually for both priming and main charge, although sometimes a separate container was used to hold priming powder. The normal procedure of loading a musket was for the soldier to half-cock his piece and to snap open the steel of the lock, thus opening the pan. He then bit off the end of the paper cartridge and poured some powder into the pan as priming, shut the steel pan cover and lowered the gun butt to the ground. He then poured the rest of the powder into the muzzle, dropped in the bullet, and inserted the paper of the cartridge as a wad to prevent the ball rolling out again. Finally he drew out his ramrod and rammed the charge down the barrel. The musket was ready to fire as soon as he drew the flint-carrying hammer back to full cock. Actually what we today think of as the hammer of a gun was then called the "cock" and the steel piece which also covered the pan was known as the "hammer" or the "frizzen." This entire operation could be carried out much more quickly than one would think. Trained soldiers were able to load and fire as many as four shots a minute, and after the Prussians had replaced the wooden ramrod with one of steel, they claimed to have even achieved five, but that was exceptional.

The paper cartridge continued in use until the time of our Civil War, by that time ignited by a percussion cap instead of a flint. Throughout the years of its use, it was necessary that a soldier should have good teeth to enable him to bite off the end of the cartridge. And so one of the ways of avoiding military service was to break off one's front teeth. In the days of wholesale conscription, such as that decreed by Napoleon, the loss of a few teeth was a cheap price to pay for avoiding military service.

The soldier was taught little or no marksmanship. He was usually instructed to point his firelock straight ahead, nearly level with the ground, but pointing slightly downward, and he was told to look in the direction in which he was firing. In formal European warfare the enemy line normally presented a continuous lateral target that could hardly be missed, and vertical control of the fire was all that really mattered. It is obvious that a soldier trained in such a method as this had a lot to learn before he could hit a running Indian or one largely concealed behind a tree. By 1754 we find at least one French military treatise speaking of target practice at a range of some fifty yards against a fifteen-inch-square target. This was considered an excellent exercise to develop sharpshooters and skirmishers, but the encouragement of individual marksmanship was still in its infancy. British orderly books of the 1750s sometimes mention that each soldier shall fire two or three shots at a mark. Those relatively few colonials who had hunted game and Indians on the frontiers of America had developed their own skill, but in many cases it was severely limited by the crudeness of their weapons. On the more southern frontiers where the Pennsylvania rifle was in use it was a different matter, but the colonial wars were largely fought on the northern borders by regulars and militiamen to whom the rifle and its much greater accuracy were practically unknown.

We need say but little about the manual of arms and the process of loading and firing by command. Part of this of course was intended to develop parade-ground perfection and to inculcate the automatic obedience of orders necessary to the type of discipline required in that day. Moreover it made the operation of loading and firing an almost automatic one that could be continued without conscious thought during the stress of battle. The manual varied somewhat in different countries and at different times, but it was a logical one, and it achieved its purpose. The Prussians instituted methods which led to the highest rate of fire, but the British carried theirs to perhaps a still more effective level. Throughout history the final clash of the line of battle has always called for the maximum amount of fire power per yard of front. In the days of Crécy and Agincourt this was achieved by ranks of British bowmen, in World War II machine guns and artillery concentrations were the answer, while in the future it seems probable that the atomic bomb will rule. But from the late colonial period onward for many years the British infantry battalion reigned supreme, with its three ranks of trained soldiers firing four volleys per minute from smoothbore muskets. Those who once had faced the fire of such a battalion and lived to tell the tale never forgot the experience.

At one time four ranks of men closed up tightly into one line and all fired at once, but by the later colonial wars the use of three ranks was normal, the front rank kneeling, the other two closing up and firing over the heads of the front rank. Some, including Marshal Saxe, even advocated only two ranks but this did not become general until many years later.

Military drill and evolutions basically were methods of getting columns of men marching perhaps four or more abreast deployed into a firing line three deep, and the reverse operation of getting the firing line back into a column. There were, of course, many other formations for maneuver and for the parade ground but they need not concern us here. In the forests of America few of these evolutions and formations were of any practical value except in those rare cases, such as the two battles of the Plains of Abraham, when trained European troops met in the open field. Too often small bodies of soldiers with little training met others of similar background, and each potted away at the other through the obscurity of trees and powder smoke. Most of the major clashes were those of an expedition against a fort or at least against makeshift defenses, and Wolfe's battle at Quebec and Murray's subsequent defeat on the same field were the only examples of formal open-field battles which followed European procedure.

The rifle was known and in common use during the colonial period, but its military employment was very limited. It was at this time primarily a civilian weapon of the frontiers of the middle colonies. Developed into its American form in Pennsylvania, it spread westward and southward but only to an extremely limited extent to the north. The barrel of a rifle is cut with spiral grooves inside its bore, and these cause the bullet to spin in flight, which greatly improves the accuracy. On the other hand a rifle was slower to load, and demanding of precise ammunition. It was a weapon for the scout and the sharpshooter, not for the true infantry soldier. The British had copies of the Pennsylvania rifle made in England, and during the last French war they were issued in small quantities to some of the regular regiments, but the basic weapon of the colonial wars was always the smoothbore firelock. An exception to this generalization was the case of the Pennsylvania troops in the southern campaign of 1758. These men, coming from the region where the Pennsylvania rifle had been perfected, brought many examples of this weapon to General John Forbes' army and each carried the mold which made the special bullet suited to his individual piece. The incursion of these guns into the expedition forced the provision of a special finer grained powder, more suited to the rifle than the coarser musket powder then issued.

Once a musket had been fired, it was of use only as a club at close quarters, where there was no opportunity to reload. At some time, perhaps early in the seventeenth century, an unknown genius thought of making a knife with a handle that could be jammed into the muzzle of a musket, thus converting the weapon into a short pike. Then toward the end of the century another inventive soul put the blade on a socket which fitted around the end of the barrel instead of plugging it, and by offsetting the blade he had produced a bayonet which allowed the weapon to be loaded and fired while the blade remained in position. Throughout the period of the muzzle-loader the bayonet was a most important adjunct to the military musket and this lasted down into the days of the single-shot breech-loader. In the colonial period regular troops always had bayonets, but the colonial troops usually lacked them. With the coming of the repeating and automatic weapons of recent times the bayonet today plays primarily a psychological role and has lost most of its place as a practical weapon, except perhaps for policing civilian mobs.

The regular soldier of the 1700s carried a short sword as well as his musket and bayonet, but the sword was often discarded in colonial expeditions, while most of the militia and colonial levies never possessed one. The lower ranks of officers carried spontoons, short spears, and the sergeants somewhat similar halberds, but these were really only symbols of rank inherited from earlier days, more suitable for parade than for colonial warfare. They were usually left behind when on campaign, and the junior officers were armed with somewhat smaller and lighter models of the standard soldier's musket.

All that has been said hitherto applies primarily to the issue musket —sporting flintlocks, and this in a majority of cases would include the light muskets of the officers, were more carefully made. Misfires would be fewer and speed of ignition materially faster. A high-grade flint gun in proper shape goes off when the trigger is pulled, without any noticeable time lag, and it is a practical and relatively dependable weapon. It can be loaded and fired in a light rain if reasonable care is taken. Of course there is bound to be some time lag while the lock performs its function, but it is so slight as to be of importance only in shooting at moving game when a somewhat greater lead must be allowed. I have shot a flying duck with a flint shotgun, granted that it was accomplished only after several misses, and I have also fired both British and French flint muskets many times. Too many misconceptions have appeared in print regarding the capabilities of the flint musket. It is obvious that those who wrote had never fired one.

Cavalry was practically useless in America during this period, and we can disregard it and turn to the other major arm, the artillery, which had three main types of weapons—cannon, howitzers, and mortars. Cannon had relatively long barrels and normally fired a solid iron ball against the walls of a fort, other defensive works, or ships, and they also could discharge a load of musket balls or iron grapeshot against personnel at short range, just like great shotguns. Howitzers were short-barreled cannon which fired either a solid ball or an explosive shell over a curved trajectory or grapeshot at short range. Mortars were very short and stubby. They lobbed an explosive shell high up into the air at an angle of about forty-five degrees so that in falling it could land behind a wall or in a deep valley. The explosive shell had a fuse, the length of which determined its time of burning. The gunner estimated the time it would take the shell to reach its target and cut the fuse to the proper length to burn that long. In the French service the shell was loaded into the mortar with the fuse up, and it was lighted just before the mortar was discharged. The English usually loaded with the fuse placed so that the flame of discharge of the mortar automatically lighted it. All these guns were loaded from the muzzle and were fired by touching a lighted slow match to priming powder held in a little cuplike depression cut in the top of the breech. A flash hole led from this into the barrel at the breech and transmitted the flash of the priming to the main charge. Cannon could fire red-hot shot to set a target on fire, and howitzers and mortars used "carcasses," incendiary shells, for the same purpose.

The size of a cannon was determined by the weight of the solid iron ball which fitted into its bore with a slight clearance, perhaps one-fifth of an inch. A three-pounder had a bore of two and seven-eighths inches, a twelve pounder four and five-eighths, while a great twenty-four pounder, which might weigh up to almost three tons, had a bore five and three-quarters inches across. When used in a fort the barrel was normally mounted on a low carriage with either two or four small solid wooden or iron wheels, while a carriage for use in the field had two much larger wheels, and its trail, the rearward extension of its body, was attached to an additional wheeled affair, the limber, when the gun was to be moved. Gun and limber were normally horse-drawn, but in the American woods oxen were sometimes used. When the expedition went by water the guns would be carried in flatboats or large bateaux and manhandled over the relatively short land travel required at portages. Howitzers and mortars were classified by the diameter of their bore, six and eight inch being typical howitzer sizes, and ten and thirteen inch for mortars, although smaller ones down to four and a half inch were very useful and easy to transport. Howitzers were mounted on a regular field carriage, while mortars had a simple flat bed without wheels, and were carried in a wagon or a flatboat and skidded into place with crowbars.

These artillery pieces of the colonial period had, practically speaking, a maximum effective range of about half a mile. The extreme range, of course, was much greater, but accuracy fell off badly. When it was desired to concentrate fire in order to break down a wall, the shortest possible range was sought, say two hundred yards or even less. Then the accuracy became such that two successive shots would land in nearly the same place. The range was adjusted by elevating or depressing the barrel by means of a sliding wooden wedge for cannon and howitzer carriages. Toward the end of this period screw elevating gear had started to come into use on the lighter field pieces but was hardly yet in general use. While mortars could also be adjusted by wedges, it was more usual to set them at approximately forty-five degrees and to vary the range by increasing or decreasing the powder charge.

Bronze made the best guns. It did not rust and made a stronger although more expensive gun for the same weight than did cast iron. Light bronze guns were much favored for use in the field, while iron ones were more normal for permanent fortifications. Some authorities felt that iron guns were better able to stand up under the long continued fire necessary to breech a wall in heavy siege work, but all agreed that for use in the open field the bronze cannon had the advantage.

Colonial forts were usually of one of three kinds. The simplest and by far the quickest to build was an enclosure formed by a stockade of vertical logs. A narrow trench was dug, some three or more feet deep, logs perhaps twelve to fifteen feet long were placed in it on end and earth tamped around them. Loopholes would be cut through the logs, and barracks and storehouses constructed inside. In carefully built forts when time was sufficient the meeting faces of the logs of the stockade would be flattened to meet snuggly together so that no enemy bullet could pass between them. A fort of this sort, if efficiently defended, was quite safe, barring accidents, from any attack which did not employ artillery. Cannon, however, could make short work of the stockade, so this type was usually employed only when time pressed, or it was believed that artillery could never be brought against it. A much stronger fort was made by building walls of timber cribbing, filled with earth and faced with timber. This kind of construction furnished an excellent defense against artillery, but had the disadvantage that before many years had passed the timbers would rot out and the whole would collapse. To guard against this in important forts where expense was secondary the walls would be faced with stone. An example of the first stockaded type was George Washington's Fort Necessity, a very hurriedly built affair. Fort William Henry on Lake George was of timber and earth construction, while Fort Carillon at

Ticonderoga in its final stage was built of stone-faced earthen walls. All these frontier forts, regardless of method of construction, usually followed the same ground plan, either that of a square or of a five-pointed star, with redoubts extending out from each corner to allow flanking fire along the length of walls between the redoubts.

The operation of besieging a fort followed quite formal rules, and consisted of bringing up heavy artillery and breaking a hole through one of the walls, thus forming a breach which could be stormed. Convention decreed that, once the attacker had made such a breach, the commander of the fort had done all that he could, and might surrender without fear of censure. If the breach had to be stormed, the garrison could expect no quarter. There also of course was always the possibility that a fort could be taken completely by surprise and overwhelmed by men swarming up over the walls on scaling ladders. Unless a garrison was very small an alert commander could always be expected to prevent this happening, at least until after the defense had been softened by artillery fire. Such an assault was expensive of the assailants' lives, and was to be avoided when artillery could achieve the same result at much less cost.

The average provincial was a poor soldier. He could not well be anything else considering his background and lack of training. Farm boys, sailors, fishermen, apprentices, and the jobless, all these were what the hurriedly raised armies drew upon to a large extent. Those who led them generally had little or no military qualifications. The chief requirement for a senior officer was a good political connection and an ability to persuade men to enlist, while the junior officers had to be popular with their men, first in order to be selected for commissioned rank, and secondly in order to hold it. All the officers to a greater or lesser extent had to be somewhat subservient to the wishes of their men, and thus it was only in a very few units that any effective discipline could be maintained. In many cases the colonel of a regiment had no more real military knowledge or experience than his men; he was merely the leader in civilian life, the squire, the tavern-keeper or the merchant, translated overnight into the military leader.

Despite this there were some, possessed of sound common sense and without illusions of grandeur, who did well. As the wars continued, experience was gained and competent leaders emerged. But the problem of maintaining discipline in a summertime army of citizen volunteers always remained a difficult if not almost impossible one to solve.

The British regulars normally drew their recruits from a segment of the population probably even less desirable than that from which the provincial armies were drafted, but they enjoyed the tremendous advantage of having skilled professional officers in command, officers who had the power to enforce the sort of discipline necessary to produce a trained and efficient soldier, yet knew in most cases how to temper this power with a certain amount of kindness and understanding. The Royal American Regiment, the 60th, raised in North America but officered by a competent commissioned body, proved that Americans could be turned into excellent soldiers, if given proper leaders endowed with the power to enforce a reasonable discipline.

In actual battle the provincial soldiers could usually do quite well, but unfortunately battle then constituted an extremely small portion of a soldier's life, and, if the long intervening weeks and months were not filled with busy active days of training, road or fort building or some other similar activity, even the best of soldiers would degenerate into lazy, dirty loafers. If the officer was slack, ignorant, or slothful, so was his command, and this condition unfortunately was all too common in the colonial armies. Lord Loudoun sent a lieutenant colonel of regulars in the summer of 1756 to inspect the provincial troops stationed in the Champlain Valley. Here is part of his report. "At Fort William Henry about 2,500 men, 500 of them sick, the greatest part of them what they call poorly. They bury from five to eight daily. . . . [They are] extremely indolent and dirty, to a degree. The fort stinks enough to cause an infection, they have all their sick in it. Their camp nastier than anything I could conceive, their necessary houses, kitchens, graves and places for slaughtering cattle all mix[ed] through their encampment, a great waste of provisions, the men having just what they please, no great command kept up . . .

not in the least alert . . . no advanced picket, no scouting party out
. . . during . . . six days. . . . The people extremely indolent. . . .
The camp [at Fort Edward] much cleaner than at Fort William
Henry, but not sufficiently so to keep the men healthy."

Lest one should think this the prejudiced report of a stiff British
regular, listen to what Chaplain Gideon Hawley of the Connecticut
troops wrote in his journal while serving at William Henry this same
summer. "One of the regulars is worth 5 of our men. They are healthy
& well—and tis because they stir and are active and keep clean. . . .
I pity our sick in their tents [lying] on the ground with but one
blanket. They are dying every day . . . putrid and yellow fevers
prevail."

The sick or wounded soldier could not expect very much from the
medical service of the armies of colonial days. Normally each battalion or regiment had its surgeon and perhaps also an assistant surgeon. Hospitals were established by the armies of both countries, in
buildings where possible, but also under canvas when campaigning in
the wilderness. British regulations allowed a certain number of women,
usually about four per company, but sometimes as many as six, to accompany each regiment in the field to act both as laundresses and as
hospital nurses, and they drew regular rations. In fact women, unless
positively forbidden, accompanied armies in those days much more
than one would have thought. Many were wives of soldiers, but others
plied other vocations. The British garrison at Quebec during the winter of 1759–60 officially included 569 women, or one for every thirteen
soldiers.

In many cases the sick and wounded were cared for by the French
in hospitals staffed by nuns, but at least some military hospitals also
had male attendants. The Newburyport shipwright, Stephen Cross,
was captured at Oswego in 1756, and carried to France. He eventually
arrived in a prison hospital in Dinan, and was pleasantly surprised to
find an Englishman in charge of one of the wards. There were both
men and women attendants. Cross was issued a clean shirt and sheets,
clean in the sense that they had been freshly laundered, but already

they were infested with lice and nitts. Throughout his captivity the shipwright was treated with as much kindness and consideration as conditions allowed. At the Dinan prison he even received a small money allowance daily, which permitted him to purchase little luxuries at the prison canteen. This welcome dole had been made possible under a provision in the will of the widow of a French admiral, a resident of the vicinity.

When possible both nations provided food suitable for the sick, and the invalid soldier was apparently given as good care as was possible in the light of the medical knowledge of the day. This was very crude and limited when judged by later standards. Too often about all that could be done for a patient was to allow him to lie down and rest in the hope that a strong constitution, weakened nevertheless by bleedings, purgings, and doses of Jesuit's bark, would at last let him recover. There was, of course, no understanding of the cause of infection in wounds and little application of the rules of sanitation, which, however, were beginning to be appreciated. A bullet or a bayonet wound in the body cavity was generally considered to be mortal, and the cure for injured limbs too often was amputation. The appearance of pus, "laudable pus" they often called it, was greeted as a sign of an approaching recovery. It did mean that the infected part was at last draining and that infection was probably not spreading. Mechanical cleanliness was sought in the treatment of wounds, and drainage was encouraged, but the medical knowledge of the day had as yet no appreciation of biological cleanliness, and would have to wait another century for its coming.

Dysentery, they called it the "bloody flux," was the commonest disease of armies in the field, and by the middle of the eighteenth century it was realized, at least by some, that failure to dispose properly of excrement was the cause of its spread, although transmission of the disease through the air was the then faulty belief. Despite this knowledge, which probably was still far from widespread, it was almost impossible to make poorly disciplined troops take proper care of their latrines, even today it remains a problem in the field. Smallpox raged at times in the armies, but it was a common civilian disease, the control of which was understood, while dysentery could be more properly called a military one. Scurvy was more of a naval than a military evil, but troops wintering in forts and western posts often succumbed. It appears to have occurred more commonly among the French. By the mid 1700s its cause was realized, and the British, at least, knew that it was prevented by eating vegetables, "potatoes, radishes & carrots to prevent scurvy, the ordinary result of a diet of salt meat."

Scurvy was too often the fatal companion of military and naval expeditions of those days, when the basic food was salt meat and biscuit. When combined with scarcity as well it caused great losses. The first French garrison at Niagara was established by Denonville in 1687, and he left a force of one hundred men there that fall. After his departure it was found that much of the provisions left behind were spoiled, and it was too late in the season to plant a garden. Scurvy and famine struck the hapless garrison. Only twelve survived. A few years later it was reported that at Fort Frontenac this dread disease carried off one hundred out of a total force of one hundred and forty in the course of the winter.

The basic food of all the armies in the American wilderness was salt pork, packed in barrels in brine, and it would keep for a long time. Civilian wagoners, however, in order to lighten the loads they were hired to carry, had a shameful trick of boring a hole in a barrel with a gimlet and thus letting the brine drain out. The pork then promptly spoiled. The French, who had ample opportunity for knowledge through their captures of British supplies during the last of the wars, claimed that their own pork was of better quality than that of the British. Perhaps this was fortunate for them, for the British had other meats, while the French, practically speaking, had nothing but pork. This salt pork was not the fat belly pork we use today in baked beans, but the solid meat of the pig preserved in salt brine. When the excess salt was removed it could be quite palatable. There is at least one instance on record where troops mutinied when poor fresh beef was substituted for the usual salt pork in their ration.

The other basic staple was bread, hard ship biscuit while in the field, but often soft bread when in garrison at a fort. The French issued dried peas and wine in addition to pork and bread, but that was all, except for salt and other condiments. Very occasionally fresh beef was issued, and special rations, such as chocolate, were sometimes handed out for winter expeditions, but these were very much exceptions. New France always hovered on the edge of famine and supplies for the troops were meager and of the most simple variety. At all permanent camps and forts, and sometimes even at temporary ones, both French and British planted vegetable gardens, both to supplement their rations and to add foods which would guard against scurvy. Just what vegetables were grown cannot be said with certainty, but a colonial who was at the taking of Fort Carillon in 1759 wrote: "Cabbage is very plenty and all sorts of greens which they got in the French garden."

The British were less Spartan in their foods. They had a longer growing season and no blockade to strangle their imports from the home country. They had more fresh meat; Braddock, for example, took live beef cattle on his expedition. Regular articles of issue were salt pork and salt beef, salt codfish, oatmeal, cornmeal, beans, peas, rice, vinegar, butter, cheese, and sugar, as well as condiments such as ginger. All of these items, of course, were not available at any one time, but there generally was a fair amount of variety on major expeditions, and, when in garrison in settled regions, the troops ate well. This was not so in Canada, where scarcity was a normal condition, and the French ration was monotonous and meager. A colonial officer's Thanksgiving dinner at Fort Edward in 1759 included roast fresh pork, mutton, venison, turkey, cabbage, carrots, and plum pudding. This of course was exceptional, but it shows what could be done in the field. There is no question, however, that the basic mainstay of all the armies was salt pork, salt beef, and biscuit.

Lieutenant John Knox of the 43rd Regiment spent two rugged

winters in Nova Scotia during the last French and Indian War, and he wrote that very often a bowl of pea soup with a hunk of pork in it was the main dish of a meal. He found that the hard ship biscuits, not unlike the plain water biscuit we have today, but larger in size, when soaked in water, split in halves and then toasted, became quite palatable. When the late Nova Scotia spring brought the first greens, they became a welcome addition to the menu.

Sutlers followed British armies in the field and sold the troops liquor and various foods and supplies. They were civilian merchants, sometimes licensed to sell specified goods at prices fixed by the commanding officer, and sometimes left free to charge whatever the traffic would bear. Their wagons contained some necessities and often a surprising number of what were really luxuries, particularly to a soldier in the field. Sutlers accompanying General Forbes' 1758 expedition against Fort Duquesne sold Madeira, spirits, sugar, soap, candles, cheese, chocolate, coffee, tea, butter, condiments, tobacco, and writing paper, as well as shoes, cloaks, and blankets. They also took over the operation of the officers' messes, drawing the issue rations and charging each officer sixpence per day. Canteens at French posts and forts were operated as the perquisite of the senior officer or of the engineer in charge of construction. The prices charged the soldiers were such as to produce great profits, but such was only to be expected in Canada. The engineer at Fort Carillon at Ticonderoga, de Lotbinière, was reported to have made 100,000 livres a year out of his canteen, equivalent to perhaps $150,000 at today's values.

The French of course had to have their wine, all of which necessarily came from France to the detriment of many other desperately needed supplies. Wine seems to have been considered first in importance, and great quantities of cargo space were devoted to it. Bougainville in his journal reported the arrival of ship after ship which were essentially nothing but wine carriers. One cannot but wonder if the French might not have held Canada if they had only been willing to drink water—certainly they could have held out longer. Brandy was issued or made available to the officers, and the soldiers usually got supplies of it, although it was sometimes forbidden them.

The British and their colonials of course had beer and rum to solace their idle hours. When supplies of their drinks ran out, as they often did, both nations had recourse to spruce beer, which not only was considered an effective remedy against scurvy, but was also a not unpleasant drink. The soldiers of those days preferred almost anything to being reduced to drinking water, an awful fate. Spruce beer was made by boiling the tips and small branches of the spruce tree until they started to disintegrate, then they were skimmed off and molasses added to the remaining liquid. When the solution had cooled, yeast was put in and nature allowed to take its course for a few days. Oddly enough, the resulting brew not only smells like beer, but tastes like it, not a very good beer perhaps, but undoubtedly beer, and it pleasantly warms the stomach of one who drinks it. I know, because I made some from a recipe recorded by General Amherst in his journal. The British issued molasses for making spruce beer, and penalties were decreed for using it for any other purpose.

Such were the usual foods of the soldiers of colonial America. There were, of course, some variations. Game was often obtained, but usually in small quantities only. The French indulged in fishing to supplement their ration, but apparently without much success. Salt cod was sometimes issued to them in times of scarcity. New France existed in a state but little short of famine, not growing enough food to support itself and its garrison of regulars. In time of war the British Navy did its best to minimize the flow of supplies from the home country and to prevent avaricious New Englanders from smuggling flour and other foodstuffs into Canadian ports.

Troops of the regular armies of both nations wore the normal uniform of their country, modified sometimes by substitutes adopted to meet shortages, such as the Indian moccasin. When uniforms wore out, they often could not be replaced and had to be patched with what came to hand. Sometimes the skirts of a jacket would be cut off and used as patching material, and trouser overalls made of sailcloth or bed ticking might be used at times. One piece of clothing developed by the Indians was worn very generally by both armies. This was the "mitasse," a legging formed by a tube of coarse woolen cloth pulled over the leg and extending up above the knee. It was made very loose, and the slack was folded around the leg and the whole lashed in place by garters at knee and ankle. A pair of "mitasses" furnished better protection to the legs in the wilds of North America than did the lighter European leggings, and they were much warmer in cold weather. Woolen greatcoats were issued to the French troops in winter, probably much like the Canadian blanket coat of today, and British troops had an outer garment called "watch coat," originally a special overcoat for sentinels, but later issued to all soldiers in cold climates.

Provincial regiments usually were supposed to be uniformed, but there is little information available on this subject, and, except for a few instances, one must resort to conjecture as to how these soldiers were dressed. Colonel Frye's Massachusetts regiment, which was captured at Fort William Henry in 1757, was ordered by the General Court to be outfitted with blue coats, the lapels faced in red. Presumably they wore their own breeches of leather or homespun. Two years previously some of General William Johnson's men had worn a similar uniform at the Lake George battle. Colonel Peter Schuyler's New Jersey regiment of the same period was known as the Jersey "Blues" because of its uniforms. George Washington's 1st Virginia in the 1758 expedition against Fort Duquesne was dressed in rifle shirts, a long garment, not unlike a dressing gown, probably of coarse linen but possibly of deerskin, reaching almost to the knees, overlapping in front, and held in place by a belt or sash. The men wore breechclouts and long leggings, probably of green cloth, as such was what Washington ordered, with white as an alternative. The Pennsylvania troops had short green coats with green lapels, probably of a different shade, while the North Carolina regiment had no uniform at all. Colonel Henry Bouquet, second in command of the expedition, advocated "making Indians of part of our provincial soldiers. . . . It would only be necessary for them to remove their coats and breeches, which would delight them; give them moccasins and blankets; cut off their hair and daub them with paint and intermingle them with the real Indians." The French, both officers and men, when on the frontier, at times also dressed as Indians.

A soldier in colonial days was not overburdened with clothing. A French regular arriving in Canada in 1755 was given a coat, a sleeved vest, often worn as an outer garment, breeches, hat, three shirts, a pair of gaiters, two pairs of shoes, two pairs of socks, a black stock and two spare soles. Sometimes he only got the leather for the shoes and had to pay for having them made up. He also was issued a blanket, a haversack, knife, fork and spoon, and a wooden comb, as well as an awl, some thread and six needles. For a razor he had the use of one of the five issued to every company of sixty men. There is no record of any sort of individual mess kit, probably the soldier was expected to eat out of a common pot, several of which were allotted to each company. At times underclothes are mentioned, but often not. Musket, sword and other accouterments of course were also issued. In the field tents or tarpaulins were generally available, and the French soldier often got a bearskin for extra bedding in cold weather. He also was sometimes given cloth out of which to make mittens.

Whether the British soldier fared better I cannot say, but nearly a hundred years later he was issued only coat, trousers and a pair of boots once a year, a cap every other year, and he had to buy the rest of his clothing through stoppages out of his meager pay. The colonial soldier received very little indeed. In 1755 Massachusetts expected each volunteer to bring his own gun, allowed a small bonus for so doing, and gave him a blanket. Two years later men were encouraged to enlist by a bounty of a blanket, a coat and a "soldier's hat," while in 1758 only the blanket was given, but with the sum of thirty shillings allowed each man to provide his own clothing.

Militia, practically speaking, never had uniforms, save perhaps for some of their officers, but turned out in everyday clothes, and surely not their best. This would also have been true for many of the provincial troops, particularly in the earlier times. One probably will not be far wrong if he thinks of all troops in colonial days, except for the regulars and a few provincial regiments, as being dressed in shabby, dirty, and worn civilian clothing, with an old rusty musket, long discarded as too obsolete or worn out for use in Europe, and no bayonet. A powder horn, a cloth or leather bullet pouch, and a blanket would have completed his equipment, although a few of the men would have carried a frying pan or a kettle of some sort slung on their muskets.

We tend to visualize the British soldier as a majestic being clad in scarlet, his crossbelts bright with pipe clay and his buttons flashing in the sun. Let Lieutenant Knox tell us what some of them really looked like in Nova Scotia in 1758. They ". . . made as droll and grotesque an appearance as a detachment of Hungarian or Croatian irregulars, occasioned by the length of their beards, the disordered shape of their hats, and the raggedness of their party-coloured cloathing; for some had brown, others blue watch-coats [buckled around their waists with a cartouch-box strap] and some were in their threadbear uniforms; in short they had very little of the British regular about them . . ." This was certainly an extreme case, but a soldier on campaign never looks the way the regulations expect, be he in the forests of North America in 1758 or the mountains of Italy in 1945.

Chapter VIII

THE FARM BOYS TAKE LOUISBOURG

U<small>NDER</small> the Treaty of Utrecht in 1713 France lost Acadia and Newfoundland, the gateway to the St. Lawrence and Quebec. Moreover the ports and shore stations necessary to the successful conduct of the cod fisheries came into British hands. The French realized that something must be done at once to make safe the sea approach to New France and to preserve the very important fisheries. Only Cape Breton—save a few little islands—remained in their hands in this region, but it occupied a most strategic position, jutting out into the Atlantic and guarding the mouth of the St. Lawrence while at the same time threatening New England's trade routes to the old country.

The French at once started a search for the best port on the island, and, after exploring several sites, selected the place then called Havre à l'Anglais, English Harbor. Work was promptly begun, fisherfolk from Newfoundland were transported to the island, and a few Acadians left their old homes in British hands and migrated to the new colony. In the fall of 1713 the future stronghold of Louisbourg was founded. Its population was but a little over a hundred souls. They had four small fishing craft, a half-dozen cannon and inadequate supplies for the coming winter. They managed to throw together shelters of a sort and survived the bitter season, although scurvy took its toll.

The little settlement grew rapidly. In 1715 it had a population of more than seven hundred, not counting the soldiers in the garrison, and a visitor of that year reported seeing forty merchant craft and six men-of-war at anchor in the harbor at one time. Many of the officials, including the governor, were engaged in fishing operations on the side, but this was soon forbidden, despite which the practice continued. Merchants moved in, and active trade soon developed. During the early days the garrison averaged perhaps five hundred, and the soldiers worked at building the fortifications, receiving additional pay for their labor.

The defenses of the citadel progressed but slowly, and in 1718 the construction work was auctioned off to competing contractors, the bidding being by "extinction of candle." In this procedure a short stub of a candle was lighted and the bidding started. The winning bid was the last made before the candle went out. It was years before the fortifications were completed, so great was their extent. By 1726 the civil population was nearly one thousand, and other little settlements on the island together contained nearly twice as many more, although these were merely unfortified fishing stations.

Somewhat before 1740 the great fortress was practically complete, the civil population was about fifteen hundred, and the town covered fifty acres of land inside the walls. Many of the houses were only one story in height, but the citadel and the hospital were both large and handsome buildings. A considerable number of farms had been settled around the outskirts of the town, and there were a few houses just outside the walls.

Despite the vast importance of the place, the number of the troops forming the garrison was inadequate, their quality was poor, and sufficient cannon were lacking. The fortifications nevertheless were of great size and strength. In 1744 there were 116 cannon in place, some of them great 36-pounders, and a garrison of about seven hundred men. An additional defense was the weather, said by some visitors to be the most unpleasant in all North America. The ice pack often did not allow access to the harbor until early May, and then there were fogs that might last for weeks on end.

New England's trade with Louisbourg was large, although almost all of it was illicit, but with hungry Frenchmen on one side and greedy Yankee traders on the other the law was certain to be flouted. Some of the leading merchants of Boston engaged in exporting food-stuffs to Cape Breton Island, even during wartime, and the French authorities encouraged them surreptitiously. Flour and axheads seem to have been most wanted by the French, while they gave in return salt cod, coal and some furs. Smuggling between French and British possessions was quite general throughout the period of the French and Indian Wars, and there evidently was many an Englishman who thought more of profits than of patriotism. Rhode Islanders were per-haps the worst offenders, smuggling goods to the French islands in the West Indies, but they had plenty of company. There is even record of British ships, operating from home waters, obtaining licenses from Paris to carry supplies to Canada while the two countries were formally at war.

The Strait of Canso separates Cape Breton Island—Isle Royale to the French—from Nova Scotia, and near the southern end the British established a fishing station which, by the 1740s was defended by a little blockhouse and somewhat more than one hundred soldiers. News of the outbreak of King George's War reached Louisbourg early in May, 1744, a month before it was known in Boston. The French at once pounced on the little fishing port with a force much greater than that of its defenders and captured it without bloodshed.

John Bradstreet, whom we shall meet again several times at criti-cal moments during the next dozen years, was then an officer in the Canso garrison. He owned a little schooner and apparently engaged in trade or fishing in his off moments, in the course of which he some-times visited Louisbourg. He was captured at the surrender, taken to Louisbourg, held there for a while and then paroled to Boston, where, he claimed, he first gave Governor William Shirley of Massachusetts the idea of seizing the French citadel. This seems rather unlikely for Shirley's active and fertile mind must already have considered the possibility of such an attempt. Bradstreet, however, was certainly able to give the governor much detailed information as to conditions exist-ing in the French fortress, information of great value. Another contender for the origination of the idea was William Vaughn, a great lumber king of Maine. Whether or not he first suggested the plan we do not know, but he certainly did much to secure its adoption, went along on the expedition as a volunteer and did well. Shirley, however, was unquestionably the man who deserves the credit for planning the expedition and getting it started on its way.

The success at Canso inspired the French to make another attempt on Annapolis Royal that summer. They invested the place and made some halfhearted attacks. The local Acadians were called upon for aid, but they refused to act openly, although they gave some undercover assistance. Colonel Mascarene, despite his small force, made a good defense which, aided by the arrival of a few reinforcements sent by Shirley when he learned of the outbreak of war, finally caused the French to give up and withdraw their forces. These attacks on Canso and Annapolis Royal drew New England's attention to the threat from the north and probably were the major causes which led to the colonists' assault on Cape Breton Island.

Early in January, 1745, Shirley asked the Massachusetts General Court to take an oath of secrecy, and then informed them of his scheme for attacking Louisbourg. The representatives showed no enthusiasm and voted against taking action, but a week or two later reconsidered the matter, largely because of a merchant's petition initiated by Vaughn, and voted approval by a very narrow margin. The secret of course had leaked out despite all promises. Several Frenchmen had been clapped into the Boston jail to prevent their getting word to Louisbourg of what was brewing, and one of them reported to the others that he had heard some members of the General Court talking freely about the expedition at the Royal Exchange Tavern. One of these Frenchmen was involved in a scheme to send two sailing vessels to Louisbourg, laden with flour and the news. This apparently was arranged through the connivance of a prominent Boston merchant who was not above picking up a dishonest dollar, war or no war. Despite an embargo on all shipping ordered by the governor the ships got away successfully, and Louisbourg was warned.

Shirley acted promptly, and the whole expedition was planned, organized and equipped in a surprisingly short time. It consisted solely of New England troops, for the more southern colonies, not exposed to the threats from the northeast, offered only excuses. Massachusetts, which then included Maine, sent 3300 men, Connecticut 516, and New Hampshire 454. Rhode Island sent a few men, but only after the fortress had fallen. The command was given to William Pepperrell of Kittery Point in Maine, whose only qualifications were a successful career as a great merchant, as a politician and as a militia officer, good sense, good will, and very considerable popularity, not bad assets for the commander of an army of citizen soldiers. Hardly a man in the whole expedition possessed any real military experience beyond that of the occasional muster day of the militia, and the officers knew little more than did the men. Never did so callow an army nor so undisciplined a one sail away to assail a great fortress, but fortunately it turned out that the defenders of Louisbourg were just as lacking in knowledge of warfare. Neither the French commander nor any of his officers had ever seen an action.

Shirley gave Pepperrell a lengthy letter of detailed instructions, many utterly impossible of execution. The Massachusetts governor obviously had a great deal of information about Louisbourg and its defenses, and he also had the good sense to realize that his precise instructions might be found impractical. So, in effect, he gave Pepperrell authority to use his discretion, directing him, however, to consult with his council of senior officers should unforeseen emergencies arise.

For once in colonial history an expedition got away on time, in fact too early, for the little fleet had to wait at Canso for the ice fields around Louisbourg to break up. The volunteers—we can hardly call them soldiers—were stowed away in a fleet of little fishing sloops and trading schooners, the first time the great majority of them had ever been on salt water. It was March, the sea was rough, and they did not like it.

Seth Pomeroy was a gunsmith of Northampton, Massachusetts. We shall meet him again in the last French war, but in late March of 1745 he was a very seasick major. "From Fryday till this day which was Tuesday [I had] nothing to eat or drink that I had any appetite to . . . sick day & night so bad that I have not words to set it forth, nor can I give anybody an idea of it that hath not felt the same thing." Another unhappy soldier reported that their "vessel was a very hospital, wee were all sick . . . [It stormed] so that we could not be upon deck . . . but was shut down in the hold; and a long dark and teadious night wee had." What appeared to be a French privateer appeared, "but we was so sick . . . that being taken seem'd no great matter."

The little transports were escorted by a dozen provincial warships, and after a miserable trip through a howling northeaster reached Canso after a dozen days of suffering. How good the solid ground must have felt to those farm boys and apprentices as they staggered ashore and again breathed clean fresh air, so different from that of the stinking ship holds they had just left! For over three weeks the army was held at Canso waiting for the ice to break up at Louisbourg. The time was devoted to attempts at organizing the various little companies into regiments and to drilling the raw recruits, to open-air preachings and to plain loafing and time-killing.

Rum and molasses ran short, but the providential capture of two French merchantmen remedied this painful situation. Once the army reached Cape Breton Island and the blockade had been established, the flow of supplies from Boston came through without difficulty, only powder and shot being sometimes in short supply. At first the only food was salt pork and hard bread, but, early in June, Seth Pomeroy reported his first meal of boiled greens, probably fiddlehead ferns, and he very evidently enjoyed it.

Shirley had sometime previously asked London for naval aid to protect the fisheries and Commodore Peter Warren on the West Indies station was directed by the Admiralty to concert with Shirley in measures to annoy the enemy. Warren could easily stretch this into supporting an assault on Louisbourg, and accordingly he brought his

squadron north to guard the rear of the land forces and their line of
supply. The commodore owned large tracts of land in the Mohawk
Valley and was an uncle of William Johnson. Warren's four warships furnished the little colonial navy a reinforcement which removed
all risk of the French making trouble at sea in the Cape Breton region,
at least for some time to come. Pepperrell was a civilian colonial soldier
without real military experience, and Warren was a British naval
officer who had spent a lifetime at sea. One might well expect the two
to clash, but on the contrary these two most contrasting personalities
were to work in almost complete harmony and with mutual regard
and respect throughout the campaign.

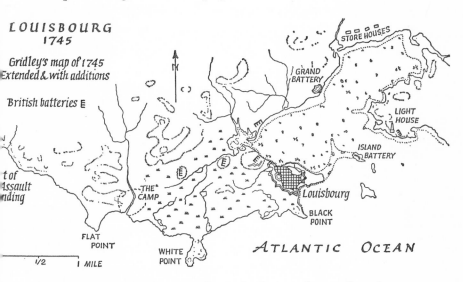

A neck of land encloses Louisbourg harbor on the south and west,
and on this peninsula the town had been built, defended on the
land approach by huge earthworks with a great stone bastion in the
center. On the mainland directly opposite to the narrow entrance
to the harbor there was a mighty battery of twenty-eight heavy 36-
pound cannon, really a complete fort in itself, while on an island a
short way inside the entrance stood an additional battery. No ship
could enter until these guns were silenced, and the land defenses
were such as would require formal siege operations of considerable

magnitude before they could be breached. As against these advantages was the fact that the great battery of 36-pounders, known to the colonials as the Grand Battery, was in the process of being modified, and the defenses in its rear had been partly torn down to make way for new construction.

The peninsula jutted out from land which was mostly a great marsh, making the approach to the town from that direction extremely difficult. Except for the harbor entrance the coast was rugged and rocky, lashed for days on end by heavy surf. Once troops and a train of siege artillery had managed to secure a landhold, they still had to face the problem of the great morass, which prevented the besieging cannon from coming within practical range of the defenses of the town. Add to this the fogs, the ice packs of early spring, and the possibility, even the certainty, of French warships arriving, one can see how very difficult and daring the operation of capturing this fortress would be. Shirley's hope of taking this French citadel of North America with an army of untrained volunteers verged on the fantastic. Parkman was certainly right when he referred to the project as "a mad scheme."

The great fleet of little transports arrived without incident on the last day of April at Gabarus Bay, a little to the west of Louisbourg. The French commander, Du Chambon, sent an inadequate force to oppose the landing, which had to be made through heavy surf onto a rocky coast. Several boatloads of colonials headed for a point on the shore to which the French rushed to prevent their landing. The real attempt was then made by about one hundred men at a point two miles farther west.

They were safely ashore before the Frenchmen appreciated the ruse and arrived, panting and exhausted, on the scene. One of the landing party later wrote in his diary: "About 100 of the French com to hender our design we had but a small schurmidg to what we expected 3 of our men wound 3 of thers found ded 12 of them was tok 4 cows 23 houses they set on fire with out the walls and sunk there vessels. . . . These scoundrel French dogs they dare not stay to fite but set there houses on fire and so ran into the city by the light [of the burning houses]."

The way was now clear for the main force to pour ashore. Half of them were off the ships by nightfall, the rest following the next day. Chaos reigned, and much of the undisciplined horde evaporated to the four winds, bent on loot and plunder. "Many . . . went . . . to plunder (and indeed! wee fill'd the country for as yet, wee had no particular orders, but everyone did what was right in his own eyes) among which I was one." Another diary, written on rough paper in an unformed hand, records: "We killed several cows and took several more som horses sheep and other suitable things for our casses rum wine molasses sider etc. but these things was soon sceyrse again. . . . We found severl of their camps fild with all sorts of goods and we liv'd upon them fowls and sheep goats calves . . . This day we found one more camp with 2 pritty gurls in it . . ."

It must have been an almost impossible task to catch all these excited, rampaging farm boys, apprentices, and seamen, and to herd them back to make some sort of an organized attempt on the great fortress. Indeed it would seem that throughout the siege only a portion of the army was ever actively engaged at one time in operations against the enemy. Too large a part, if not on the sick list, and many were, was loafing or engaged in some sort of deviltry. Frenchmen and Indians lurked in the woods and a number of careless soldiers met trouble by straying too far from camp alone or in small parties. Reverend Jeremy Belknap, the New Hampshire historian, wrote that veterans of the expedition had in later years often laughed in his hearing at the memory of their lack of discipline and their escapades "The rear [of the army] was a scene of confusion and frolic. While some were on duty at the trenches, others were racing, wrestling, pitching quoits, firing at marks or birds, or running after shot from the enemy's guns . . ." Dr. Douglass of Boston, a contemporary historian, compared conditions at the camp to those of a Harvard commencement, notorious in those days for the disorder and horseplay of the attending crowds. During World War II our artillery officers had a saying when a lucky shot was made that "The Lord has you by the hand." It is certain that this rowdy yet earnest and God-fearing expedition against Louisbourg also had His guidance.

Despite all the excitement and confusion some kept in mind the fact that capture of the French citadel was what they had come for, and that plunder, while pleasant to acquire, did not help the main purpose. The day after the landing was completed William Vaughn, now a lieutenant colonel but without a regular command, led a force of some four hundred men through the hilly country to the north of the harbor and burned warehouses filled with naval stores which he found at the eastern end of the little bay. While returning with about a dozen men to the main camp, which had been established about a mile and a half west of the town, just out of range of the enemy's artillery, Vaughn noticed that the Grand Battery seemed suspiciously silent. He just happened to have a flask of brandy in his pocket—an eighteenth-century historian claimed that Vaughn never touched it himself; possibly so, rum was probably his drink—and with it he bribed an Indian in his party to approach the works and climb in through an embrasure. The great battery was empty, abandoned by the French for no good reason and in such haste that the only damage done was the spiking of the huge guns. This operation consisted of hammering a stout, tempered steel spike into the touchhole of the cannon as far as it would go and then breaking it off flush with the top of the barrel. The gun now could not be fired unless the spike could be punched out to clear the touchhole or a new hole drilled, a simple operation but time consuming.

Vaughn's little force ran into the battery and nailed a red coat to the flagpole. A body of French shortly moved against them in boats, but the little party of colonials held them off with musket fire until reinforcements arrived and the place was secured. This achievement was of great importance for not only did it rob the enemy of one of their major harbor defenses but it furnished Pepperrell with the heavy siege guns that he lacked. This capture was not entirely unexpected, since the plans for the expedition had foreseen the possibility and a supply of cannon balls had been brought along of the correct size to fit the French 36-pounders, which by English measure were rated as of nearly forty-two pounds.

Du Chambon in his report to the home government wrote that his council of war had voted to abandon the battery because, due to the absence of defenses in its rear, it could not be defended successfully and because its garrison of two hundred men was of more value in the main works than in this detached one. One or two of his officers had advocated blowing up the battery, but for some reason this was not done. The decision to abandon cost the French dearly, for it was their own heavy cannon that now were to breach their walls.

The army started to steady down to the work at hand, although due to one cause or another probably never more than a third to a half were ever gainfully employed at any one time. All the provisions, ordnance, and ammunition had to be manhandled ashore over the surf-drenched rocks by men soaked to their waists or higher, sliding and staggering on their slippery footing and sometimes falling in all over. One can easily imagine the confusion, the noise, the shouting and the yelp as some unfortunate farm lad got a hand pinched between the gunwale of a boat and a rocky ledge. But they got it all ashore, tired and dripping wet as they were, and then lay down on bare damp ground with only a few pine branches for a bed and a wet blanket for a cover. Even after the main camp was established there was never sufficient shelter. Tents were in short supply, but huts made of turf and of pine branches furnished some protection from the weather.

Parties of French and Indians prowled through the woods to the north and west of the camp, and it was necessary to keep scouting parties of considerable size guarding the exposed flank. The threat from that direction never came to much beyond the waylaying and scalping of a few stragglers, but the colonel of French regulars, Marin, who had taken a party of about six hundred French and Indians in another attempt against Annapolis Royal, was recalled by Du Chambon, and for a time it was feared that he would attack the exposed flank and rear of the army. His force, however, was delayed through meeting British privateers and reached the scene only after the town had changed hands.

The artillery was safely landed, some 22-pounder cannon, one 13-inch mortar and some smaller guns, but it was found impossible to move anything across the great marsh. Guns and carriages almost disappeared in the mud, and the horses that had been brought along merely floundered helplessly in the sticky mire. A solution was at last found by building great sledges of 12-inch timbers, 16 feet long and five wide. One gun at a time was placed on such a sledge, and two hundred men were harnessed to it by ropes and breast straps. Either by night or in heavy fog it was hauled over the morass, unobserved by the French gunners, the sweating men sinking in the mud to their knees, slipping, sliding, and falling underfoot. The passage of each sledge left a long trail of quagmire behind it, and the next must follow a new route. Before any gun could be put into action it had to be dragged four miles from the landing place, partly over rocky hillocks and through woods, and the rest of the way over the treacherous marsh.

Within less than a week of the first landing six guns were in action against the town from a little hill something over a mile from the nearest part of the target. The range was too great to be effective, and a few days later another battery of four guns and ten small mortars was advanced almost half a mile farther. Other batteries were put in position, the last including two of the captured French 36-pounders, each hauled into position over very rough terrain by three hundred harnessed soldiers. These guns were only about two hundred yards from their main objective, the West Gate, and they delivered an effective fire, but in turn were the target upon which the French threw everything they had. At first the battery was protected only by hogsheads filled with earth, but the fire of the enemy turned the men into energetic moles, and the guns were soon dug in and well under cover from much of the enemy's cannonading. Several men were killed there, either by cannon balls or by random musket fire—random for even at this short range the muskets of the period were too inaccurate to make aimed hits possible. Captain Sherburne, the battery commander, had an experience quite out of the ordinary. He had lain down for a bit of needed rest upon a ration chest inside a house which had somehow survived both fire and cannon shot. Suddenly he was wakened by an awful crash and found that a French cannon ball had gone through the wall of the house and right through the chest upon which he had been napping.

The French fire of course was directed almost entirely against the colonial batteries, but it was only partly effective. Many of the bombs failed to explode, and some when examined were found to be loaded only with sand and dirt. Nevertheless the fire kept the colonists busy digging deeper and repairing damage. One lucky shot disabled one of the attackers' guns by hitting it directly on the muzzle, and several other cannon were split because enthusiastic but entirely inexperienced gunners double-loaded them, a procedure almost certain to produce a burst piece. The big 13-inch mortar, in many ways Pepperrell's most effective weapon, was split by one of its shells exploding while still within the gun. Despite all this the amateur artillerymen kept pounding away at Louisbourg's defenses and gradually wore them down. They often ran out of powder, and had to suspend fire until more could be procured either on loan from the British fleet or from new supplies forwarded by Governor Shirley.

The fire of the besiegers' batteries was directed largely at the West Gate and its adjoining walls. Much of this was knocked down, but the French ventured out each night after dark and managed to repair the worst of the damage before daylight. Eventually two breaches, each almost fifty feet long, were made near this gate. Some of the colonists' fire also fell inside the town, smashing the houses of the civilian population and enfilading the streets so that the inhabitants had to remain in cellars and casemates. "Women and children [were] heard to screach and cry out in the city when our bums came amongst them." Nevertheless the civilians suffered few if any fatalities. Red-hot shot was fired into the town, and several fires were started, but they were extinguished before serious harm was done. The cannon had to cease fire many times through lack of powder or shot, but the colonists threw against the defenses of Louisbourg in the course of the entire siege some nine thousand cannon balls and six hundred explosive shells. A good average day's fire for a siege gun was a little over thirty rounds, while the great mortar might lob its 13-inch explosive shells high up into the air perhaps a score of times in the course of the day's operations.

Meanwhile the fleet blockaded the port, and in the third week of the siege had the good fortune to make a real capture, the French 64-gun ship *Vigilant*, whose name her commander failed to apply to his own actions. Approaching the fortress with the mission of getting much needed supplies ashore, he spied a little English snow and sought to capture her, but the wily Yankee skipper managed to slip away and decoy the Frenchman within range of the British fleet. After a brisk defense the *Vigilant* was captured, damaged in her masts and rigging but otherwise unhurt. Speedily repaired and furnished with a scratch British crew, she became a material addition to Warren's fleet, as she flaunted the British ensign in sight of the discomfited French. Through good luck and inattention on the part of the besiegers one or two small French vessels managed to slip into port and find safety, but their reinforcements were too meager to affect the final result.

The siege dragged on, to the vast disgust of both Pepperrell and Warren, while the latter wrote kindly if somewhat barbed notes to the commander of the land forces, urging action and offering advice, yet never in a way to offend. Throughout a difficult and somewhat irritating operation the two commanders maintained excellent cooperation and mutual understanding of the other's problems. The heavy fog often rendered communication between the land and sea forces difficult or even impossible, and of course it also hampered the operations of the artillery.

There was always the fear that naval aid from France might force the raising of the siege, for Warren's fleet was really not very powerful, and the little ships of the provincial navies were incapable of meeting real warships. About a week after the landing Pepperrell and his council of war decided upon a night assault, but, as soon as the word got around to the lower officers and the soldiers, such a protest was raised that the project was at once dropped. It certainly was a truly democratic army of vocal New Englanders, who did not hesitate to express their opinions, and the commander, popular leader that he was, was immediately responsive.

As the siege dragged on it was realized that, if it were to be expedited, the navy must be brought in to assist in the assault. The Grand Battery, the major defense of the harbor, was no longer a threat, but the Island Battery, nearer to the entrance, was a powerful one and Warren's council of captains agreed that it must be reduced before the warships could be risked near enough to the town to deliver effective fire. There appear to have been several minor attempts on this battery, which consisted of twenty-one heavy guns behind breastworks on a rocky little island only 150 yards long and about a third as wide. Near the end of the fourth week a major attempt was made. Four hundred volunteers were assembled at the Grand Battery, and boats had been dragged three miles from the landing place to this point. "The hardest service I've ever undergone" wrote one of the hauling party. The volunteers included no officers and instead elected their own leaders. To get into a proper spirit many of them apparently consumed two or three of their daily rations of a gill and a half of rum. After dark they enthusiastically rowed to their objective. Part got ashore without being discovered by the French, but then foolishly shouted rum-scented hurrahs at their accomplishment. The French awoke to their danger and promptly slaughtered many of the assailants and captured more than a hundred of the rest. The attack was a complete failure and a disgraceful one, and it was due to lack of planning and lack of command. But we must always remember that this was an army of volunteers who to a great extent "did what was right in . . . [their] own eyes," and their commanders had to accept the fact to a very considerable degree or lose their ability to command at all.

By now the siege had dragged on for almost four weeks, and, except for the capture of the Grand Battery and some material damage done to the West Gate and to the houses of the civilian population, little had apparently been accomplished. It was realized that the Island Battery must be taken or at least neutralized. Since there was little reason to believe that another assault by water would be any more successful than the last, it was decided to erect a new battery on Light House Point only a bit over a thousand yards from the island. After great labor this new battery was established on the rocky point, and its fire at once became effective, causing much trouble for the garrison on the little island.

In a situation such as the French were now in, closely assailed by artillery which was systematically breaking down their defensive works, the military doctrine of the day called for a sortie to destroy or at least spike the guns of the attackers' batteries. Partly through lack of men—Bigot later wrote that there were only 1262 men to man defenses which needed at least 3000—and partly through lack of confidence in the troops, for they had mutinied only the previous fall, Du Chambon failed to take such action. He proposed a sortie to the council of war, but was voted down. One of his subordinate officers, however, executed a daring feat which, fortunately for the colonists, ended in failure.

Lavallière de Beaubassin, formerly an ensign of the Louisbourg troops, secured permission to lead an expedition of about a hundred men out of the harbor in longboats and around eastward to the little settlement of Lorembec. The party landed there and attempted to get at the rear of the colonials on Light House Point. The latter, however, were on the alert, and the attempt failed. The French believed that the security of the English main camp was poor. In fact one of Beaubassin's officers had penetrated into one of the huts of the camp and brought away a large kettle as a souvenir. An attempt to burn the colonists' supply dumps seemed worth trying, so the party swung

north and then west through the woods, at last arriving west of
Gabarus Bay, but only after losing some of its number in a skirmish
with colonial scouting parties. Then, with success almost in his grasp,
Beaubassin was foiled. One of his men deserted to the enemy and
warned them of the coming attempt. Beaubassin led the remnants of
his party back, now and then fighting little rear-guard actions with
pursuing colonial soldiers. At last he regained Louisbourg, wounded
and with only about a dozen of his followers.

Toward the middle of June the Island Battery was practically out
of action. It was now the sixth week of the siege and the way at last
seemed clear for a joint assault by both land and sea forces. Warren
had meanwhile been reinforced by more warships, and there was now
little fear of the French being able to raise the blockade. Conditions
inside the town had become almost impossible, the civilian population
cowering underground, and supplies running short. The powder was
practically all expended, only enough remaining for some three shots
per gun, and there was nothing for Du Chambon to do but surrender.
This he did on the fifteenth of June and he was granted generous
terms, which, however, did not please the New Englanders, still hope-
ful of plunder. "They came to termes for us to enter the sitte and
poore terms they be two," so a disgruntled and disgusted soldier wrote
in his diary. The British Navy through its captures enjoyed large
amounts of prize money, but the army got none of this. Months after
the surrender there was a distribution of so-called "plunder money,"
and, since Seth Pomeroy, a major, got only a bit of £8, it is obvious
that a private soldier got little indeed.

There was one man who wanted something other than loot, and
he was the oldest man in the entire expedition, Parson Samuel
Moody, Pepperrell's chaplain and a tough, despotic and fanatical old
fellow of seventy years. He was the minister of York, Maine, and he
was accustomed to having his way and usually got it, by force if
necessary. Moody was a zealot of the old Puritan school and what he
wanted was the destruction of the images and altar of the Louisbourg
church. He is said to have taken along a special ax for this purpose,

and after the occupation of the town was seen hacking away to his heart's content.

The rewards to the leaders were generous. Pepperrell was made a baronet, and he and Shirley were each given a regiment, source of ample pay and perquisites. Commodore Warren was made an admiral and is said to have refused an offered baronetcy.

Considering the magnitude and the difficulties of the operation, the losses in men on both sides were surprisingly few. The colonists had about 130 deaths in all, while the French reported 50 killed and 95 wounded. The besieging forces had many laid low by camp diseases, chiefly dysentery. At one time some 1500 were on the sick list, and the camp was really one great hospital, but almost all recovered.

The English evacuated the French soldiers, but kept the French flag flying, and several unsuspecting ships came into harbor to add to the Navy's prize money. The army now became the garrison for the town, an unhappy garrison which liked neither the climate, the duty nor the lack of diversions in the dismal, battered place. Disease rode rampant among the soldiers. Dr. Douglass recorded that "putrid fevers and dysenteries [broke out], which at length in August became contagious, and the people died like rotten sheep." In the course of that fall of 1745 and the following winter nearly a thousand New Englanders died and were buried in the soil of Cape Breton Island. In the spring of 1746 British regulars took over and the colonists who had survived the siege and disease at last got home again.

After peace was signed the great fortress was returned to the French, who at once rebuilt it and made it stronger than ever. Thus New England's great efforts and her immense expenditure of funds seemed wasted. The money, however, eventually was refunded by England, and Boston saw over two hundred chests of coin trundled through its narrow streets. This money was used to re-establish the devalued currency and thus restore Massachusetts finances to a sound basis. This wise expenditure was the result of the activities and urgings of Thomas Hutchinson of Boston, who, save for General Thomas Gage, was to be Massachusetts' last royal governor.

The Louisbourg expedition achieved something else beyond the
capture of that great citadel and the removal for a time of the threat
to New England from the northeast. It gave the Yankee colonists
confidence in their own abilities, and it was a training ground for
the leaders of the two wars yet to come, the last French war and the
Revolution. Some, like Seth Pomeroy and John Bradstreet, were already officers and leaders, but there were also many youngsters who
here got their first taste of war, and soon would furnish the leadership
the colonies would need. For example take Seth Turner of Wey-
mouth on Massachusetts Bay, in 1745 a simple youth of eighteen
years. Later he made a successful career in his everyday life as farmer
and merchant, but he turned out whenever there was need for volunteers. He marched as a sergeant to the relief of Fort William Henry
in 1757, was a trusted lieutenant the next year on Bradstreet's expedition against Frontenac, was present when Wolfe scaled the
heights of the Plains of Abraham, was a captain at the siege of Boston
in the Revolution, a major in Washington's army, and finally a colonel. Such was the history of many a colonial who eventually was to
form part of the backbone of Washington's command.

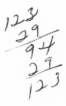

Chapter IX

DIVIDED CONTINENT

Not only was our continent divided in two by the great mountain mass, but equally sharply was it divided into two violently different civilizations.

To the east and south stretched the British colonies, each almost an independent and self-sufficient little nation, in theory tied to Britain and ruled by royal governors sent out from the mother country, but actually left relatively alone to work out its own salvation. Laws and regulations were decreed by London from time to time, but often they were flouted or given only lip service. There was no union of any sort among the various colonies other than that resulting from the fact that they had a relatively common origin and owed their allegiance to and had much of their trade with the same European power. Each colony had its special interests and problems, and attempted to meet them in its own way without outside help. Only when it came to defensive action against French and Indian inroads did some of the colonies share a common cause, and one vital enough to lead them to band together for military action. Even this was only temporary, assumed to meet the immediate need, but dropped once the emergency was over.

The French threat of course was greatest to northern New England and New York, while it was practically nonexistent to Rhode Island and New Jersey. Farther to the south Pennsylvania suffered under an assembly that would do little or nothing to guard its frontiers, but Virginia took care of her own. Naturally the southern colonies had little or no interest in what happened in New York or Maine. On the other hand Connecticut, almost completely protected by Massachusetts and New York, on occasion sent some of its troops to garrison Massachusetts forts in the Connecticut Valley.

One then should think of the British colonies during the first half of the eighteenth century as a group of nearly independent little republics, owing allegiance to a common overlord, who to a large extent left them to their own devices. The colonies were friendly to one another, had many common bonds and interests, and from time to time engaged in co-operative ventures, but there were no formal ties. To a large extent, except for protection of their merchant vessels at sea and a market for their exports, the colonies asked nothing of Britain but to be left alone to follow their own fortunes. Each had a representative assembly which made its laws, subject to the approval of London, assessed its taxes, and allocated its expenditures.

North and west of the mountains lay a vastly different land, an autocracy minutely and rigidly ruled by a despot, the King of France. There was not the slightest vestige of self-government, officials appointed by the King carried out his policies and directives regardless of the wishes of the inhabitants. Canada was a colony built on a feudal base, the land held by seigneurs and leased out to tenants, though the actual system was very different from that which then existed in France. The Canadian tenant lived a far happier life than did the wretched peasant of the homeland. The Canadian never thought of himself as a peasant but called himself a habitant. In practice, beyond paying a quite moderate rent to his landlord, he led a life essentially free. In theory he was subject to the *corvée,* the requirement that he give a certain number of days of service to his feudal proprietor, but this appears often to have been waived or leniently applied. The habitant could fish and hunt to his heart's content, a pleasure and source of food entirely forbidden to the peasant across the seas.

There was, of course, an upper class in New France—the noblesse they called it—but it was not at all a nobility by modern definition.

Nor did it correspond to the class which existed in the homeland under the same name, although there was much in common. Gentry is perhaps the best English word to describe this class, which sprang from three main sources—officers of the Carignan Regiment who had settled in Canada, government officials, and successful merchants and traders. The seigneur of a manor might be of the noblesse, but might also have sprung from very humble sources. Additional patents of noblesse were granted by the King from time to time, many of them as rewards to successful officers. Even in France, rigid as the social system was, favored plebeians could hope to receive a patent giving entrance into the favored class. In the home country title went with the land, but not in Canada. Probably half of the seigneurs were not members of the noblesse, and many drew little rent from their lands, were poor and enjoyed a prosperity but little better than that of their tenants. A seigneur had no more say in government than did his tenants and except for possibly holding court to hear petty cases, he had no inherent official standing. Many of the rich seigneuries were held by the Catholic Church; that of Montreal, for instance, belonged to the Sulpicians.

While in the British colonies religion was divided into many sects, each by this time free to worship as it wished, Canada had a state religion, the Roman Catholic, whose power was great in the land. We have heard much of the kill-joy rules of the New England Puritans, which actually were self-assumed and had been greatly eased by the eighteenth century, but little has been said of the equally rigid rules Canadian bishops attempted to enforce. Secular books were sometimes seized and destroyed, mixed dancing was forbidden, and theatrical performances were banned. There was much opposition to these restrictions and they of course could never be completely enforced, but the Canadian clergy in the latter years of the seventeenth century attempted quite as Puritanical a rule as did any New England divine. Moreover they had a powerful weapon not available to the clergy of the Protestant colonies—refusal of the sacraments and excommunication. These weapons were sometimes used by the Catholic Church in purely secular matters, as for example when a bishop, believing that a captain was cheating the men of his company of part of their pay, threatened excommunication.

Letters from Canadian governors to Paris reveal a constant succession of petty little squabbles, matters that in New England would have been squelched by the village selectmen. The French governor solemnly referred them all to his minister, some for information, but others for a ruling from the King. One man sat above his proper place in church, another wrote "esquire" after his name when he was only the son of a lawyer, or a soldier failed to salute his officer. Silly little matters were solemnly reported to Paris, covering page after page of the official reports. One, however, has only to read St. Simon's story of life at the French Court at this period to realize that pettiness did not all arise in the New World.

New France was governed by two chief executives, who usually were at loggerheads with each other. The governor, commonly a naval officer since the colony was under the jurisdiction of the Ministry of Marine, was the official head, yet his real powers consisted only of command of military operations and of dealings with the Indians. The intendant possessed all other economic, executive and police powers. There was a council, initially presided over by the governor, but in later years operated under the intendant with the governor seldom present. It consisted in the early 1700s of the intendant, the bishop, and a dozen councilors appointed by the King. The council saw to it that the King's orders were carried out, issued decrees, and, as the final court, gave judgment in civil and criminal cases which came before it. Although it was the high court of Canada, many of the cases it heard were trifling.

New France lived under a completely arbitrary government, one not of laws but of the will and the whims of an absolute monarch. No one whosoever had any voice or vote, even the highest officials had merely to execute the orders they were given. This, of course, did not result in all the King's wishes being carried out; time and space worked against this, and it was impossible with the means at hand to enforce unpalatable orders throughout the colony. In theory little latitude was allowed the Canadian officials, but the time required to report an action to Paris and to receive approval or condemnation was so great, often well over half a year, that a governor or intendant at times might indulge in considerable discretion.

Despite laws and ordinances a Frenchman could always be practical and let common sense outweigh the regulations. At Chambly on the Richelieu River there once was a dog who had a dog friend at the post of La Prairie, a dozen miles away and just across the St. Lawrence from Montreal. So the Chambly dog used to visit his friend at La Prairie at frequent intervals. This was soon discovered and the dog was promptly turned into a postman, carrying letters tied to his collar every time he made the trip. Moreover he was put on the roll call of the fort and issued an official ration.

The intendant held a position of great power, and he was in effect a spy over the actions of the governor, reporting in detail directly to Paris. He usually was of the lawyer class, that middle class that produced the professionals who carried on the business of government, while the noblesse played. Expenditure of public money was under his control, and his orders covered a broad field. Regulations of inns, the sale of liquor, weights and measures, value of coins, building of churches, road construction and the sweeping of chimneys, all these activities and many more were under his direction. The intendant was the real ruler of New France; the governor, save when military operations were under way, was largely a figurehead. The intendant's opportunities for graft and peculation were immense, as was shown when Bigot, a capable and utterly unscrupulous man, held the post. He was the last intendant of Canada, and the gang of thieves which operated under his protecting wing did much to speed the fall of the unfortunate colony.

Graft had been rampant in New France long before Bigot and his machine commenced their terribly effective exploitation of the land. Governors came out from France hoping to restore their fallen fortunes, and the fur trade offered ample possibilities. Canada was a country of high prices and a devalued currency. Officers coming from home found that they could not live on their pay, and they were practically forced to secure additional funds in order to exist. Thus graft and peculation became accepted as normal among the great majority of Canadian officials.

There were many ways of securing some of the King's money, even if one were not a member of the lucky few who enjoyed positions which favored illicit gain. An officer might, for instance, draw full-strength rations for his diminished company, and sell the excess. Should an inspector by chance appear, spare soldiers could be borrowed from a neighboring company or any handy *coureur de bois* or trader could be shoved into the ranks to pass a muster. Perhaps he commanded a post in the west, then he could sell to the Indians the trade goods sent from France as gifts of the King. One intendant was refused sufficient baggage stowage on the warship assigned to take him to Canada because the captain had filled the hold with wine and brandy he was taking to Quebec on his private account. Graft, peculation, and thievery were common and accepted by Canadians as something to be taken for granted. Officers of the regular troops who came to Canada with Montcalm were shocked by the extent and the amount of these irregularities. One of them recorded in his journal that the Grand Vicar of Canada told him that most penitents at the confessional believed that stealing from the King was only a peccadillo, and that the King every Easter made them a present of what they had stolen during the previous twelve months. New France had always been a drain on the mother country. Its exports never covered its expenses, and as the graft increased over the years this deficit became much greater. Bigot and his evil crew carried their thievery to so great an extent that the financial drain could no longer be endured, and New France, had it not been lost in war, might well have been abandoned by the mother country and left to its own resources.

Education was sadly lacking in New France. To be sure a real center of learning had been established by the Jesuits at Quebec, but

only a few were able to attend the institution. There was also a
seminary and a college at Montreal. Such education as existed beyond the very elemental was primarily designed to train for the priest-
hood. Few Canadians could read, probably only one in about five
hundred, but they did not feel the lack of this ability for there were
no newspapers, no printing press, and practically no books other than
those of a religious nature. A report of 1737 stated that most of the
children of officers and of the gentry could scarcely read or write, and
that they were ignorant of the first elements of geography and history. Even in Montreal, it stated, only the rudiments of grammar were
taught.

In New England almost every man could at least sign his name,
and reading was required to be taught in every town in Massachusetts. Inventories of New England estates of the less well-to-do show
that many owned a surprising number of books in the early 1700s.
Education was perhaps not so far advanced in the other colonies, but
it certainly exceeded that provided the average Canadian.

During the last of the colonial wars Canada had three kinds of
soldiers in addition to her Indian allies—militia, the Canadian regulars of La Marine Regiment, and French soldiers of the regular army.
In each parish a captain of militia was appointed, responsible for
the local company. When the militia was called out, little bands of
ill-equipped and untrained men appeared, and it was necessary to
organize them into some sort of battalion or brigade before they could
be of any use at all. Like all untrained militia, that of New France
proved to be of dubious value.

The colony's regular army consisted of twenty-eight companies of
La Marine Regiment, stationed in various parts of the country in
company units, and sometimes even in lesser strength. The companies
were small, averaging perhaps thirty men and there was no higher
organization. Each of the three major centers, Quebec, Montreal, and
Three Rivers, had a major stationed there, and a few of the western
posts had one. The major took over command of the units of La
Marine stationed at his post. When the soldiers took the field, an

extemporized organization was established. Governor Vaudreuil in the 1750s tried to introduce a permanent assignment of the companies to battalions, but Paris refused to permit the innovation.

While in theory the soldiers of this regiment were supposed to be competent professionals, actually they were far from it, recruited as they often were from the slums of Europe. Governor de la Jonquière wrote home to the Minister of Marine in 1750 that the recently arrived recruits for La Marine were "cripples from birth, men 60–70 years old . . . married men with women and children, foreigners . . . mostly Spanish who neither speak nor understand French, rogues and scoundrels who should be in the gallies." A slightly later report stated that it was useless to try to teach La Marine the new drill since the majority of the soldiers could not understand French. The officers were better men, many were drawn from the sons of the Canadian noblesse, while others came from regiments disbanded in France after the Peace of 1748. The training of the soldiers of La Marine was better than that of the militia, but the poor quality of the men, their lack of battalion organization and the small experience of many of their Canadian officers made it impossible for them to be really effective troops. They probably were really more policemen or gendarmes than combat soldiers. The Marquis de Vaudreuil, who succeeded to the governorship in 1755, was Canadian-born and of course was proud of the soldiers of La Marine. He boasted that they knew how to make bloody war on the British, while Montcalm's French regulars, he said, fought in too gentle and conventional a manner. The soldiers of La Marine numbered less than a thousand in all.

Until the last of the colonial wars Canada had only militia, La Marine troops and Indians for her offensive and defensive operations, but in 1755 French regulars crossed the ocean and furnished that striking force of trained and efficient soldiers which allowed Montcalm to wage an effective war against the heavy odds that gradually mounted against him. With these troops came an excellent staff and

competent subordinate commanders, essential tools hitherto lacking
in Canada.

Canada possessed another useful class of men, the *coureurs de
bois*—fur traders, explorers, and forest adventurers. The life of restraint which existed in New France, orders of the King, ordinances
of the intendant, restrictions by the Catholic Church, all these tended
to drive some of the best of Canada to the west. The son of the
habitant who did not favor a farmer's or a tradesman's life could find
escape in the forests. Many sons of the noblesse, lacking a commission
in one of the companies of La Marine—almost the only possible
career open to one of that class—sought their fortunes in the far west
as fur traders or Indian leaders. On one side lay the absolute authority
of King and Church, a conventional life and at best genteel poverty,
on the other the open forest, profit, adventure, and an unknown
future. Is it any wonder that much of the best of the youth of Canada
took to the North American woods? Every attempt was made by the
authorities to stop this flow of Canadians away from the settled lands,
but it was ineffective. The experience these men gained and the life
they led produced from among them incomparable leaders of Indians,
as the frontiers of New England learned to their sorrow.

The population of the British colonies outnumbered that of New
France nearly twenty times, and the colonists were prosperous and
self-sufficient. In 1754 about 40,000 people lived in the little colony
of Rhode Island, while in all Canada there were but some 55,000.
How was it, then, that these colonies were nearly overrun by the
French and allowed themselves to suffer for so many years from the
incursions of the enemy and their savage allies?

New France, although small in population, was a tightly controlled and centralized despotism, with a definite objective in view—
the extinction or at the very least the containment of the intruders
south and east of the mountain barrier. The British colonies on the
other hand were a group of decentralized states, each concerned primarily with its own affairs, with no wish to harm New France, and a
primary desire to be left alone. Only when goaded by thrusts from the

north would they attempt retaliation, and that would be a disjointed action only by the colonies directly affected. Although the French were greatly outnumbered, they could call to their service hordes of savages, some from the missions but many others from the far west, and it was with these bloodthirsty allies that they kept the British frontiers in ferment. To oppose them the colonists had almost nothing except militia or scattered farmers attempting to guard their little homesteads, for they were able to secure but little help from the Indians living within their borders. The Canadian habitant himself was only slightly involved in the colonial wars. When the final clash came, the battle was taken over by regular troops from France and Britain, and the colonial troops on both sides became on the whole of minor importance. Thus the great discrepancy in manpower had relatively little effect on the final result. Militia of both countries turned out from time to time, but the regulars usually bore the brunt of the battle. The last war was fought largely by European armies fighting on the American soil, assisted by the fleets of the two powers. Only to a relatively minor extent did the colonial troops and militia participate in active battle.

There seems little reason to believe that the British colonies initially had any intentions against Canada; they were content to live and let live and to engage in trade with the French. This was particularly true with respect to New England and New York. When the two nations clashed in Europe, colonial privateers of course took advantage of the opportunity, but it seems unlikely that any attempts against New France by land would have been initiated by the colonists except in retaliation for Canadian assaults on the British frontiers. While the French incursions were often those of Indian raiders led by a few white men and were made against the scattered civilian population, the retaliatory efforts of the colonists were almost always conducted by armies of white men, and they usually bogged down and got nowhere. I have been unable to find any record of a British raid against the civil population of New France either by Indians or by colonists. Sometimes, as in John Schuyler's raid of 1690, a few habitants were killed, but this was merely an unfortunate incident in an attempt against the little Canadian fort at La Prairie. The failure to raid Canadian settlements probably was not because the colonists had moral scruples; it was because of distance and inability to persuade their Indians to make active war on the French. The British raided hostile Indian settlements, such as Norridgewock and St. Francis. In each raid the French mission priest was killed, in the first case undoubtedly with intent, for Father Rasle was feared and detested by the dwellers along the coasts of Maine, but at St. Francis it seems to have been accidental.

The policy of Britain toward her colonies was initially that known as "mercantilism." The colonies were considered to exist for the economic benefit of the mother country, and, generally speaking, were expected to look after themselves. Military costs for their defense or for a possible expansion of their extent must be measured against the mercantile benefits to be gained. Unproductive lands served no economic purpose and hence were not to be sought. Commerce should be expanded, not territory. Applying this policy to the American colonies gave little encouragement to expansion beyond the Appalachians. Many of the furs of the west were coming to Albany through direct trade, and an additional quantity was smuggled from Canada, and, moreover, this latter trade furnished a market for English-made Indian trade goods. The colonies produced food, timber, and other supplies for the West Indian plantations, which in their turn poured out sugar and other money crops. Thus the North American colonies by the early 1700s were fulfilling the purpose which a policy of mercantilism prescribed. Britain as yet had no desire for empire or further westward expansion, but a need for the protection of existing conditions had appeared.

For a century a wide band of forest land had separated the French and the British settlements, and direct contact between them hardly existed. As the British pushed up the river valleys and westward toward the mountains, and as the French advanced their missions and trading posts, this relatively neutral ground, inhabited only by Indians, became more narrow and contact more frequent. At the same time the French, having successfully resisted the Mohawk invasions and having consolidated their position along the St. Lawrence, became more aggressive, and incited their Indians against the frontiers of the colonies. This new condition led to a modification of the previous policy to one which called for an active defense by the occupation of regions which could assure better protection to the long and narrow band of colonies by securing their extremities. The establishment of British regular troops in Acadia to the north and in Georgia to the south was the result. The earlier clashes of the 1750s had resulted from attempts to maintain a status quo, and to eject French incursions from lands held to be British, not from attempts to seize territories from the French. Soon William Pitt was to initiate a new concept of empire and a policy of expansion would follow, but that was still in the future.

The French attitude toward Canada was even more materialistic than that of Britain toward her colonies. New France was supposed to produce raw materials and food for her own consumption, and furs, fish, and naval supplies such as tar for export, while her industrial activities were restricted to some shipbuilding and the production of iron. Basically this was perhaps not a very different approach from that of Britain, but the latter nation left trade almost entirely free to set its own prices and maintain its own economic balance. The French Court on the other hand not only exercised a tight control on all economic activity, but also granted privileges and monopolies to the favored, which resulted in excessively high prices, graft, favoritism and an unhealthy economy.

It would be hard to visualize two lands more different from each other. In New France a sturdy race of contented farmers, unlettered and ignorant of the world beyond, bound together by a common ancestry and a common religion, had been accustomed for many years to be ruled and to obey. A few had revolted and taken to the woods to become the *coureurs de bois* who were to push the frontiers of Canada far to the west, to gather the crop of furs and to become most effective leaders of Indians. Then, of course, there were the dwellers in the towns, but more than three quarters of the Canadian people lived on their farms along the St. Lawrence and the Richelieu.

Farmers certainly comprised a majority of the population in the British colonies, but here the economy stood on a broader base. There were many sailors, shipbuilders, merchants, and skilled artisans, and all were accustomed to think for themselves, to govern themselves, and to do as they wished without orders from anyone. The vastly greater number of the disunited and self-interested British colonists was balanced by the uniformity of interest and the centralized control existing in Canada.

North and west of the mountains were hordes of Indians, many of whom could be led to war against the British, and there was also a standing army of nearly a thousand, far from the best of quality, no doubt, but still full-time professional soldiers. The British in effect had no Indians, no standing army beyond a company or two of King's troops, and had to rely upon militia and hurriedly raised forces of volunteers to guard their borders or to wage offensive war. Such were the two greatly contrasting civilizations which were to engage in the duel for North America.

Chapter X

THE ACADIANS ASKED FOR IT

T HE capture of Louisbourg in 1745 removed the major threat to Acadia, although there was a narrow escape from trouble the following year, when a great fleet gathered at Brest to wipe away the stain of the disaster France had suffered at Cape Breton. The Duke d'Anville sailed in command of threescore warships to restore the fortunes of the French King. He had a difficult crossing, dead calms alternating with stormy seas, and pestilence struck the crews of some of the ships. As they neared Nova Scotia a terrible storm scattered the great fleet over many miles of ocean. The shattered remnants finally worked their way into the safety of Chebucto Harbor, where in a few years the town of Halifax was to be founded by the British. D'Anville died, probably because of despair combined with a bad heart, and his successor soon took his own life. La Jonquière, later to be a capable governor of Canada, then succeeded to the command. The fleet remained in the great harbor, large enough to hold all the navies of the world of that day, and refitted as best it could. The pestilence raged unchecked until over a thousand men of the fleet were buried in the Acadian soil. At last, after abandoning and burning some of the remaining ships, the remnants of the fleet sailed back to France, and the threat to Nova Scotia was over.

In this same year of 1746 the competent de Ramezay led a little army to the head of the Bay of Fundy, where Abbé Le Loutre and his Micmacs were then lurking. Mascarene, as a counter to this threat, sent Colonel Noble and nearly five hundred Massachusetts men to winter at Grand Pré on the Minas Basin. Ramezay had paid this place a visit shortly before, and the governor thought it wise to let the Acadians of that region have a sight of English soldiers.

Noble's force bedded itself down for the winter in the best comfort it could find and relaxed. All precautions were not forgotten; scouting parties were kept active, but the British commander believed that no enemy would be so foolhardy as to attack him in the dead of winter. He had yet to learn the capabilities of Canadian raiders, and he learned too late. The French were informed of the arrival of the British at Grand Pré by an Acadian messenger, and an attack was at once planned. Ramezay himself was disabled by an injured knee, and the command was delegated to Coulon de Villiers. He it was who only a few years later was to corner George Washington in makeshift Fort Necessity and force his surrender, and others of his officers were to achieve fame in the course of the last French war. In bitter February, Coulon led his men from Beaubassin on the Isthmus of Chignecto to the vicinity of Grand Pré. It took them nearly three weeks to make the one-hundred-mile trip, but they picked up increments of Indians and Acadians on the way with the result that the force totaled over three hundred in the final count.

The British were quartered in little groups in various houses scattered over a considerable area, and local Acadians pointed out the places where the principal officers lived. The French split up into a number of little parties and made a night attack on these houses, killing Colonel Noble and others of his officers. For a short while the French and the Indians had it all their own way, and many English were tomahawked in their beds, never realizing what had happened. Soon daylight came, and the scattered English gathered together in a stone house and presented a firm defense. The fight soon tapered off into a stalemate, and Noble's men finally signed a capitulation and marched back to Annapolis Royal as prisoners on parole. About eighty had been killed and nearly as many wounded. The English soon learned that Acadians had assisted Coulon and a black mark was chalked up against the account of that unhappy people.

By this time Governor Shirley had become convinced that the only real solution to the problem of Nova Scotia would be to remove and exile the more dangerous of the Acadians and to replace them with British settlers. Mascarene, on the other hand, believed that, given time, these so-called neutral French could be converted into Englishmen. Very likely he was right, but time was the one element that was lacking, and the sands were running out for these unfortunate people. The attack on Grand Pré, proving as it did that some at least of the Acadians were actively pro-French, hardened the hearts of the British and hastened the end of French Acadia.

The English had now held the unhappy land for over thirty years, and had neglected it almost completely. The population was entirely French, except for the Indians, and only at Annapolis Royal did the flag fly to show that this was part of the far-flung British Empire. Suddenly London awoke from its apathy. The great citadel at Louisbourg had been restored to the French by the peace treaty, to the vast disgust of the New Englanders to whom it had fallen. It was realized at last that action must be taken to neutralize this great seaport, and a British base in Nova Scotia was decreed by London. In 1749, Colonel Edward Cornwallis was sent to replace Mascarene as governor, and he started to build the naval base of Halifax in the harbor of Chebucto where d'Anville's fleet had found shelter and left a great graveyard three years before. Moreover he brought colonists with him, some 2500 of them, supposedly all good Protestants, including Cockneys, French, and Germans. Soon British settlements were to dot the southern shores of Nova Scotia. This was a real change. Financial aid was forthcoming, and a stiffer policy was decreed. The Acadians were to be required to take the oath within three months, and, if any wished to leave, they must forfeit their houses and lands.

These stubborn and foolish people failed to realize that this time the British had really determined upon a stiff policy, although the sight of Halifax and the new settlers should have made them appreciate that the old days were over. The Acadians maintained their refusal to sign the unqualified oath, and waited on events. These were somewhat long in coming for the Board of Trade dallied, not wishing to drive these people into the arms of the French. The Acadians for their part believed that they had again called England's bluff and had made permanent their status as the neutral French.

In 1749 the fanatical Abbé le Loutre returned from France and proceeded to make mischief. There was a considerable settlement of Acadians at Beaubassin near the Isthmus of Chignecto which was informally considered the border. Le Loutre secured arms for his Indians from the French, and set them to raiding against the English, as well as threatening the Acadians with dire punishment if they should take the oath the English required. In the spring of 1750 a British force sailed to Beaubassin to occupy and fortify the little village and thus guard the strategic isthmus. Before they could set foot on shore the fanatical priest and his Indians set fire to all the buildings. The British soon managed to land but found themselves opposed by a much greater force of French and Canadian troops, as well as a large body of the so-called neutral French, who had turned out at the call of the missionary priest. The British fell back to their boats and returned to Annapolis Royal, while the homeless Acadians of Beaubassin sadly left the ashes of their homes and crossed over into Canada, where further unhappiness awaited them.

The French now built Fort Beauséjour at the isthmus and the British started Fort Lawrence on the opposite side of the Missaguash River. Soon the two rival forts glowered at each other across the intervening marshland. Theoretically there was peace between France and England, but there was no peace on the Acadian frontier. The French troops held to a meticulous neutrality, but Le Loutre's Indians, armed by the French and aided by some of the Acadians, continued to harry the British fort with nuisance forays.

The Acadians on the whole blew hot or cold just as the Abbé le Loutre fanned the flames, and, despite English attempts to meet them part way, they still, with a few exceptions, steadfastly refused to take the basic unmodified oath, even though it was softened somewhat so that it would be more palatable. According to a contemporary Canadian writer most of the Acadian priests had taken a simple oath that they would commit no direct or indirect act against the British, but Le Loutre persuaded some of them to break this pledge. Le Loutre continued to put pressure on the Acadians, threatening them with divine vengeance and even with excommunication.

A new governor took over from Cornwallis, Colonel Charles Lawrence, a high-minded professional soldier without greed and without hatred, but conditions failed to improve. Finally by 1754 Lawrence became convinced that the Acadians could never be made into useful citizens. Neither leniency nor harsh measures had any effect upon their complacent stubbornness. He advised the Board of Trade that the only solution was to force a showdown, and, if the Acadians would not take the oath, to exile them from the colony. Thus matters stood in Acadia when the last of the French wars burst upon the continent. A strong-minded governor faced a stubborn little people who, after forty years of life under the British Crown, still remained aliens. Each group had made up its mind as to the action to take and the final contest was at hand.

By the end of 1754 the French had a strong fort at Beauséjour and another at Baye Verte, the two together covering the isthmus effectively, and there was also a post on the St. John River. Within Acadia itself there were Le Loutre and his Micmacs, as well as perhaps fifteen hundred Acadian men who openly favored the French, and there was always the threat that in case of war all the Acadians might become active enemies. Against this the British had some three hundred and fifty soldiers at Fort Lawrence, just across the marshes from Fort Beauséjour, and about three hundred more at Annapolis Royal and Fort Edward on the south side of the Minas Basin. The British position could be called precarious at best.

Governor Lawrence fully appreciated the risk to the province, and in the late winter of 1754 he proposed to Governor Shirley of Mas-

sachusetts that a force of two thousand volunteers should be raised in
New England and brought to Acadia to drive the French from the
isthmus in the coming spring. War had not yet been declared, but
George Washington had already surrendered Fort Necessity to the
French, and London had decided to send Braddock and his regulars
to America. Shirley clearly appreciated the threat that a French
Acadia would hold over New England, both as a base for privateers
and as a source of trouble for the cod fisheries in its nearby waters.
A firm hold on the isthmus would not only make Acadia safe, but it
would cut Louisbourg off from all land access to Canada. Shirley was
always a man to look on colonial affairs from a broad viewpoint, and
he at once fell in with Lawrence's scheme and started raising troops.

Late in 1753 an interesting Frenchman went to Fort Beauséjour
in charge of the commissariat and also as secretary to the commandant.
His name was Thomas Pichon, and he was a spy and a traitor. We
cannot here go into his earlier history except to say that it was
checkered. He was an able and essentially honest person who had
become disgusted with the French service, embittered by the peculations of Bigot's evil crew, and disillusioned as to France's actions in
North America. Pichon determined to go over to the English, and he
seems to have been led to this extreme largely by conscience rather
than by hope of reward. In the winter of 1753–54 Captain George
Scott was in command of the British Fort Lawrence. We shall meet
him again later in the course of the war, one of its unsung heroes, an
unusually able soldier and a merry companion. There still was peace,
and visits between the two forts were common, so Pichon made contact with Scott. From that time on the British knew all that happened
at Fort Beauséjour.

In June of 1755, Shirley's New Englanders, reinforced by two hundred and fifty British regulars, crossed the marshes and invested the
French fort. Its commandant, de Vergor, was an incompetent—it was
said that he could not even read—who owed his position to his friend
Bigot, and he will appear again in another critical situation in which
he failed his country for a second time. De Vergor summoned the

Acadians of the surrounding area to come to the aid of the fort. Several hundred turned out willingly against the English, requiring, however, that it should be made clear that they came only under compulsion. About half of them deserted before the British started the attack. The little village which adjoined the fort was burned, along with its church, the first of the many sad works of destruction that Acadia would see in this unhappy year. The attack got under way. The defense was feeble. Beauséjour soon surrendered, but not before, it was said, de Vergor and other officers had looted and sent away to a safe place a considerable amount of the French King's stores. The other French fort on the isthmus at Baye Verte surrendered as soon as English troops appeared in its vicinity, and the post on the St. John River was abandoned. The victors strengthened Beauséjour and called it Fort Cumberland. Not only did the British now have a firm hold on the important isthmus, but they also had clear proof of how at least a part of the Acadians would act in case of open war.

Lawrence, after consulting with his council and the two British admirals then at Halifax, and without further informing the Board of Trade, decided to transport all the Acadians out of the province. New England troops were assigned the invidious task and coastal shipping was hired for transport. The Acadians were collected and herded on shipboard, including, most unfairly, those few who had taken the unqualified oath. Many took to the woods and escaped.

Some six thousand Acadians, men, women, and children, were distributed to colonies along the coast as far south as Georgia. Some were better received than others, some were even refused permission to land, and had to be taken to a more receptive region. It is little wonder that the southern colonies, with Braddock's defeat still much in their minds and French led Indians harrying their frontiers, failed to wax enthusiastic over receiving and supporting large numbers of Canadian Frenchmen. New England, also, had bitter memories of scalping parties on her borders only a few years before.

Eventually, after the peace, a considerable number of the exiles were taken back to France. Nearly fifteen hundred had fled to Canada where their board and lodging was farmed out to one of Bigot's clique. They were horribly exploited by the contractor and died off like flies from famine and exposure during the bitter Canadian winter of 1755–56. Those that were landed in the American colonies appear to have fared much better. Except for a few unusual cases, they certainly were not overwhelmed with welcome, but they were treated at least as well as were the poor and indigent of their hosts, and in many cases somewhat better. Eventually a material portion of the exiles were assimilated into the British civilization, while many others, either shortly after their exile or after the peace, found their way back to Nova Scotia and were accepted as citizens. Still another group finally reached Louisiana, then a French colony, and became the ancestors of the Cajuns of today.

No displaced people in history have ever been treated as kindly as were the Acadians that were sent to Massachusetts. Thomas Hutchinson, a most prominent citizen, later to be royal governor of the province, met the transports when they reached Boston and did all he could to ease the hardships of the Acadians. They received free medical care at public expense, a privilege no citizen of the colony enjoyed then or since.

Poets have wept over the fate of the Acadians, and many crocodile tears have been shed by those who should have known better. The basic truth is that an alien people who for forty years had lived and bred, free, untaxed, and unfettered under the British flag, refused to abandon their allegiance to an enemy nation. As a wartime measure for the safety of the province these people were removed, without intended harshness, but under conditions admittedly far from ideal, and dispersed elsewhere in parts where they could do no harm. Canadian authors have claimed that this expulsion was motivated by the greed of New Englanders for the lands of the exiles, but, if this were true, why were all the houses, barns and crops destroyed instead of being reserved for Yankees? The dispersal was an act of war, hard and unpleasant, which the commander on the ground, an able professional soldier to whom the King had delegated powers of decision and of action, had decided was a military necessity.

Chapter XI

BRADDOCK DESERVED BETTER LUCK

Sir,

The lands upon the river Ohio, in the western parts of the colony of Virginia, are so notoriously known to be the property of the crown of Great Britain, that it is a matter of equal concern and surprise to me, to hear that a body of French forces are erecting fortresses and making settlements upon that river, within his Majesty's dominions. The many and repeated complaints I have received of these acts of hostility, lay me under the necessity of sending, in the name of the King my master, the bearer hereof, George Washington, Esq; one of the adjutants-general of the forces of this dominion, to complain to you of the encroachments thus made . . .

ROBERT DINWIDDIE

Williamsburgh
October the 31st, 1753

T HUS did the governor of Virginia by the hand of the future President of the United States notify the French commandant at the newly built Fort Le Boeuf on French Creek on the upper waters of the Ohio of his displeasure. Dinwiddie, perhaps unwittingly, in this way initiated the events which led to the last of the French and Indian Wars. The clash, however, was inevitable, for the possession of the great Ohio Valley was at stake, and only armed action would determine it. For years British traders had been penetrating into this country, bringing out the furs and alienating the Indians from the French, who in their turn were establishing a chain of posts aimed at sealing off the English penetration and confining their settlements to the regions east of the Alleghenies. Each nation claimed that the other was encroaching on its territories, and each decided to take action to make the other desist. The Seven Years War in America might well be called "The War for the Ohio Valley."

The Ohio Company was a group of land speculators, many of them of the best Virginia families, organized to exploit and colonize the Ohio Valley. Early in 1754 the Company was establishing a trading post at Redstone Creek, only some thirty miles short of the Forks of the Ohio. William Trent, a Pennsylvania Indian trader, had charge of this post for the Ohio Company, and Governor Dinwiddie commissioned him to raise a body of volunteers and build a fort at the Forks of the Ohio. Dinwiddie was himself a member of the Company, and his action could hardly be called disinterested. Trent promptly left Redstone with such men as he then had or could enlist and commenced work at the Forks of the Ohio, where Pittsburgh stands today. By mid-April he had a small fort well under way.

We must now go back a few months and follow Washington's actions after he delivered the Virginia governor's message. He suffered various adventures and one near escape from assassination by his Indian guide, and returned to Williamsburg in January, 1754, with the French commander's answer. This in effect told Dinwiddie that he was writing to the wrong man, as his own orders came from the Marquis Duquesne, governor of Canada. The Virginia governor, after starting Trent to the Ohio, proceeded to raise a further body of troops to reinforce him, and the first portion moved westward in April. George Washington, a lieutenant colonel at twenty-three, was their commander.

Meanwhile a thousand Frenchmen had suddenly descended upon Trent's little force. The British were ejected, quietly and peacefully, but with extreme firmness. On their way back to tidewater they met the little body of Virginia troops which was hurrying to their aid. Washington's force clashed with a reconnoitering body of Frenchmen who falsely claimed to be under a flag of truce and their leader,

Jumonville, fell dead. The French later made much of this incident, and accused Washington of murdering one who came in peace. The French survivors brought up large reinforcements, penned Washington's force in the hurriedly built Fort Necessity at the "Great Meadows," and gave the future general his first taste of combat and of the bitterness of surrender. This was the first battle, although a petty one, of the last great French and Indian War, a war which was to endure for six years, bring great disasters to the British and ultimately, after trials and tribulations, cause the fall of New France.

Washington was forced to give two hostages to the French, one of whom was Captain Robert Stobo. This officer was taken back to Fort Duquesne and while there made a plan of the fort which he succeeded in some way sending back to Virginia. It was given to Braddock before the start of his expedition and captured along with the rest of his papers, greatly to Stobo's future peril.

There was now to be a short period of quiet. Each nation knew that war was inevitable, and each began its preparations. Canada could invade the British colonies most easily through the Champlain Valley, or less so through the Mohawk, but there was still a third possible route, one which threatened eastern New England. This route ran through Maine. From the St. Lawrence it ascended the Chaudière River in Canada, crossed the Notre Dame Mountains and descended the Kennebec to the sea. It was a most difficult route, as Benedict Arnold's little army was to learn to its sorrow in 1775, but it was practical for a fast-moving raiding party, and Governor Shirley decided that it must be closed. In this same summer of 1754 he sent John Winslow, of Pilgrim ancestry, to do the job. Winslow was a kindly man, the next year to have the invidious mission of collecting and shipping away the unfortunate Acadians of Nova Scotia, and then, as a major general, to command the New England troops at Lake George during the do-nothing summer of 1756. Winslow's expedition moved up the Kennebec to the head of navigation at present day Augusta, the capital of Maine, where he built Fort Western, and then went on upstream by bateaux and whaleboat to where Waterville now stands and there built Fort Halifax, around which later grew up a little town to be named after him. Thus Shirley blocked off any threat from the east and New England could breathe easier and look only to the west.

For a number of years before 1754 the French had been making serious inroads upon the loyalty of the Five Nations to Britain. The English had given the Indians causes for grievance, one of which was the unjust appropriation of some of their lands. London realized during that winter of 1753–54 that steps must be taken to regain the friendship of the Indians, and Governor De Lancey of New York was directed by the Board of Trade to invite the several colonies to send representatives to meet and confer with the Iroquois at Albany in an endeavor to smooth out the various differences which existed. The Virginia governor was engaged in a conference of his own with the Ohio Valley tribes, and New Jersey sent no representatives, but all the other northern colonies dispatched special commissioners, and included among them were some of the best minds of North America. The difficulties with the Indians were smoothed out, and the Albany Congress took up another problem, one which they initiated themselves and not at the suggestion of the Board of Trade. That was the matter of establishing a union of all the colonies for three major purposes, the control of all Indian affairs, regulation of new settlements in the west, and the raising and maintaining of troops and the building of forts to protect the frontiers. Taxes were to be levied to finance these operations, and there was to be a colonial congress composed of representatives from each colony proportionate in number to the tax raised by the colony. Benjamin Franklin was most active in promoting this union. It was approved by the various commissioners at Albany, but when referred to the colonies for ratification the plan was defeated. So ended the first attempt at a real union of the American colonies.

Despite the fiasco of Washington's expedition and Fort Necessity, Governor Dinwiddie still believed that the French could easily be driven from the Forks of the Ohio, and he tried to raise troops for another attempt, but the project was abandoned. The serious condition existing in the Ohio country was, however, soon realized in London, and in the fall of 1754 two regiments of regulars were ordered to Virginia. Two more were to be raised in this country by Shirley and Pepperrell to whom they had been given as a reward for the capture of Louisbourg in 1745. These two regiments had been broken up after the peace of 1748, and now they were to be reconstituted. Major General Edward Braddock was chosen to be commander in chief in North America. A long-time career officer, he had an excellent record. A strict disciplinarian, he at the same time was humane, considerate, and appears to have been well thought of by the rank and file. The new commander and the two regiments from Ireland reached this country in the early spring of 1755. Virginia's little war with the French had now become that of Britain.

Paris, of course, had an ear to the ground and realized what the English were doing. In November 1754 the French Minister of Marine had written Governor Duquesne that, while His Most Catholic Majesty was pained at Jumonville's death at the hands of the Virginians, he did not believe that a break with England was justified or desirable. The Canadian governor was warned against giving the English any grounds for complaint, and against in any way appearing to be an aggressor, but he was told that he was free to use the Indians against the British colonies if he believed it wise.

Early in the following year the French Court decided to reinforce Canada, and nearly four thousand regulars were loaded on transports and put to sea. Their commander was German-born Baron von Dieskau, a skillful officer of considerable reputation. The British learned of this troop movement and tried to prevent it, but without much success. The fleet sent to intercept the convoy missed its major objective and succeeded in capturing only two of the transports, warships with most of their guns removed. Some five hundred French soldiers were on the two prizes. Only later in the year will these French reinforcements enter into our picture, and we shall leave them for the moment to regain their shore legs and enjoy the Canadian scene, while we return to General Braddock and affairs farther south.

The British general's instructions stressed the fact that the purpose of the campaign was to recover territories belonging to Britain, or in other words to remove French encroachments rather than to invade their land. Such action might be considered to be a police operation rather than an outright act of war, and both nations were to maintain the pretense of peace for another two years. Braddock was ordered first to drive the French from Fort Duquesne, then to dislodge them from Niagara, and to seize and hold control of Lake Ontario, by building a fleet if he deemed it necessary. Next he was to capture the fort at Crown Point on Lake Champlain, and finally to destroy the French fort at Beauséjour in Acadia.

Of all these projects only the last was to be accomplished, and that had been done by a New England expedition almost as soon as Braddock had arrived in Virginia. The British Ministry failed to realize that by concentrating on the third objective, securing control of Lake Ontario, the French lifeline to the West would have been severed and Fort Duquesne and Niagara would have fallen without any further action. Shirley and some other far-seeing Americans knew this, but the point was missed in London. An expedition up the Hudson and out the Mohawk to Lake Ontario would have moved along the natural communication routes of North America, and a real concentration at Oswego with the construction of a powerful little navy would have been relatively simple and inexpensive. Instead, London's orders violated all the laws of geography, and sent an army into the wilderness on a route directly across those land formations which would retard progress to the maximum. The objective was only the finger tip, but a finger tip at the end of one of Canada's natural routes of communication, a relatively long one but a clear water route, interrupted only by a few portages.

One of the new commander's first acts was to summon a conference of the governors of Massachusetts, New York, Pennsylvania, and Maryland to meet with him and the Virginia governor at Alexandria and discuss plans for the coming campaign. The governor of South

Carolina was not invited, probably at the instance of Dinwiddie of Virginia. It was a sad mistake for only he could have produced the force of Indians that Braddock required. Attacks on the French forts at Niagara and Crown Point were discussed and it was agreed to strengthen Oswego on Lake Ontario. Shirley was to lead the Niagara attack, William Johnson that on Crown Point, while Braddock would march with the two newly arrived regular regiments and some colonial troops through the Allegheny Mountains against the French at the Forks of the Ohio.

The expedition against Fort Duquesne assembled at Will's Creek on the Potomac, where Fort Cumberland had been built. Progress up the Potomac Valley from tidewater to this point had been relatively easy, but this was the jumping off place. From here Braddock faced "an hundred and ten miles . . . thro' an uninhabited wilderness over steep rocky mountains and almost impassible morasses." He had an army consisting of 1445 regulars fit for duty, 262 men in three independent colonial companies, 30 sailors to assist with block and tackle in hauling the cannon over the mountains, and 449 Virginia, North Carolina, and Maryland troops, as well as a small detachment of gunners.

The artillery train consisted of ten six- and twelve-pounder guns, four big howitzers, and fourteen small mortars. The heaviest piece weighed well over half a ton not counting its carriage, a discouraging object to haul over mountains where no road existed. In addition to the guns themselves shot and shell had to be carried, as well as powder. There was, moreover, a host of necessary artillery supplies that must be taken, about 269 separate items, many of them in several sizes, and ranging from a small derrick down to candles and carpet tacks. Then there was the food for more than two thousand men for at least a month and forage for the horses, for there would be little or no natural feed in the deep woods. No horse could maintain its strength on leaves alone, but part of the time they were to be reduced to that. All this meant many wagons, and, despite promises from Virginia and Maryland, none appeared. In despair Braddock sought aid from Benjamin Franklin, and that good man succeeded in producing one hundred and fifty heavy wagons and five hundred pack horses. Another serious void was caused by the failure of the promised Indian scouts to appear. Instead of the hundreds that the Virginia governor had said he could produce, only a handful showed up, and the expedition finally had but eight at the time when they were most to be needed.

George Washington had resigned from the Virginia troops shortly after the surrender of Fort Necessity, when a reorganization took place and he would have reverted to the rank of captain. Braddock invited him to serve on the staff as a volunteer lieutenant colonel without pay, and he accepted. As a soldier Washington still lacked experience, but his knowledge of the country and of local conditions could be of considerable value. The two men developed great respect and liking for each other.

The expedition at last got under way and moved ponderously through the primeval forest. The wonder is that it was able to move at all. Braddock appreciated the hardships of the work ahead and equipment was lightened as far as he felt it wise. The soldiers, all of whom at that time normally wore swords, left them behind, as well as some of their other heavy accouterments. The work involved was terrific. A road had to be hacked out through a wilderness, rock ledges drilled and blasted, swamps corduroyed and streams bridged. Moving a military expedition along one of the great waterways of North America, involved as that might be, was child's play compared to this struggle against the valleys and mountains of the Alleghenies. Braddock's march to Fort Duquesne, despite its tragic ending, was actually a monumental achievement in military logistics.

The expedition advanced slowly. Small parties of French and Indians hovered around it and skirmished with the flank guards, but did little harm and caused no material delay. The march was well conducted, security was maintained by ample advance and flank guards, and considering the ruggedness of the terrain traversed, the operation deserved the highest praise. Braddock, however, soon real-

Quebec

Trois Rivieres

Montreal

Fort Orange

Boston

New Amsterdam

St. Mary's

Jamestown

ATLANTIC

OCEAN

The COLONIES in 1660

The colored areas represent the generally settled regions.
Trappers, traders, and frontiersmen moved farther west,
but they were a roving and not a settled population
and hence are not included.

British and Dutch   French

Quebec

Trois Rivieres

Montreal

Fort Frontenac

Albany
(Fort Orange)

Bosto

New York
(New Amsterdam)

St. Mary's

ATLANTIC

OCEAN

The COLONIES in 1675

British   French

Charleston

Quebec

Trois Rivieres

Montreal

Fort Frontenac

Oswego

Niagara

Albany

Boston

Detroit

New York

ATLANTIC

OCEAN

The COLONIES in 1725

British   French

Charleston

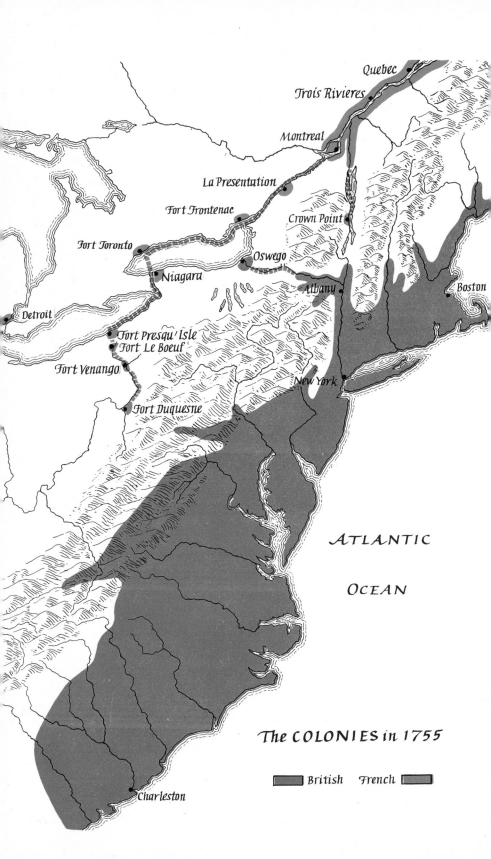

Quebec

Trois Rivières

Montreal

La Presentation

Fort Frontenac

Crown Point

Fort Toronto

Oswego

Niagara

Albany

Boston

Detroit

Fort Presqu'Isle

Fort Le Boeuf

Fort Venango

New York

Fort Duquesne

ATLANTIC

OCEAN

The COLONIES in 1755

British   French

Charleston

ized that the rate of advance was far too slow. It had taken five days to move the first fifteen miles from Will's Creek to a place called Little Meadows. A council of the senior officers was held there and decided to detach a part of the force, lightly equipped, to proceed forward as rapidly as possible, while the remainder, with most of the wagons, followed at a slower pace under command of Colonel Dunbar, the officer next in seniority to Braddock. The striking force consisted of some 1400 men with eight cannon, four howitzers, and three small mortars, and only about thirty-four wagons. This speeded the advance up considerably, but even then it required nineteen days to march the remaining one hundred miles.

Progress was nowhere opposed except by the forces of nature, and on July 8 the little army crossed the Monongahela for the second time and found itself within a scant ten miles of the French fort. Up to that time the march had been conducted admirably, and excellent security had been maintained. It was after midday when the last river crossing was completed. The worst was over, and there remained merely a matter of investing the fort and putting the artillery in position. The expedition seemed a success, and everyone was cheerful. As one survivor later wrote "[we] hugged [ourselves] with joy at our good luck in having surmounted our greatest difficultys & too hastily concluded the enemy never wou'd dare oppose us." Evidently there was a general let down of tension and probably some slackening in security.

It was almost axiomatic in colonial days that, once relatively heavy artillery had been brought within range of a colonial fort, the fort would fall. And here was British artillery almost on the doorstep of Fort Duquesne. Contrecoeur, the French commander, had a total force of about 1600 men, of whom eight hundred were Indians, excitable and unpredictable. His intelligence must have been somewhat at fault, for, while he knew that the expedition was on the way, he was somewhat surprised to find it so near at hand on this day of battle. It seems almost certain that he must have believed that he would have to surrender the fort after making something of a token resistance to fulfill the conventions, and he probably was just as amazed at the final outcome as was poor Braddock.

Contrecoeur at about midmorning sent out as large a force as he could spare to try to intercept or delay the British advance. It consisted of 108 regulars, 146 militia, and 600 Indians. Most of the force, and certainly the officers, were in Indian dress. They advanced eastward and met the head of the British column a little after noon at a point about half a mile beyond the river crossing. The surrounding forest at this point had become surprisingly open. ". . . We came into an open wood free from underwood with some gradual riseings, this wood was so open that carridges could have been drove in any part of it."

The British advance guard suddenly saw a white man, dressed as an Indian but wearing a shining gorget, darting among the trees ahead of them, then Indians, and suddenly they were struck by musket fire. They deployed, got the artillery of the advance into action, and returned the fire. At almost the first shot all the Canadian militia ran away, led by their two cadet officers, and the cannon fire greatly deflated the courage of many of the Indians. But the French officers soon rallied the redskins and deployed the remaining force into a U-shaped line which enveloped the head of the British column and flanked it on both sides. The British advance fell back, and the reserve, rushing up to see what was wrong, collided with it.

All became confusion. Near to where the two parties met was a little hill by the side of the road. It would have formed an excellent base upon which to take up a temporary position, reorganize and plan to recoup, but the British failed to act promptly and the Indians got there first. To make the confusion complete, the wagon convoy and the rest of the artillery, instead of halting and waiting for orders, continued to march forward and piled into the rear of the melee ahead. The British force thus found itself surrounded on three sides by Frenchmen and Indians, hidden from their view by trees and powder smoke, and behind by horses, wagons, guns, and ammunition carts. There was no opportunity to deploy into a firing line and no really visible enemy to shoot at, though musket balls were hitting them from three sides at once. Small wonder that discipline collapsed, and the little army broke down into a milling mass of scared and bewildered soldiers. Many of the officers were killed or wounded early in the fight and those who remained on their feet could do little or nothing to restore order. Yet the fight continued for nearly three hours, the British wasting their ammunition into empty space and sometimes hitting their own people. Finally the breakdown became complete. Everything was abandoned, including all of General Braddock's papers, and the survivors fled the field in blind panic, despite all attempts by the general and his surviving officers to stop them. Only 459 soldiers out of nearly 1400 escaped death or a wound, while less than a third of the officers came out unscathed. When the French came to examine the field of battle, they discovered the bodies of eight women among the British dead. The defeat was total. Braddock had five horses shot under him before he finally received the wound which was to prove mortal. Washington lost two horses but escaped unwounded.

The rear echelon which had been left behind under Colonel Dunbar was at this time about fifty miles to the rear, in the vicinity of Laurel Hill. The remnants of the defeated army fell back in disorder to Dunbar's camp, abandoning everything to the enemy. When the wild-eyed and panting survivors reached Laurel Hill and Dunbar learned of the catastrophe, he, too, was seized with panic. All the remaining artillery, except for four light guns and four little mortars, the ammunition and one hundred and fifty wagons, were destroyed or buried. Whether this was done by order of the dying Braddock or by Dunbar is not known. Retreat was ordered at once, and that night at the Great Meadows, near where Fort Necessity had stood, the unfortunate Braddock died of his wound. Dunbar continued the retreat to Fort Cumberland at Will's Creek, caught his breath, and then cravenly marched his two regiments of regulars to Philadelphia, leaving the defense of the frontier to the few remaining colonial troops. He shortly was removed from command and never again took the field. Braddock's great expedition to drive the French from the Forks of the Ohio had collapsed in utter defeat and senseless panic.

Many a writer has blandly explained the defeat by saying that Braddock was incompetent, stubborn, and scornful of all colonials, and that if he had only taken Washington's advice and made his troops fight from behind trees like frontiersmen all would have been well. This is much too simple and easy an explanation. Nor is it true, for the march which preceded the defeat is proof of Braddock's competency.

I believe that the blame for the debacle rests primarily on some of Braddock's subordinate officers rather than on Braddock himself, although as commander he was responsible. Gage, for one, failed to occupy the little hill which might have saved the day, and he let the advance guard retreat instead of holding its ground or even moving ahead into the more open country where it could have deployed more effectively. Sir Peter Halkett allowed the trains to continue to advance, instead of halting to await clarification of the situation. Washington blamed the British soldiers, and this was probably true, but only because command broke down and they did not know what to do.

Another factor which has perhaps been largely overlooked was the quality and the state of training of the British regulars. The regiments had been stationed in Ireland before being ordered to America, and they then contained a little more than three hundred men each. Drafts were made on several other regiments for sufficient men to bring the 44th and the 48th each up to a strength of five hundred men. When the commander of a regiment is called on for men for a draft, it is only natural that he should send his worst soldiers, his misfits and bad actors, and one may be sure that such was done in this case. Then, when the troops reached America, they were recruited up to their practically full strength of 727 from colonials. Thus the two British regiments that fought in the battle contained about 43 per cent regulars of average quality and training, 26 per cent regulars of poorer quality, and 31 per cent American recruits, whose training was of the shortest.

The final result of all the errors and misadventures was that the

British, instead of deploying when taken under fire, did the reverse and allowed themselves to become jammed into a tightly packed mass of dismayed soldiers, caught in a fire from three sides to which they could make no effective reply. Many of the officers were killed or wounded early in the fight and command soon broke down and with it discipline. The inevitable followed.

Another serious handicap had been the lack of Indians who certainly would have been of material help. The British commanders still had much to learn about fighting in North America, but they were willing to learn and before long they would begin to prove their growing competency. This was their first and perhaps their hardest lesson.

Chapter XII

BARONET OF THE MOHAWK

Before Braddock arrived in this country, Governor Shirley had recommended that William Johnson should lead an attack on Crown Point, and this was approved at the Alexandria Conference. The troops were to be solely colonials, drawn from New York and the New England colonies, and to secure unity and guard against any question of doubt each colony commissioned Johnson a major general over its troops. Phineas Lyman of Connecticut, an able lawyer but so far no military man, was made second in command.

The expedition assembled on the river flats at Albany and in mid-July, 1755, started up the Hudson, a force of perhaps 3500 farmers, tradesmen, and artisans. A few of the officers had seen service in the earlier war, and there was one excellent captain of British regulars, William Eyre, who doubled as engineer and artillery commander. Throughout this last French war Eyre was to continue to prove his worth, and then, the war at last over, he started home on leave and was lost at sea.

A powerful artillery train went with the little army, six great 18-pounder cannon, each weighing nearly three tons, and two even larger, but somewhat lighter 32-pounders, which carried a ball more than six inches in diameter, or half a gallon of musket balls or grapeshot, fearful missiles at short range. There were also two eight-inch and one 13-inch mortars, the last a huge and ponderous piece of iron. This expedition and that of Braddock present an interesting contrast. Braddock with the greatest of difficulty led an army of professionals across the mountain ridges, flouting all the rules of geography, and he just managed to drag with him cannon weighing somewhat over half a ton apiece. Johnson followed a route of communication decreed by nature, up the Hudson waterway and then across the relatively easy portage to the waters of Lake George. He had an army of amateurs, yet he took with him—and there is nothing on record to show that he had any particular difficulty—great cannon weighing five times as much as those which gave Braddock such trouble.

In late August the little army moved north up the Hudson. A scant fifty miles above Albany there is a sharp bend in the river, and here began the two portages which led to the north, one to Lake St. Sacrement, the other to Wood Creek, the site of abandoned Fort Anne, and on to Lake Champlain. Here at "The Great Carrying Place" was the trading house of John Henry Lydius, son of a Dutch dominie of Albany, "perfidious Lydius" to some, a trusted employee of Shirley, anathema to William Johnson and the Five Nations and probably a spy for the French—an interesting and devious personality about whom too little is known. Johnson started construction of a fort at the strategic carrying place, which soon became known as Fort Edward. For many years to come it was to be a rallying point for colonial and revolutionary armies.

Lieutenant Colonel Seth Pomeroy of Colonel Ephraim Williams' Massachusetts regiment was an old campaigner who had helped Pepperrell take Louisbourg ten years before, and twenty years later he was to appear at Bunker Hill, musket in hand, there to greet another famous old man, Israel Putnam, with the usual interchange of scurrilous banter that old soldiers have used since the days of Julius Caesar. In 1755, however, Pomeroy was in his middle years, and Putnam was a private in one of Johnson's Connecticut regiments, although, still unknown to him, his commission as lieutenant was being signed in Hartford. Both Pomeroy and Putnam were to become generals in the Revolution.

Pomeroy one hot August day was marching along the road toward the north when he found General Johnson and some other officers

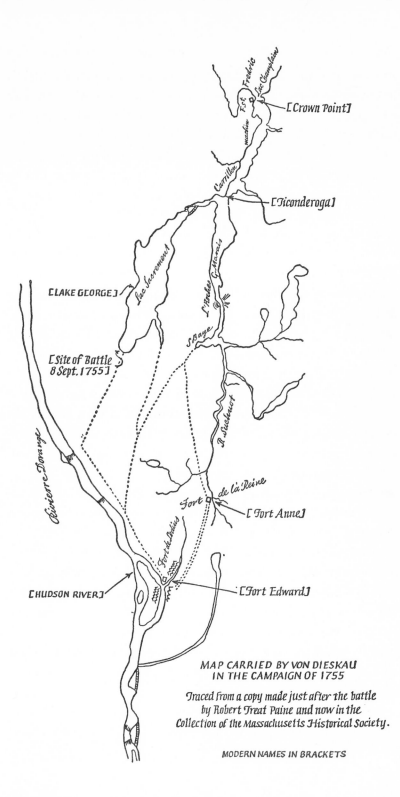

[Crown Point]

[Ticonderoga]

[LAKE GEORGE]

[Site of Battle
8 Sept. 1755]

[Fort Anne]

[HUDSON RIVER]

[Fort Edward]

MAP CARRIED BY VON DIESKAU
IN THE CAMPAIGN OF 1755

Traced from a copy made just after the battle
by Robert Treat Paine and now in the
Collection of the Massachusetts Historical Society.

MODERN NAMES IN BRACKETS

picnicking by the side of the road, and he was invited to stop for lunch. The party tarried for about an hour and enjoyed a meal of ham, bacon, peas, bread, cheese, a fine lemon punch, and some wine. Hardly campaign rations, one would say. At the next day's nooning he found the general established in the shade of a tree alongside of a little brook, and at this meal venison was added to the menu. Pomeroy liked Johnson, and wrote home to his wife that the general "appears like a gentleman: & with a grate deal of modesty yet free & pleasant . . . and resolution good enough to prosecute this grate affair . . ." Johnson evidently got along well with his officers, perhaps almost too much so, for he called the senior officers to council almost daily to consider and to vote upon actions to be taken. He seems almost to have acted more as the chairman of an executive committee than as a commanding general. This was his first military command; he had to feel his way along, and some of his subordinates had seen active service. Later in the year, after the battle had been fought, the relations between Johnson and his senior officers became strained, but at first the high command seems to have been a happy family.

Johnson left a party of five hundred men to build the new fort and took the rest northward over the divide whose few miles separate the waters of the Hudson from those of the St. Lawrence. Never a man to miss a chance, Johnson changed the name of Lake St. Sacrement to Lake George in honor of his king, and saw that word of his act reached London. The southern end of the lake was virgin country. Over a century before Father Jogues had passed by to his martyrdom, and so had traveled many Indians, fur traders, and Frenchmen in the years that followed, but this was the first British expedition to reach this lovely lake. The party started clearing land for a camp and for a fort, meanwhile portaging their bateaux up from the Hudson, and preparing to move north down the narrow waters of the lake. By the end of the month it became apparent that the French, too, were on the move, and that Johnson might not have to go to Crown Point for his fight.

Some months ago we left Baron von Dieskau and his French regulars marching ashore after a long sea voyage to taste the delights of Quebec. By the end of August, Dieskau had his force of nearly eight hundred regulars, twelve hundred Canadian militia, and more than six hundred Indians at Fort St. Frederic at Crown Point, and he had learned that the British were up to no good at the head of Lake George. On the second of September he was told that there were only five hundred men at the new Fort Edward and that its defenses were far from complete. Reinforcements were, however, expected in the near future. Dieskau at once initiated plans for a surprise attack on the fort. He still had much to learn of the capabilities of militia and Indians, and he left most of his regulars behind. He took only a few more than two hundred of them with him, in addition to six hundred and eighty Canadians and some six hundred Indians. The French left Crown Point about the fourth of September, dropped off part of the force at Ticonderoga, where as yet there was no fort, and reached the vicinity of Fort Edward three days later with a striking force of some fifteen hundred men. The Indians promptly refused to attack the still unfinished fort and its adjoining camp. By this time Dieskau had learned of the presence of Johnson's army at the head of Lake George. He thought that the English numbered about three thousand, yet he marched to attack them with a force he believed to be only half their size, and one which consisted largely of untried militia and temperamental Indians. Dieskau had much to learn, and he was to learn it the hard way.

Johnson in his turn was to make his mistake, an unfortunate but not a fatal one. His scouts reported the French advance against Fort Edward, and he sent a force of a thousand men and some Indians to its assistance. Old Hendrick, Mohawk chieftain and friend of Johnson, protested that this party was too small to be of real value and too large to sacrifice, but his advice was disregarded. A few miles south of the lake, near the top of the divide, the colonials ran into an ambush set by the French. It was not wholly effective, for some of the Iroquois with the French sprung the trap too soon, in order, Dieskau afterward claimed, to spare their Mohawk brothers who were with the

English. Be that as it may, the ambush was only too successful and many of the survivors pelted hotfoot back to the lake in panic.

Colonel Ephraim Williams had led the party, a Massachusetts officer of considerable military experience, but not enough to save him on this day. He fell dead while trying to rally his men, but his name still lives through the college which resulted from provisions in his will. Chief Hendrick of the Mohawks also met his death in this affair. He had been one of the four chieftains who were taken to the British Court by Peter Schuyler in 1710, and he had visited London again in about 1740, when he was presented to King George II. An engraving of this old Indian that has come down to us shows a rather repulsive and terribly scarred face, but he had been a firm friend of the English all his days, and died because his sound advice was thrown away. Despite the surprise and the wild-eyed flight of many a man who lived to be ashamed of his action, part of the force maintained its discipline and formed a fighting rear guard which covered the retreat. After the battle Dieskau told Johnson that the withdrawing action was beautifully handled. Only about one hundred men took an active part in it, but this little body delayed the French advance most effectively and gave the force at the lake much needed time to complete their defenses. Hendrick's Indians either were the first to flee, or else they made the best time, for they rushed into the Lake George camp well ahead of any of the white survivors.

Dieskau advanced to the lake and found Johnson's men established in a hurriedly arranged defensive area surrounded by a rude barricade of tree trunks, wagon bodies, and bateaux, armed with cannon, some of them those great 18- and 32-pounders whose murderous load of grape and musket balls would cut a fearful swath through an attacking force. The military art of the day held it most unwise to attack entrenched troops unless artillery could be brought into play, but, when the defenders had powerful artillery and the attackers none, it was madness. Dieskau sent his men in to charge the breastworks, the colonials let go with their cannon, and the Indians and part of the Canadian militia promptly fled. The little band of French regulars went on, some two hundred against almost ten times their number, but their charge was hopeless and they suffered fearful casualties.

During the winter of 1755–56 the Marquis de Vaudreuil, appointed governor of Canada the previous spring, somewhere secured a journal kept by an unnamed British officer who was at the fight. In it the latter wrote that when the French first appeared no one was sure whether they were friend or foe, until they had advanced within about sixty yards of the British line and opened fire. Johnson's men replied with everything they had, but our journalist reported that the French were brave men who seemed to pay no attention to the British fire. "I dare say," he wrote, "that there never has been in America a more fearless and vigorous attack, nor a stronger defense than [in this battle]." The French risked all and came on with the bayonet, but the cannon fire decimated them.

Many of the English ran and hid or suddenly developed severe stomach aches, but about seventeen hundred of Johnson's men stood to their guns and beat off the French. The Canadian Indians and the militia drifted back into the fight, which dragged out into intermittent musket fire for several hours. The French finally withdrew, leaving their badly wounded general in the hands of the enemy. The British made one sortie late in the engagement, and it was then that von Dieskau was captured. They had no bayonets, but charged with their camp hatchets in hand, finding these weapons most effective.

Johnson himself had been wounded early in the fight by a musket ball in the thigh. It was reported that he retired to his tent, leaving the conduct of the battle in the hands of General Lyman, to whom, however, he gave no credit whatsoever when he made his report of the battle. Other witnesses claimed either that he kept the field despite his wound, or that he was wounded only toward the end of the battle and remained in active command throughout. The stories vary, depending upon whether the reporter was pro-Johnson or pro-Shirley. Certainly Johnson was responsible for establishing the defenses, placing the cannon and the early conduct of the battle, but the evidence for the early wounding and the withdrawal to his tent seems to have the greater weight.

At last the French fell back, but they were not pursued, nor was any attempt made to seize their boats on South Bay of Lake Champlain, which should have been relatively easy, so disorganized were Dieskau's men. Some of the muskets they left behind were found to be British firelocks captured at Braddock's defeat. On their retreat the French met a party of British reinforcements near the scene of the morning ambush and were roughly handled. The French fell back to Ticonderoga, where they started to build Fort Carillon, while the English continued their work on Fort William Henry.

Johnson's decision not to push on against Crown Point was probably wise. His troops had on the whole had a hard day, and they were, after all, only untrained militia, while the French still had a considerable body of regular troops in reserve. On the other hand the failure to attempt to cut the badly disorganized French off from their boats represented a lost opportunity. All in all the day's actions offered little honor to either side. The faulty generalship was Johnson's, while the successful defense must at least partially be credited to Lyman, yet Johnson got all the plums. To England, still stunned by the news of Braddock's debacle, the defeat of a French army, even so small a one as this, and the capture of its general was tremendous news, which went far to lessen the sting of the defeat on the Monongahela. Johnson was made a baronet and was given a purse of £5000 by Parliament. Throughout the entire history of British North America only three baronetcies were awarded to colonials, to Robert Eden of Maryland, to William Pepperrell for the Louisbourg victory of 1745, and to Johnson. Eden's and Johnson's today are borne by their descendants, but Pepperrell's has become extinct.

Johnson's wound kept him in his tent for a few days, and then he was hit by "a violent inflamation in my head and ear" that left him little taste for action of any sort. Reinforcements came in after the battle, and there were soon ample troops to continue the expedition against Crown Point, but the supplies were far from sufficient. Johnson referred to a council of war for advice, and it agreed with his own belief that no further advance should be made. He was in the unenviable position of a Yorker commanding Yankee troops, and he was most careful to consult with his subordinate officers, probably more than was desirable.

The campaign was a failure in that Crown Point had not been taken, but it produced a major achievement nevertheless, because the construction of Fort Edward on the Hudson and Fort William Henry on Lake George effectively advanced the British frontier farther north along the great Hudson-Champlain waterway and provided protection to Albany and Schenectady, no longer assured the safety they formerly enjoyed under the benevolent neutrality of the Five Nations.

Chapter XIII

A NEW STAR RISES

T HE other great throughway of colonial America, the east-west highway of the Mohawk, Lake Oneida, and the Oswego River, tenuously tied the Great Lakes region to Albany. The Dutch fur traders of that city drew some of their furs from the north through the Champlain Valley, but the rest came down the Mohawk from the west. For many years the trade came to Albany, and any expansion of trading posts to the westward was resisted. The Five Nations wished no posts in that direction, lest their position as the middlemen of the fur trade should be endangered.

The westward pressure, however, became constantly greater and could not be resisted. Probably the first British attempt in that direction was the establishment of a post on Irondequoit Bay on Lake Ontario, near the present Rochester, New York. This did not last, but by 1721 there were active traders at the mouth of the Oswego River, the western end of the Mohawk thoroughfare. This trade was almost certainly on a seasonal basis, but in 1727 a fortified stone house, really a redoubt, was built by Governor Burnet of New York at his own expense, because the province would not make the funds available. He never was fully repaid. The place was garrisoned by a few soldiers, and traders' huts and storehouses soon sprang up around it. On hearing of this the first reaction of the Canadian governor, de Beauharnois, was to order out the militia for an expedition to remove this thorn in the side of New France. Better judgment, however, prevailed, and a strong protest was sent to the governor of New York.

The French only the year before had built at Niagara a similar stone house, actually a fort but masquerading as a peaceful trading post, and they were in no position to cast stones. There was a sharp interchange of letters and nothing more.

For a generation Oswego was to remain a threat to Canada, and a double one at that. As a post guarding the great western thoroughfare it gave the British a spearhead on the Great Lakes from which Canada might be attacked, and through its fortunate location and its cheap and excellent trade goods it diverted many Indians and their furs away from Montreal. For years it was lightly held by small garrisons of only a handful of men. Its fortifications never amounted to much, and they rapidly became dilapidated. It was a post of vital importance, yet it remained largely neglected. In 1742, for instance, it was reported to be in a defenseless condition, occupied by a lieutenant and a command of only twenty-two men, and some of the walls were laid in clay instead of mortar.

One of the enigmas of our colonial history is the failure of the British, despite their long tradition of the importance of sea power, to utilize the inland waters of North America effectively. Lake Ontario, guarded on the east by Fort Frontenac and on the west by Fort Niagara, was the lifeline of the French west. With the foothold which Oswego gave them the British had only to build a sufficient fleet to dominate the lake, and the hinterland would be effectively blockaded. True there was still the Ottawa River with its portages into Georgian Bay and Lake Huron, but this was well to the north, and the road to the vital Ohio Valley ran through Niagara. Not much of a fleet would have been required to control the waters of Ontario, though once winter came shipping was solidly locked in the ice, most vulnerable to the torches of a raiding party. Hence there was need for a fortified harbor where the warships could be safely held and guarded until the ice went out in the spring thaw. All this, of course, would run into money, much more than would have been provided in time of peace. When war came, and funds could be made available, time was then the element that was lacking.

Throughout all the early years of the last of the colonial wars the British devoted their energy in the west to attacking the tips of the French tentacles, Duquesne, Niagara, Crown Point, and Ticonderoga. Good strategy would have dictated striking where the tentacle joined the body or at the body itself, and this was appreciated by Shirley. The initial British policy, however, was only to remove encroachments on what they felt to be their territories.

A little fleet on Lake Ontario and a sufficiently guarded harbor at Oswego would have solved the entire problem and made the British masters of the French west. As early as 1741 Governor Clarke of New York, an able and farseeing man, recommended just this procedure, but his advice fell on deaf ears, and for years futile expeditions were to march off into the wilderness and expend themselves in utter waste. Washington, Braddock, and Abercromby exhausted themselves against the tentacles and never touched the body. It was only when Bradstreet in 1758 captured Fort Frontenac with his waterborne force that the lifeline of Canada was severed, cleanly, expeditiously, and cheaply.

Despite its military potentials Oswego was used only for mercantile purposes. What fort and garrison there was served as a purely defensive force to protect a great trading post. Politically, of course, it was of great importance in showing the British flag to the western Indians, letting them realize that France was not the sole owner of the west. From the point of view of Canada the situation was intolerable. Built on what the French claimed as their territory, it not only offered a constant threat as a base for military action, but, and even worse, it was a leech sucking and fattening on the lifeblood of New France, the furs of the far west. As early as 1709 the French realized that any British establishment on Ontario would be most damaging to their interests. Yet when the post was built in 1727 the French took no action, despite vehement talk, and Oswego was allowed to go its way in peace for a generation. In 1741 the Marquis de Beauharnois again planned an expedition against the British fort, but the preparations dragged and the idea was abandoned. Throughout these years the fort was something of an orphan child of New York, the province which fathered it, but could not afford to maintain it properly. By the time the last French war was looming up on the horizon the place was in a hopeless state, the works too small, commanded on two sides by high ground, and the ill-built walls starting to crumble. In 1752 Duquesne, the French governor, was advised by his king that while the French of course could not attack Oswego in peacetime, he should exert himself to persuade the Iroquois to seize the fort, taking great care that the French should not appear to be involved in any way.

At the Alexandria conference with the colonial governors Braddock had advised among other projects the strengthening of Oswego, and this was heartily approved by all. In the late spring of 1755 reinforcements arrived at the post. Shipwrights also came. Soon more than three hundred men were at work building little warships, and the first British vessel on Lake Ontario, an undecked 40-foot row galley armed only with the lightest of cannon, was launched by the end of June.

Oswego was in a most exposed position, over 160 long wilderness miles from its nearest base, Albany, and exposed to French vessels on the lake as well as to the Indians who often lurked in the surrounding forests. It was only fifty water miles from Canada's Fort Frontenac. Even under favorable conditions a bateau required at least three weeks for the round trip from Albany. The fort existed on the far end of a precarious lifeline. Probably only the benevolent self-interest of the Five Nations allowed this little post to survive through the years.

At the Alexandria Conference, Braddock had given Shirley the task of leading an expedition against Niagara in that summer of 1755. The troops assembled at Oswego. It, of course, was essential that this base should not be captured in Shirley's absence in the west, and steps were at once taken to strengthen the post. The Oswego River flowed into Lake Ontario through a narrow stretch of low-lying ground bounded on either side by quite steep bluffs. The stone redoubt and its surrounding wall were built at the river's edge but a short way back from the lake shore, and they were commanded on three sides by materially higher land. The construction of two new forts was started, one on each side of the river on the high land. Fort Ontario on the east side was a conventional four-sided, star-shaped, palisaded structure, built of 18-inch logs, eight or nine feet high. It was surrounded by an eight-foot deep ditch, and could be considered entirely safe against musketry and perhaps even light artillery fire. Wooden barracks were built against the inside of the palisades. Fort Oswego on the west side of the river never progressed very far and became more a collection of huts than a fort.

Shirley's Niagara expedition never got started because of delay, bad weather, and lack of proper shipping, but he was fertile in his plans for the following year, and Oswego was to remain his base.

In the fall of 1756 Lydius made a formal deposition at Albany concerning events of the summer of the previous year. In accordance with Shirley's instructions he had assembled a party of Indians and Albany men and proceeded to Oswego. He sent scouts to look over the French fort at Niagara and one of them, Aaron, an Indian, even succeeded in spending two nights inside the fort. He reported that the garrison was only a hundred and that the posts of the stockade were so rotten that they had to be held up with props. Lydius claimed that he begged for permission to add three hundred men from the garrison at Oswego to his own party of two hundred and fifty, to borrow a vessel and proceed against Niagara, which he was sure he could capture without difficulty. This was refused, and he then asked only for the vessel, for which he would give a bond, and permission to go with only his own little party. Again he was turned down and was accused of trying to steal the glory. The inference is that Shirley wanted it all for himself.

Efforts were continued throughout that fall to strengthen the Oswego post. Two regular regiments, the 50th (Shirley's) and the 51st (Pepperrell's), were left to continue work on the forts and to guard the place. While these regiments were rated as regulars, they had been raised in America, and most of the men and many of the officers were colonials without any real battle experience. Moreover, their muskets were very poor, the locks badly worn, with the frizzens of such soft metal that they often failed to strike a spark. The guns of the 51st were old captured Dutch weapons and the cartridge boxes of both regiments had compartments too small to hold the regulation British cartridge. This sad condition was reported to Shirley but no better weapons were then available in America. Throughout the colonial period it was the custom of the War Office to send all the cast-off and otherwise inferior muskets to America, while rearming the troops at home with newer weapons. One of the other regular regiments in America was equipped for a period with French muskets captured at Louisbourg in 1758.

The problem of supplying the large garrison was handled quite incompetently, and provisions soon became in short supply. At one time during the winter, and winter was indeed rugged on the shores of Lake Ontario, the daily ration was down to two ounces of salt pork and eight of bread. One company of fifty lost thirty-nine men before spring came to lessen their suffering. Each of the eight companies of the 50th lost some thirty men during those freezing months of hardship. The carpenters fared better, since they were paid and fed by a contractor, but they could not work on the shipping because the soldiers were too weak to furnish a guard against the prowling Indians. By the end of March, 1756, the garrison was destitute, and it was decided to abandon the post and to attempt to struggle eastward to the settlements. Just at this critical moment aid at last arrived. Oneida Lake was still frozen, and the barrels of salt pork were rolled by hand for its entire length of some twenty miles. The garrison had only just managed to exist through the winter, and nothing had been accomplished on the fortifications or on the little warships.

Early in the spring of 1756 Shirley placed Captain John Bradstreet in command of a force of forty companies of bateaumen, two thousand men in all, and gave him the entire responsibility for building boats and operating the supply line to Oswego. Bradstreet was one of the great men of the last colonial war, though scant justice has been done him. We first met him eleven years before at the siege of Louisbourg, for his part in which he was rewarded with a company in Pepperrell's new regiment and made lieutenant governor of St. John's, Newfoundland. He continued to serve in that region until the spring of 1755, when he brought two companies of his regiment to reinforce the Oswego garrison. An officer of regulars, he nevertheless could handle colonials, even such rugged individuals as the boatmen of the Mohawk. Bradstreet quickly organized his group, built bateaux, and got his first convoy out to Oswego. On the return trip with the empty bateaux he was jumped by a party of French and Indians, but drove them off with little damage to his party. The French always exaggerated their achievements and this was reported in the French newspapers as resulting in the destruction of two hundred "vessels" and the killing or capturing of five hundred men with almost no loss to the Canadian party. Bradstreet actually saved all his boats, lost sixty or seventy men and brought eighty French muskets back to Albany.

Indians padded through the heavy woods, and anyone who wandered much beyond the immediate vicinity of the Oswego forts was asking for trouble. Sentries were sometimes found dead and scalped at their posts and scouting or wood-cutting parties might fail to return. A member of the garrison recorded that "one of our soldiers came in [this morning] from the edge of the woods, where it seems he had lain all night having . . . got drunk . . . [and] found he had lost his scalp, but could not tell how nor when." The man survived.

Work was resumed on the forts and the ships, but things dragged. A sufficient supply of cannon and rigging was lacking for the two rather sizable craft still on the ways, the *Halifax* snow of eighteen guns and the *London* brigantine of sixteen. Had these two been completed the British fleet would have outmatched the French, but they never got into action. At the time of the French attack Oswego was guarded by only two little warships, each carrying ten small guns, while the French had three ships of greater tonnage armed with thirty-four guns, most of which were of materially larger size. Small wonder that the British squadron accomplished nothing; it was beaten before the start. Oswego was a plum ready to fall as soon as any reasonably sized force could shake the tree, and this the French proceeded to do in the summer of 1756.

A new character, and a great one, now makes his entrance on the Canadian stage. Louis Joseph, Marquis de Montcalm de Saint-Véran was a career officer of the French Army. Forty-four years of age, he had served his king since early youth and fought in many campaigns. A Provençal, he was excitable, nervous, impetuous, quick to anger and also quick to cool, but most capable and a man of complete integrity, a quality then not too common. The Indians, who had heard great things of him, were amazed at his small size. He was to prove himself far and away the best general that New France ever possessed. Montcalm reached Canada in May of 1756, and he brought some able assistants with him—Brigadier Lévis, who was to die a duke and a marshal of France, and Colonel Bourlamaque, another able officer.

As aide-de-camp Montcalm had an extraordinarily gifted young man, Louis Antoine de Bougainville, a half-pay captain of dragoons, but fated to die an admiral of the French Navy and a peer of France. After the fall of Canada, Bougainville was to transfer to the navy and become a famous explorer, predecessor of Captain Cook in the South Seas. He it was who brought the bougainvillea flower to Europe. While still in his twenties he had written a book on the integral calculus which gained him election to the British Royal Society, a signal honor for one so young. Bougainville had served for a period in the suite of the French ambassador in London and had learned to know the English and their language. Now he had come to Canada, an observer with a brilliant and inquiring mind, one who lived with Montcalm and knew all that took place. He was short and plump, almost fat, and he suffered from asthma, but not when at sea, and this perhaps explains his later shift to the navy. He must have been a delightful companion, and he and Montcalm became close friends. Bougainville kept a journal, and one much out of the ordinary, which tells us frankly and honestly what he did, saw, and heard. For the period which it covers it is by far the best single piece of source material known to exist. He also wrote many letters to relatives at home which are even more frank and revealing than the diary.

Pierre François de Rigaud, Marquis de Vaudreuil, was the Canadian-born son of a former governor of New France, and was fated to be the last governor of the French colony. A naval officer, he had been governor of Louisiana, and in 1755 he came to Quebec to replace Governor Duquesne. He was a man of unusual character, pleasant, mild, and affable, but weak, ill-informed, vain, easily led by evil influences, ambitious, and intensely jealous. His only military experience had been on an expedition with Indians, when an old man was captured and burned at the stake. Vaudreuil was said often to have laughed at the memory of that burning, because the Indian made such funny faces as he died! Vaudreuil was a true patriot and loved Canada and its people. He also was excellent in dealing with the Indians and persuading them to his way of thinking. He was closely associated with Bigot and the clique who were so openly robbing Canada, and must have known what they were doing, yet he himself apparently never benefited from their immense operations. An unusual man, with some abilities and many faults, he dearly loved his country, yet was to do it great harm.

Montcalm was an officer of the regular army and as such commanded all the regular troops in Canada as well as any Canadian formations that might be assigned to him in addition, but he was subordinate to Governor Vaudreuil. Relations between the lively, impulsive Provençal and the jealous, egotistical Canadian soon were strained, and Montcalm's position became a difficult one. Vaudreuil at times issued orders and allocations purely out of spite, and was continually sending lying letters home to the authorities in an attempt to undermine their confidence in Montcalm. The governor wished to have Brigadier Lévis, who was more congenial to the Canadians, put in command. Throughout the rest of the war Vaudreuil was to continue intriguing against Montcalm, but the victories won by the French general were to tell their own story. Eventually Montcalm, although he always remained under Vaudreuil's orders in theory, became practically independent in military matters, and the governor, to his vast disgust, was even ordered to consult with the general on all administrative matters that in any way concerned the defense of the colony.

Montcalm's first move after his arrival in Canada was a trip to Fort Carillon at Ticonderoga, the southern outpost in the vital Champlain Valley. He soon returned north and in accordance with orders from Vaudreuil marshaled his forces and moved up the St. Lawrence against Oswego. On the way he stopped for a night at the mission of La Presentation, the Ogdensburg, New York, of today, and met Abbé Piquet, the militant priest of that mission. Let Bougainville tell of the mission and its founder. "The Abbé Piquet, able missionary, known for a voyage he made to France with three Indians, obtained a 12 arpent [about 18 acres] concession above La Galette. Five years ago he built a fort of squared posts, flanked by four strong bastions, palisaded without and with a water filled ditch. Beside the fort a village of a hundred fires [families] of Iroquois chiefs, all warriors. . . . They have made a clearing, have cows, horses, pigs and hens. They plant Indian corn . . . Abbé Piquet teaches them and drills them in the French military exercises. His assistant is Abbé Chevalier Terley, called Chevalier Terley because of his warlike disposition. There is in the fort a captain of colonial troops as commander, but all real control is ecclesiastical." Abbé Piquet came along later to Oswego with some of his Indians but did not arrive before the forts fell.

The French had control of Lake Ontario, and could go where they wished in their lake-type bateaux. These were large enough for the often very rough waters of the lake and would carry a dozen or more soldiers, who could stand and fire their muskets without overturning. The British river bateaux were small and tipped over easily. Without the slightest difficulty Montcalm was able to assemble his little army of three thousand men, mostly regulars, but including some Canadians and two hundred and fifty Indians, near Oswego and to land them safely a little to the east of Fort Ontario, the recently completed star-shaped stockade. He brought an ample train of artillery, some of which had been taken from the English at Braddock's defeat.

The forest had never been properly cleared away to the east of the fort, and Montcalm established a battery of heavy guns, partly concealed in the edge of the woods only two hundred yards from the fort. The British cannonaded the battery with their little guns but hardly delayed the progress of its construction. Soon it was seen that the French cannon would shortly open fire on the weak stockaded walls of the fort, and the decision was made to abandon the east side of the river. The guns were spiked, the powder thrown down the well, and the garrison was ferried across the river, marching into the unfinished Fort Oswego. It was soon realized, however, that this place too was in no condition to be defended, so the men moved down into the old stone redoubt and its surrounding walls. Hardly a man had been lost.

The French, who had not yet fired a single cannon, placed a new battery in position on the bluff east of the river and opened fire on the old redoubt with its mud-laid walls. The British position, being practically at water level, was almost entirely open to the fire of the French. The walls on the exposed side were raised by a row of pork barrels, but to little purpose. The British commander was cut in two by a cannon shot, and the fort promptly surrendered. The losses had been minor, but after the surrender the Indians broke loose, finished off and scalped all the sick and the wounded and massacred a number more. Both Montcalm and Bougainville were most reticent about this phase in their journals, but there seems to be no doubt about it. The total number butchered was perhaps a hundred, but this may be a little high. The fact remains that the French took too few precautions against a massacre, and one took place, dire forewarning of what was to happen in a much greater way next year on Lake George.

All the prisoners were ordered into Fort Ontario for safekeeping and for protection from the Indians, who soon scalped those who lagged behind. At the fort the British were put under the protection of the French regulars. Stephen Cross was one of the shipwrights, a Newburyport man, and he kept a diary throughout the campaign. He recorded that some of the British filled their canteens with rum just after the surrender and got drunk as soon as they reached Fort Ontario, "singing, dancing, hollowing, and cahooping, [so] that it appeared more like a Bedlam, than a prison." The Indians also got drunk, and "hearing the confused noyes of those within [Fort Ontario]; united their hideous yells and rushed the guards exceeding hard, to git in among us, with their tomehawks; and it was with great difficulty the French, could prevent them." This madhouse continued "until the operations of the liquor, together with the strong exercions, began to dispose boath parties to sleep . . . and . . . all was quiet." That must have been a night to remember. The French treated the prisoners well. Cross was taken to France, eventually returned safely home and lived to become a builder of warships for our navy during the Revolution.

The French carried away great spoils of war, although much fell into greedy private hands. Captain Pouchot, commandant of Fort Niagara, saw a fish seine most suitable for the use of his garrison, and asked to have it saved. It disappeared nevertheless, but next year he saw it again at Ticonderoga, sold to the king for some 1100 francs by some speculating looter. Montcalm burned and destroyed all that remained and departed, abandoning the place to the wolves. A few days later English scouts found an empty site, covered with ashes and debris, and guarded by a great wooden cross, raised by Abbé Piquet to the glory of God and the memory of Montcalm's first triumph in North America.

The loss of Oswego was a shock to England. Too late was its vital strategic importance realized. Only the year before had Admiral John Byng lost the great naval battle off Minorca, which resulted in the fall of that important post in the Mediterranean. Only recently had that unfortunate admiral, scapegoat to political pressures, been executed on his own quarterdeck as responsible for the loss of the island. Incidentally it was the fall of Minorca that caused England to declare war on France in the late spring of 1756, changing the informal colonial war of the past two years into a formal one. Braddock's defeat and Johnson's victory on Lake George took place during a period when the two countries pretended to be at peace.

The great trading post of the British west was gone, and with it all hold on Lake Ontario. The smaller forts between the Mohawk and Oswego were soon abandoned and burned, and the frontier fell back to German Flats, halfway to Albany, and itself doomed to destruction by the French the following year. The great throughway to the west was closed and it was to remain so for two years to come.

A cabal, consisting of Lieutenant Governor James De Lancey and Sir William Johnson of New York, and Lieutenant Governor William Pownall of New Jersey had been working against Shirley, and they had powerful friends in England, not the least of whom was Pownall's brother, secretary to the Board of Trade. Shirley had befriended Johnson earlier, and had recommended his appointment to the command of the 1755 Crown Point expedition that earned him his baronetcy. Johnson seems to have been largely responsible for initiating the unfortunate relations which existed between the two men. In the late summer of 1755 Shirley had asked Johnson, in charge of the northern Indians under a commission issued by Braddock, to procure him some Indians to guide and scout for him on the way to Oswego. Johnson told him that he did not need any Indians, hardly a diplomatic manner of answering the request of the man who had just succeeded to the North American command. Shirley then commissioned Lydius to raise the Indians that Johnson had refused, and this naturally irritated the baronet, who wanted no interference with his Iroquois.

This initial friction between the two greatest Americans of their times had been further magnified and encouraged by other self-seeking men until it became a real quarrel.

Shirley was recalled in the spring of 1756 and he turned over the command to General Abercromby at the end of June. Lord Loudoun arrived shortly thereafter and replaced Abercromby, who remained as his subordinate. Abercromby was warned by Shirley through his engineer officer of the weakness of Oswego, but the new commander dallied, and no reinforcement reached the threatened fort.

The Marquis de Vaudreuil of course took full credit for the fall of Oswego, as he was perhaps entitled to, since he ordered the expedition, although no brilliant mind was needed to produce the idea. He was most popular with the Canadians, who were only too willing to credit him with all the glory of the victory. Someone wrote a ballad which was sung in the streets of Canada, greatly to the governor's pleasure. The first verse went:

> *Nous celebrons du grand Vaudreuil*
> *La sagesse et la gloire.*
> *Toute l'Angleterre est en deuil*
> *Au bruit de sa victoire.*
> *Chouagen* [Oswego] *n'est plus. Nos soldats*
> *L'ont forcé de se rendre,*
> *Et ses morts ne sont plus qu'un tas*
> *De poussière et de cendre.*

Chapter XIV

LORD LOUDOUN TAKES COMMAND

Jᴏʜɴ Cᴀᴍᴘʙᴇʟʟ, 4th Earl of Loudoun, a Scottish peer, was selected as the new commander in chief in place of Shirley. He was a capable and meticulous soldier, painstaking and prone to immersing himself in paper work, which in those days was just as deeply involved in red tape and complications as army paper work seems always fated to be. Loudoun was well qualified for the command, and he had a broader background than most soldiers. He was a member of the Royal Society, no mean honor for any man, and especially so for a soldier. A wealthy man, he was accustomed to living in style. He established a headquarters such as America had never before seen. It required nearly one entire ship to carry his personal baggage overseas. He reached New York late in July, 1756, bringing a suite of sixteen servants and a mistress as well. Loudoun liked to set a good table. During Christmas week of 1756 he and his guests consumed fifty-two dozen bottles of various wines, not to mention the spirits they must have drunk in their punch.

The new commander evidently had formed an antipathy for Shirley before the two ever met, and this soon grew into a violent dislike on the part of Loudoun. The professional soldier was shocked by the confusion in Shirley's handling of army finances, and of course was at heart scornful of the amateur soldier, while the latter, with a clear picture of the North American problem in his mind, was more impatient of detail than was desirable. Shirley turned over the command to Loudoun at once but showed little haste in obeying his orders to return to England, although it was intimated that he was to be given the governorship of Jamaica, quite the plum of colonial appointments. His delay gave his enemies further time to work against him. It was even hinted that he had been engaged in traitorous dealings with the French. In the fall of 1756 the late North American commander went home to an unfriendly welcome in England, and America lost the services of a good man. Shirley narrowly escaped court-martial, and the governorship of Jamaica went elsewhere. Several years later Shirley was made governor of the Bahamas, and in 1769 he returned to Boston to live out the last two years of his life.

Shirley was accused of being the cause of the fall of Oswego, of irregularities in his accounts and worse, and he narrowly escaped being sent home under arrest. In many ways he was the greatest of all the colonial governors, the one possessed of the broadest strategic concept of the British empire. He had advised London that Fort Frontenac was the key to the west, and that its capture would have the same result as that of Niagara, but that it would be cheaper and easier. Three years later events were to prove him right.

He was not a military man, and he neither understood nor had patience with the involved military administrative procedure of his day. One of his harshest critics among modern historians sums him up as: "careless in financial matters, too trusting of subordinates, ignorant of army routine, a bungler but not a thief." Others have taken a more charitable view. One very wise contemporary wrote: "For though Shirley was not bred a soldier, he was sensible and sagacious in himself, and attentive to good advice from others, capable of forming judicious plans, and quick and active in carrying them into execution." A statement such as that coming from Benjamin Franklin should go far to assure us of Shirley's worth. Never again were any of the colonies to see a governor like him. He understood and got along well with the Americans, appreciated their viewpoint as well as that of the mother country, and could reconcile the broad empire interests of the one with the much more local concerns of the others. He deserved well of this country, but there is no memorial to him among us, save for a little Massachusetts town bearing his name and the sad remains of his once great mansion house, now falling into final disrepair in a crowded Boston slum.

The new commander in chief reached Albany at the end of July, 1756, but he had been preceded by two of his subordinates, Generals Abercromby and Webb. The former had assumed temporary command pending the arrival of Loudoun, who almost at once was greeted with the news of the fall of Oswego. This of course was blamed on the former commander, not perhaps without some justice. Shirley in his defense claimed that he had put a sufficient garrison into Oswego to defend it and had given orders that the forts were to be strengthened. His plans and orders were usually quite sound, but they were not always carried out by his subordinates, and he tended to be lax in ascertaining their satisfactory execution. He also stated—and here he had a rather good case—that Abercromby was basically responsible through his discharge of nearly half of Bradstreet's capable bateau-men, men most useful both for transport and for battle, and his holding the remainder in idleness at Schenectady for a month. They should have been carrying troops forward and moving from "The Great Carrying Place" at the headwaters of the Mohawk to Oswego the cannon necessary to arm the two largest British vessels, now complete save for their armament. These little warships, Shirley claimed, would have given the British command of Lake Ontario and prevented the disaster. Possibly so, but it was cutting matters very fine, for time would still have been necessary to mount the guns. Nevertheless he had a point, for there is no doubt that Abercromby slowed up the reinforcing of Oswego once he had arrived at Albany.

Shirley had promptly informed the new acting commander of conditions at Oswego, and had made certain that he also received the engineer's report on the unsatisfactory state of the forts. In early July, Bradstreet returned to Albany and told Abercromby that he had definite intelligence that the French would shortly attack Oswego. The British general then ordered the 44th Regiment to prepare to move to the threatened point, but their departure was delayed for a month, due partly to lack of provisions resulting from the new command suddenly canceling contracts for supplies.

The Massachusetts governor had no idea of any attack on Oswego—he was still thinking of it as a base for an advance against Niagara. Nor did either Loudoun or Abercromby have any fears, despite Bradstreet's clear warning. The truth is that all the senior commanders were caught completely unawares. A new star had appeared in Canada, a general who pounced while others pondered, and Oswego was lost despite anything the British could have done in this summer of 1756.

What good could one or even two regiments of trained regulars have done to save a frontier post whose walls could not resist a cannon ball? Taking full advantage of New France's great waterway, Montcalm brought siege artillery to forts whose defenses were useless against even light cannon. What could the defenders have done, unless they greatly outnumbered the French, an impossible condition at this time? Their cannon were too small to damage the French batteries, and Montcalm had his trained battalions of regular troops to guard against a sortie. Oswego was a perfect example of the fall of a frontier fort through the successful transport by the assailant of relatively heavy artillery to the immediate vicinity of the objective. It was sound logistics, not fighting, that caused the fall of the British post.

Lord Loudoun set his capable hands to work on the problem of producing an army from the various separate colonies. Eventually he was able to achieve the start of an effective military union, an objective sought by the Albany Conference but not accomplished. Loudoun was never successful in battle in North America, but through his organization of the military administration and supply and his innovations in troop training he laid a firm and solid base for those who were to follow him. Some, at least, of the fame and rewards won by his successors rightfully belonged to him.

Loudoun apparently enjoyed pleasant relations with the colonists and his office door was always open to visitors. He must have had a sense of humor, something many senior officers often lacked. A report buried deep in the Paris Archives tells of the examination of a British soldier captured in North America, who said that he had heard the following story about the commander in chief. A certain prominent colonial politician asked Loudoun what his plans were for the coming year. The Scot replied, "Can you keep a secret?" The politician assured him that he could. "And so can I," said Loudoun. This same story has been told about Stonewall Jackson, and it is probable that it was enjoyed by Caesar's centurions, but it is amusing to read it written in the French of two centuries ago.

Lord Loudoun introduced some important innovations into the training of British regulars. First of all, however, it was necessary that they should be fully trained in the standard European procedures, because sooner or later they must expect to meet French regulars in formal battle. But, once this type of training had produced a sufficient degree of competency, it was possible to add variations suitable to the woods fighting for which they would also have to be prepared. For a supposedly tradition-bound British regular Loudoun prescribed some surprising procedures. European practice required soldiers to fire standing while closed up in tight ranks, but this Scottish general ordered that his men should be taught to fire while lying prone on the ground and also must learn to load their firelocks while in this position, a rather difficult feat and a shocking idea to many a stiff British guardsman. He also saw that flanking parties were so taught that when they ran into an enemy they separated, took to trees and fired from behind their trunks. It was found that the safest form of road through the wilderness was one where a thin screening fringe of trees and underbrush was left standing close along each side of the road, and then all growth cleared away on both sides for at least thirty yards beyond. Anyone who says that the British never tried to adapt their tactics to woods fighting is gravely mistaken.

It had become increasingly apparent to the British high command that dependence could not be put on Indians to act as scouts and security agents. At best the Indian was undependable, at worst a liar or a spy for the French. Moreover one could never tell how many, if any, Indians could be bribed, cajoled or otherwise persuaded to accompany an expedition, or, if some did, how long they would remain. Yet some agency was necessary to meet the Indians or the French on their own ground, and this need was ultimately filled by the ranger, an irregular soldier skilled in fighting Indians and in watching over the activities of the French. Certain men living along the frontiers had gradually developed the special characteristics necessary for this purpose, and in 1755 rangers first appear as a distinct part of the colonial armies, employed by Johnson after the Battle of Lake George to watch over the activities of the French.

The most famous of these people was Robert Rogers, a man of a dubious past and an unsavory future, but at this period a most useful servant of the Crown. Much romance has been written around him and his men, and he has been glorified as one of the great of the period at the expense of better men. There is no doubt that, save for one or two lapses, he was an incomparable woods fighter and leader of irregulars, though other aspects of his character were less praiseworthy. When Shirley took over the North American command from Braddock, Rogers made a trip back to Boston to see him and came away with a commission to raise a company of sixty rangers on a pay base materially above that of the British regular. Rogers' Rangers soon began to make a name for themselves in the Champlain region, reconnoitering the French forts, killing and scalping an occasional sentry or Indian and now and then engaging in minor battles. Their services became so essential that Abercromby authorized a second company, and later in 1756 two more, as well as one composed of Stockbridge Indians under their leader, Captain Jacobs. With five additional companies Rogers went with Loudoun on the 1757 attempt on Louisbourg, and he was made a major in the spring of 1758.

Despite their undoubted value the Rangers soon showed various weaknesses, particularly a deplorable lack of discipline and occasionally outright insubordination. The companies were largely composed of rugged and self-sufficient adventurers who took unkindly to control of any sort, particularly in the intervals between periods of action. One scouting expedition of Rangers was surprised by the French because it was so careless as to stop to shoot pigeons. Rogers, very much of a rough diamond himself, could handle his original company in excellent fashion, but as the corps expanded his control diminished, partly because the quality of some of the new officers was poor. Many of the men recruited for the Rangers left much to be desired. Lord Loudoun described the two new companies of Rangers formed in the fall of 1756 as composed of Irish, sailors, and Spaniards, and it is obvious that he did not think much of any of them. Nevertheless, he realized that they met an essential need, for he wrote to Pitt: "[Rangers] are a species of troops we cannot be without, now that, I may venture to say, we have no Indians, and the enemy has so great a body of them." Throughout the last French War the services of rangers were essential to the British effort, but it became increasingly apparent that, while these services must be continued, they might equally well be obtained from a corps more susceptible to discipline and less expensive to maintain. Lieutenant Colonel Thomas Gage, later to be the last royal governor of Massachusetts, offered to raise at his own cost a regiment of light infantry, British regulars but trained to serve as rangers. Early in 1758 Gage's Regiment, the 80th, was organized, composed largely of American woodsmen but carried on the regular establishment. This was the first body of light infantry ever to be included in the British Army. Gage initially raised the regiment out of his own pocket, but he was more than repaid when as colonel he received the various perquisites connected with the ownership of a regiment.

Rogers led his Rangers into many petty fights and skirmishes during four years of conflict. In most they attained their objective, but occasionally they went down in defeat. Their most famous exploit was the raid on the town of the St. Francis Indians near the St. Lawrence River in the fall of 1759, in which they executed their mission of destroying the town but suffered terrible punishment on their 230-mile-long retreat back to the British settlements on the Connecticut River near today's Bellows Falls in Vermont.

In the early 1750s another similar body of scouts and woodsmen existed in Nova Scotia, where Captain John Gorham led a company of hard-bitten New Englanders, and a little later Major George Scott, former commander of Fort Lawrence at Chignecto, most successfully commanded a body of light troops both at the 1758 siege of Louisbourg and a year later at Quebec.

The Duke of Cumberland, son of King George II, had for some years been head of the British Army, but in December 1756, not many weeks after the news of the fall of Oswego reached London, William Pitt, later to be Earl of Chatham, came to a position of power in the British government, and Cumberland retired to private life. Pitt at once started dictating details of operation to the military leaders to a much greater degree than had been customary, and to some extent he tended to restrict their authority unduly. In the spring of 1757 he was thrown out of office, but three months later was back in the saddle, more firmly in power than before. Throughout the rest of this last of America's French wars he was to guide the British effort firmly and with great success. It was due to his energy, genius, and able direction that the British Empire emerged victorious from this great struggle, which in Europe was called the Seven Years' War. It was fought by a coalition of most of the European powers against the rising state of Prussia and the ambitions of Frederick the Great, supported by Britain alone. This was a mighty war which ravaged central Europe for years until both sides were well-nigh exhausted. It extended to the east as far as India, where Clive's victories led to the inclusion of that land into the British Empire.

It is easy to become immersed in the French and Indian War on this continent and to wonder why this or that thing was not done, why more troops were not sent, or why certain essentials were lacking. One must remember that the American campaign was only a side show to the great struggle going on in Europe, on the high seas and in the Far East. Pitt had to consider all theaters of operation, to evaluate their importance, and to parcel out generals, men, supplies, and money, none of which were by any means in inexhaustible supply, where they were most needed in the mighty struggle. The early operations of the war in America all occurred during a theoretical peace, but once the Continental strife got under way North America became of secondary importance, and both of the opposing sides had to make out with what could be spared from the more vital field of operations.

The plans for the campaign of 1757 called for an attack on the re-established French base of Louisbourg, assisted by additional troops from England and an ample fleet, while a defensive position was to be taken along the rest of the North American front. Loudoun was to take with him to Cape Breton a large part of the British troops now on the American continent, thus leaving the covering forces for the Champlain and Mohawk frontiers on the scanty side. Should the French make trouble in those regions recourse would have to be made to the colonial militia for support.

The Louisbourg attempt was a complete fiasco due to several causes, none of which could be charged to Loudoun. The naval force and the transports carrying the troops from England were long delayed by bad weather and did not reach Halifax until early July. Loudoun held the American contingent at New York waiting news of the arrival of the British fleet in American waters. At last, tired of waiting, he risked sailing for Halifax with a quite inadequate naval escort and arrived there at about the same time as the ships from England. The bad weather continued. Fogs usually blanketed Louisbourg in the late spring and early summer, while the northerly winds of spring later changed to southerly and raised heavy surf on the rocky shores upon which any assault must land. That year the fogs were exceptional and lasted with few intervals well into the fall. More serious still the French had managed to send off their naval forces early and succeeded in getting seventeen warships and several frigates into Louisbourg Harbor before the British arrived.

Loudoun held his troops at Halifax for most of the summer, and planted a great garden to keep the men supplied with fresh vegetables, while the fleet was held at sea in Cape Breton waters. It soon became evident that nothing could be done against the French citadel that year. This was still further emphasized when a great hurricane—a line storm the New Englanders called it—came on September 24, scattered the British fleet, with one ship sunk, and twelve dismasted. The commander called off the expedition and led his men back to New York. In this he showed good judgment but great courage as well, for he directly disobeyed Pitt's orders and risked the fate Admiral Byng had bravely met on his own quarterdeck but the year before.

Loudoun soon was relieved of his command, partly no doubt because of his lack of success, but also for political reasons, as he had been a protégé of Cumberland. Moreover he had been guilty of indiscretion in some of his unofficial correspondence. Had he been left as the North American leader he might ultimately have achieved the success which came to others, even if he was no genius in the art of war, for the ultimate victory was to be gained by one who was also a sound and conscientious plodder rather than a brilliant exploiter of opportunities.

Lord Loudoun returned to England, to his gardening and tree planting, and to the lady friends he is reputed to have left behind. Some five years later he was made second in command of British troops in Portugal and did well there. He was unfortunate in that the period of his North American command produced two major disasters, Oswego and the William Henry massacre, as well as the failure of the great Louisbourg expedition. This has caused historians to overlook the fine work he did in pulling the colonies together and in building up the supply system, the methods of training troops, and the intelligence service, all of which together were to make more easy and certain the task of his successors.

Chapter XV

MASSACRE ON LAKE GEORGE

The southern end of Lake George is a straight shore two-thirds of a mile long. At its westerly end there were in colonial days a little brook and a marshy hollow, to the east of which lay the vegetable gardens of Fort William Henry. Then came the fort itself, covered on its easterly side by a marsh of some size, with a nose of higher ground dividing it from a second marsh which extended to the easterly shore of the lake. A road led along the lake shore easterly from the fort, crossed the marsh on a bridge, and then climbed the slope of the nose and went on south to Fort Edward on the Hudson. The fort was an irregular square with four bastions, built of timber cribbing, filled with earth and gravel, and faced with logs. The ramparts were armed with cannon, both large and small, swivels, and mortars. Within the walls there were wooden barracks for a garrison of perhaps four hundred men, storehouses, casemates, and a magazine. It was a standard frontier fort of the place and period, sufficient to resist an attack by infantry, and even by light artillery. Against heavy siege artillery skillfully employed it would stand little chance. A British military engineer had visited it in 1756 and reported that it was weak on the western side and that a ravelin, a wedge-shaped outer work, should be built there, and that the walls should be raised another three feet, bringing them to a height of nearly twenty feet. This was never done.

In late February, 1757, the Marquis de Vaudreuil sent a raiding party south against Fort William Henry, hoping to take it by surprise at a time of year when no attack would be expected. Sixteen hundred men, French regulars, Canadians, and Indians, were put under command of Rigaud, governor of Three Rivers and brother of Vaudreuil. To them were issued special food and winter equipment, all of which had to be dragged on sledges made like a giant's skis. Many of the officers bought dogs, and in some cases even horses, to drag their sleds. Dogs sold for up to one hundred livres, nearly a month's pay of a captain. At the last minute there was a thaw, horses and dogs were abandoned, and even the senior officers had to haul their own equipment and supplies. The expedition tarried at Fort Carillon for several days to make scaling ladders with which to storm the fort, and then continued south over the ice of Lake George. Whenever I go along the shores of that lake in the dead of winter I think that I can see them, a long line of little black specks plodding their way along the glaring surface of the ice and snow covered lake. They reached the vicinity of William Henry at night, but through carelessness were discovered, and lost the chance of surprise.

The fort was manned by about three hundred and fifty men under a competent commander, Major William Eyre, and it successfully resisted the French attack, made by musket fire alone. Artillery could hardly have been brought along under these winter conditions. The attackers hung around for a few days and succeeded in burning a couple of sloops, many bateaux and whaleboats, and various outbuildings of the fort. No major damage was done, but the loss of the boats was to be a handicap when summer came.

The French slowly dragged their snowshoes northward, exhausted by weeks in the open without tents or shelter from the winter winds. Some woodsman genius had devised a method of sleeping which is said not to have been uncomfortable. It was probably thus that they passed the long winter nights. A circular depression, perhaps twenty feet in diameter, would be dug down a foot or two into the snow which was piled up into a surrounding wall. A roaring fire would be built in the center and the men would lie down like the spokes of a wheel on a layer of fir branches, their feet to the fire. Many of the party suffered from snow blindness on the homeward march and had to be guided by their comrades. The expedition could hardly be called a success, although it was reported as such by Vaudreuil in letters back to France.

General Webb expected a French movement up the Champlain Valley in the summer of 1757, and to guard against it he sent a considerable number of troops to the southerly end of Lake George. By August the fort was garrisoned with fifty regulars and 385 Massachusetts and New Hampshire troops, and commanded by a captain. All the rest of the 2200 men under Lieutenant Colonel Monro were penned up in a hurriedly constructed barricaded camp on the nose of higher ground almost half a mile to the rear of the fort, and all the senior officers seem to have been stationed there. At this camp they had a few pieces of artillery, too small to be very effective against besieging troops.

The capture of a colonial fort in the final analysis depended almost entirely upon logistics, the operation of getting a reasonable amount of fairly heavy artillery, and, if at all possible, a 13-inch mortar, within effective range of the fort concerned. It was almost axiomatic that once this was accomplished the fort would sooner or later have to surrender. An analysis of all the various French and British expeditions against frontier forts during the colonial period shows that this rule held, without exception, and in the cases where artillery did not arrive or was not employed the fort was successfully defended. Thus an expedition such as Montcalm brought against Fort William Henry consisted of a striking force of heavy artillery, escorted by infantry, who would also furnish the labor to emplace the guns, and would guard them against possible sorties from the fort or the advance of a relief force. Finally in this heavily wooded country the reconnaissance mission, fulfilled in more open and civilized lands by cavalry, was here to be carried out for the French by Indians, who had all the capabilities for scouting and intelligence save for two. They were apt to go where they wished, regardless of orders, and one could not depend upon what they reported. Thus the French found it necessary to supplement them in many cases by adding a few Canadians to each party.

Montcalm brought eighteen hundred Indians on the expedition, some eight hundred Christian redskins from the missions, accompanied by Abbé Piquet and two other priests, and almost a thousand wild Indians from the region of the Great Lakes, with one priest and several partisan leaders and half-breed interpreters in their train. Father Roubaud, the Jesuit missionary at St. Francis, went along with this Indian contingent, and left a graphic account of their experience. "Imagine a great congregation of savages decorated with all those ornaments most capable, to the European eye of disfiguring one's appearance, vermilion, white, green, yellow, black made with soot or the scrapings of cooking pots; the face of a single Indian unites all these colors methodically applied, with aid of a little grease which serves as pomade. Behold the paint which goes to work on these dress occasions to embellish not only the face but even the head, almost all close shaven except for a little tuft of hair saved on the very top as a point of attachment for bird feathers or some bits of wampum or some other such trinket. Each part of the head has a special ornament, the nose has a pendant, there are others for the ears, which are hung there from childhood and have by their weight so elongated the ear lobes that they reach to the shoulders . . . a shirt smeared with vermilion, a wampum collar, silver bracelets, a great knife hung on the chest, a belt of varied colors, but always burlesquely assorted, shoes of moose hide, that is the dress of the savage."

Now let Bougainville take up the story. In a letter to his brother he wrote: ". . . Indians, naked, black, red, howling, bellowing, dancing, singing the war song, getting drunk, yelling for 'broth,' that is to say blood, drawn from 500 leagues away by the smell of fresh human blood and the chance to teach their young men how one carves up a human being destined for the pot. Behold our comrades who, night and day, are our shadows. I shiver at the frightful spectacles which they are preparing for us." Such were the allies that Montcalm was leading against the British.

The French army of some eight thousand men assembled at Fort Carillon at Ticonderoga in late July, 1757. The six thousand white men were divided almost equally between French regulars and Canadian militia. The soldiers left their vests behind, taking only coat, blanket, and weapons. Each company of regulars was allowed three tents, while every two officers could take a small tarpaulin as a shelter. Montcalm took no mattress himself, but conceded that some of the older officers might do so if they wished. Despite this Spartan equipment some of the pleasures of life went along for the officers, since, while chicken coops were forbidden, one might take live fowl if lashed together or otherwise tied up, and each officer might carry seven and a half quarts of wine with him.

The expedition was divided into two parts. Lévis took about a third of the army overland down the west side of Lake George, rough and rugged country, starting a day ahead of Montcalm's main force, which proceeded up the lake in canoes and bateaux. The two forces met as planned at the head of the lake and landed without opposition.

What followed was the normal routine of besieging a fortress. Montcalm did not have men enough to invest the place on all sides, but the terrain was such that relief could come only by the road from Fort Edward. He at once sent Lévis with a sufficient force to block approach by that route, and directed the Indians to throw out a reconnaissance screen to the south. Meanwhile the artillery arrived and was put ashore. The main force camped near the west side of the lake perhaps three quarters of a mile from the fort in what today are the northern outskirts of the village of Lake George, and the first trenches were opened seven hundred yards from the fort.

The siege proceeded in the usual fashion, the British attempting with their artillery to delay the digging of the trenches and the emplacement of the enemy guns, the French trying to get their cannon and mortars into sheltered positions from which they could start battering down a wall of the fort. Their fire was concentrated on the weak point about which the engineer had given warning the previous year. All this was normal and conventional in the eyes of a European-

trained soldier, even though carried out in the wilderness against a
fort with walls of wood rather than of stone. The Indians, of course,
furnished the discordant note. Instead of sending out scouting parties
as they had been told, they all trooped into the vicinity of the fort,
excitedly watching the French fire their guns, and hid in the gardens
to take potshots at the British. This did little good except to waste
powder. Their scouting did, however, produce one prisoner and a dead
man, whose waistcoat concealed in its lining a letter from General
Webb at Fort Edward to Colonel Monro telling him that he could

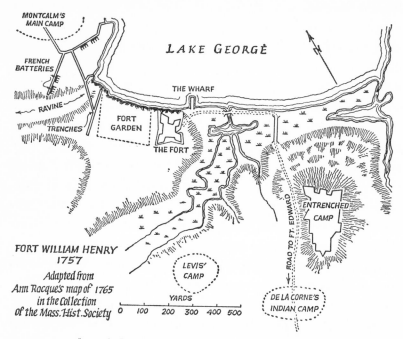

expect no aid, and that he had better make the best surrender terms
he could. This put the game right into Montcalm's hands, but he held
the letter for a day or two before sending it to Monro under a red
flag of truce.

General Webb had reinforced the fort before the attack, leaving
himself only sixteen hundred soldiers at Fort Edward. He has been
accused of being a craven for not coming to the rescue. He originally
had intended to, then becoming more cautious, felt that he must as-

semble more militia for the defense of the Hudson corridor before he
dared move forward. He had some justification. An advance through
that wooded country had grave dangers and there is some question
what he could have done once he got near the fort. The final surrender
was occasioned to a considerable extent by the bursting of most of
the fort's heavy guns and mortars, and only a new supply of artillery
or a powerful sortie could have saved the day. The former, Webb
could not have gotten to the fort, the latter would have been almost
impossible to carry out, so well did the terrain protect the attacking
French. Moreover it would seem from reports of the battle that the
active defense was left almost entirely to the little garrison in the fort
itself, while the very much larger body in the barricaded camp on
the high ground did little but watch. Would the presence of another
thousand or two English have saved the fort? There seem to be grave
doubts. Nevertheless Webb probably should have tried to do something, but he was the man on the ground, and the decision was his.
He believed that Montcalm had an army of eleven thousand men,
and his own little force at Fort Edward was, save for some scattered
regulars and untrained militia levies, the last defense of the Hudson,
of Albany, and perhaps even of New York City itself. Had he been
able to visualize some of Montcalm's problems, lack of food and supplies, a jealous and carping governor, and militia and Indians both
frantic to go home, he might not have been so cautious. One is always
prone to think of his own troubles and seldom of those of the other
side.

There was one man, however, who had no doubts at all about the
need of going to the help of the beleaguered fort, and that was Sir
William Johnson, Mohawk baronet and firm friend of the Iroquois.
Here is a colorful incident saved for posterity by Bougainville's busy
pen:

"I learned from the Sault St. Louis Indians, who keep up contact
with their Mohawk brothers, of a fine scene that happened during
the last campaign. While we were besieging Fort William Henry,
Johnson, Dieskau's conqueror, arrived at Fort Edward at the head of

800 provincials, Mohawks, and Moraigans [Mohegans] a sort of bastard tribe, all in war paint like his troop, tomahawk at his side, halberd in hand. He proposed to General Webb to march at once on the French lines. Webb said he would not, that he did not wish to expose himself to a complete defeat in woods already red with English blood. Johnson replied that these same shores of Lake George would be as fatal to Montcalm as they had been to Dieskau, that French bones would cover this battlefield where, he swore by his halberd and tomahawk, he would conquer or die. General Webb was not moved. Johnson then called to witness the Belgian lion, tore off one of his leggings and hurled it at Webb's feet. 'You won't do it?' said he. 'No.' Tore off the other legging. 'You won't?' Hurled a garter. 'You won't?' Hurled shirt, tomahawk and halberd down, and galloped off with his troop who had imitated his actions entirely. Where is Homer to paint such scenes more Greek than Greek?"

The siege proceeded in the conventional manner. The French worked their trenches forward, advanced their artillery and pounded away at the fort. The British shot back at them, but their guns burst one by one. Smallpox raged, and the garrison became discouraged, all the more so when it was learned that no relief was to come. After three days and nights of cannonading by the French the fort had shot its bolt, and the white flag was raised. Articles of capitulation were drawn up, and they were liberal. The French did not want prisoners, it was difficult enough to feed their own people with the scant crops and the modicum of supplies that managed to evade the British warships. So Montcalm decided to parole the troops and send them home. The British were to march out with their arms and baggage and retire south to Fort Edward, leaving to the French the fort and all its supplies, which included food for six thousand men for six weeks, manna for starving Canada. The soldiers retained their muskets, but, according to one who was there, they kept no ammunition.

Before the terms were finally completed Montcalm had a conference with the Indian chieftains, and secured their promise to restrain their young men from any action against the English. It seems hard to believe that after the experience he had had with Indian promises and his knowledge of the inability of the French to control the savages, he was still naïve enough to put trust in this pledge. He must have remembered what happened after the surrender at Oswego the year before. Certainly he should have taken more positive measures to see that the now defenseless British were amply protected. At the start of the siege he had reminded Monro of Indian cruelty in a letter which can be called nothing but threatening. "[I have] all the Indians from the higher parts of this country the cruelty of whom a detachment of your garrison have lately too much experienced. . . . I have it yet in my power to restrain the Indians . . . which will not be in my power . . . if you insist on defending your fort."

Now let Bougainville speak again, this time through a letter to his godmother, Madame Herault, written before the expedition started: ". . . your son shudders with horror at what he is going to be forced to witness. It is with great difficulty that we can restrain the Indians of the far west, the most ferocious of all men and cannibals by trade. Listen to what the chiefs came to tell M. de Montcalm three days ago: 'Father, don't expect that we can easily give quarter to the English. We have some young warriors who have not yet drunk of this broth. Raw flesh has led them here from the ends of the earth; they must learn to wield the knife and to bury it in English hearts.' Behold our comrades, dear mama; what a crew, what a spectacle for civilized man."

The moment the English left the fort and retired to the barricaded camp, the Indians rushed in and tomahawked the wounded in the barracks and casemates. Despite this most pointed warning Montcalm provided out of his force of six thousand regulars and militiamen only a detachment of four hundred to guard two thousand British with empty muskets from eighteen hundred murderous savages. Once the massacre started he undoubtedly did what he could to stop it, but his lack of precautions cannot but make one wonder. It is the one blot on an otherwise stainless reputation.

Some of the French officers had warned the British to make sure that the Indians got no rum or brandy, and strongly advised that they destroy all that they had with them. There is disagreement as to whether or not this was done, but it seems most likely that at least some of the soldiers had rum-filled canteens, which soon were filched by the savages and greedily swilled down their thirsty throats. All the British had been concentrated in the barricaded camp on the hillock. Seventeen wounded men had been turned over to the French surgeon and a guard placed over them, but before dawn on the day the English were to march away the guards were withdrawn. The Indians immediately dashed in and finished off the wounded, in the presence of the British and in full sight of several Canadian officers and a French guard, but nothing was done to stop the slaughter.

The escort of four hundred Frenchmen had now arrived, and the column started to leave the camp. The Indians demanded plunder, and the French officers advised that all baggage must be given them, or the consequences would be dire. This was done, but the Indians were not appeased. As the column moved out they burst into it, snatching guns and clothes and applying the tomahawk to all that resisted, including a number of women and children who had accompanied the troops. Then a Christian Abnaki of the Penobscot Mission shouted the war whoop, and the whole maddened pack, hitherto mainly interested in plunder, turned to butchery. Montcalm and other French officers dashed up and did their utmost to quiet the savages, but only after between fifty and a hundred British had been killed and hundreds carried off as prisoners. Many of the latter were recovered through the efforts of Montcalm, but about two hundred were taken north by the Indians. The remainder, many of them stripped of everything save their breeches, divided into two groups, one fleeing to the fort for protection by the French, the rest making the best of their way to Fort Edward, either by road or through the woods. The group collected at the fort were given protection at last and several days later sent to Fort Edward under a heavy escort.

Father Roubaud wrote down in his story of the expedition: "The party of 400 of the French regulars, assigned to protect the retreat of the enemy, arrived and placed themselves in line. The English commenced to file out, misfortune to those who formed the end of the line of march, or to stragglers whom indisposition or some other cause separated by every so little from the rest of the body. There soon were many dead whose corpses lay scattered on the ground and covered the outside of the entrenchments. This butchery, which at first was the work of only a few Indians, was the signal which turned almost all the rest into ferocious beasts. They let fly right and left with great blows of their hatchets at those who came to their hand. The massacre, however, was not of long duration, nor as great as its fury made one fear; it amounted to scarcely 40 or 50 men. [The best opinion today puts the figure at three times this at least.] The patience of the English, who were content to bow their heads beneath the steel of their executioners, suddenly appeased them, but it did not lead them to sense or to justice. Uttering loud cries they set about taking prisoners. In the meanwhile I arrived [on the scene]. No, I do not believe that one can be human and remain insensible to such sad circumstances. The son snatched from the arms of the father, the daughter from her mother's bosom, the husband separated from the wife, officers stripped to their shirts, without respect either for rank or decency, a crowd of sufferers who ran hither and yon, some toward the woods, others toward the tents of the French, these toward the fort, those toward those places that seemed to offer protection; such were the pitiful sights presented to my eyes; the French, however, were not passive and insensible spectators of the catastrophe. The Chevalier de Lévis ran wherever the tumult seemed to appear hottest to try to calm it, with courage animated by a clemency most natural to one of his illustrious blood. He dared death . . . a thousand times . . . Of what use could [a guard of] 400 men be against some 1500 furious savages, who did not distinguish us from the enemy?"

Father Roubaud met a wild Huron Indian from the far west carrying a very young baby he had picked up somewhere, and he tried to secure the child. The Indian refused. Finally, after much dickering, the savage agreed to exchange the baby for a scalp, and the priest ran to one of the Abnaki and told him his need. The Christian Indian opened his war bag and told the Jesuit to take his pick. He took a scalp and, followed by a curious crowd of Frenchmen and Indians, he again found his Huron and made the exchange. A little later the good father had the great pleasure of returning the baby to its mother. In later years Father Roubaud led a checkered life, abandoned his faith and married. As late as 1777 he was still trying to collect 6800 francs from the British government for ransom he claimed to have paid out of his own purse to the Indians at William Henry for 103 of their captive Englishmen. One would wonder how a Jesuit priest would have such a sum at hand, but both Montcalm and Colonel Monro seem to have attested to the truth of his claim. Toward the end of his life Roubaud returned to the Catholic Church and died in a monastery in Paris.

Colonel Frye of the Massachusetts Regiment wrote a journal of the siege and its aftermath. He said that after the massacre started, when officers of the French escort were asked for protection, they refused help and advised the English to take to the woods.

Jonathan Carver, whose stories cannot always be trusted, wrote in later years that, when being robbed by the Indians, he sought the aid of a French sentry who called him an English dog and thrust him back into the hands of the Indians.

Montcalm blamed the whole affair on the English for having given rum to the Indians. In a report sent to the French Ministry he wrote: "I cannot conceal from you that the capitulation has unfortunately suffered some infraction on the part of the Indians. But what would be an infraction in Europe cannot be so regarded in America . . ."

Bougainville was sent to Canada to report the capture as soon as the capitulation was signed, and he missed the massacre. Hence the record in his journal is a hearsay one. Nevertheless he was an honest and very intelligent reporter and we may be sure that he was certain of his facts. He wrote: "A great misfortune which we dreaded has happened. Apparently the capitulation is violated and all Europe will oblige us to justify ourselves . . . at daybreak the English, who were inconceivably frightened by the sight of the Indians, wished to leave before our escort was all assembled and in place. They abandoned their trunks and other heavy baggage . . . The Indians had already butchered a few sick in the tents which served as a hospital. The Abnakis of Panaomeska [Old Town] . . . commenced the riot. They shouted the death cry and hurled themselves on the tail of the column which started to march out.

"The English, instead of showing resolution, were seized with fear and fled in confusion, throwing away their arms, baggage, and even their coats. Their fear emboldened the Indians of all the nations, who started pillaging, killed some dozen soldiers and took away 5 or 600 . . . a great number of English soldiers, hoping to put them in a good humor, had given them rum which, despite all our warnings they had kept in their flasks. Finally [after Montcalm and other officers had rushed into the fray to stop the Indians] the disorder quieted down and the Marquis de Montcalm at once took away from the Indians 400 of these unfortunate men and had them clothed. The French officers divided with the English officers the few spare clothes they had, and the Indians loaded with booty, [and some 200 English prisoners] disappeared that same day.

"Would you believe that this abominable action of the Indians at Fort William Henry had accomplices among those people who call themselves Frenchmen; that greed, and the certainty of getting all their plunder from the Indians at a low price are the primary causes of a horror for which England will not fail to reproach us for a long time? Thank heaven our [French] officers are without stain in this respect; several risked their lives on this occasion; they shared all that they had with the unfortunate English, who said that if they should ever besiege us and capture us, there would be two terms of surrender, one for the French troops, and the other for the Canadians. These are frightful truths, dear mama."

Bougainville was in Montreal when the Indians and the miserable party of English captives reached that town. "Meanwhile the Indians arrived [at Montreal] in a crowd with about 200 English. M. de

Vaudreuil scolded them for having violated the capitulation. They excused themselves and put the blame on the mission Indians. They were told that they must give up these English, who were captured unfairly, and that they would be paid for them, two kegs of brandy apiece. But this ransom was not greeted with enthusiasm. The Canadians bought the English plunder from them.

"They did not spare the brandy, and this liquor, the god of the Indians, abounds in their camp. They swill it, and the English [prisoners] die a hundred deaths from fear every day.

"At two o'clock in the presence of the entire town they killed one of them, put him in a kettle and forced his unfortunate compatriots to eat him. . . .

"Will they in Europe believe that the Indians alone have been guilty of this horrible violation of the capitulation, that desire for the negroes and other spoils of the English has not caused the people who are at the head of these nations [Canadian leaders of the Indians and the interpreters] to loosen the curb, perhaps to go even further? The more so since one today may see one of these leaders, unworthy of the name of officer and Frenchman, leading in his suite a negro kidnapped from the English commander under the pretext of appeasing the shades of a dead Indian, giving his family flesh for flesh. That is enough of the horror the memory of which I would hope could be effaced from the minds of men."

Such was the massacre of Fort William Henry. It was not intentional, but Montcalm failed to take the measures necessary to prevent it. His aide-de-camp Bougainville feared the worst, and in view of the close friendship and understanding existing between the two it is most unlikely that he did not communicate his fears to his general. Why Montcalm did not take the precautions he must have known were necessary is something we shall never learn. The whole affair clearly brings out the inability of the French to control their Indians or to utilize them effectively. You could persuade an Indian to go off to war with you, you armed him and fed him and pampered him. He was flighty and temperamental and gluttonous. When at last you gave him orders to fight, he did what he wanted to, not what he was told. Finally, once you had unleashed him, you lost him, and as soon as he had taken some scalps and plunder his only desire was to go home.

Richard Saltonstall was a captain in Colonel Frye's Massachusetts Regiment. After his death in 1800 his nephew, Leverett Saltonstall, in clearing up his papers came across a long epic poem. A few of the many verses will serve to close this account of the massacre. The poetry is hardly such as can be praised, but the author was present and this is an eye witness account.

> For now behold Hell's swarthy allies dire!
> With visage foul, and horrid awful grin!
> Red, black, and green besmear'd their mighty fronts!
> With snaky braids, and dreadful ornament!
> And pitchy feathers platted on their hair!
> Obscene, and naked! daubed with various paints!
> With aspect dire, and fell Canadian rage!
> And murd'rous shafts, presage of awful death!
> Like fiends of Hell, or rather tenfold worse,
> With fearful yell, to raise the Hell below,
> To the assistance of the Hell within 'em;
> Rush on their unforwarn'd unguarded prey!
>
> . . . .
>
> See! weltering in a sea of blood; the babe,
> The hapless, harmless babe by savage fiends
> Torn from its mother's arms, and with a stroke
> Against the craggy cliffs, deprived of life!
>
> . . . .
>
> See discompos'd the naked flying troops!
> Seek asylum in woods and miry swamps
> On bended knees implore the Gallic aid
> Remind them of their honour—but in vain!

And so on for a total of 179 lines of perfectly terrible poetry.

Such were some of the stories of the massacre at Fort William Henry, but one must also look at the event in its broader aspects. As the most advanced post of the British on the great colonial thoroughfare, it was the base for practically all action against the French. Its existence meant that despite bungling, mismanagement, and inept commanders, the British were at last seriously threatening New France. Some foresighted Frenchmen realized this, and Montcalm was one of them. His attack on the British fort was really a defensive act, an offensive raid aimed at removing a threat, not of occupying ground and advancing farther into the British colonies. The French were much too weak in supplies and transport to be able to move on against Fort Edward. The destruction of Fort William Henry set the English back and preserved Canada for at least another year. There was always the hope of peace in Europe, and Montcalm was soon to realize, if he did not already, that only peace could save New France.

There was one final and grisly aftermath that needed a little time to make itself evident. After the massacre some of the western Indians, still mad for blood and scalps, discovered fresh graves in the English camp. They dug the bodies up and scalped them. It was only later that they learned that they had been resurrecting victims of the smallpox! The disease went home with them and wrought havoc that fall and winter, for smallpox was a disease to which the Indian was most susceptible. Almost the entire Potawatomi nation was wiped out. Thus some of the victims of the campaign at last gained an indirect revenge.

Chapter XVI

TICONDEROGA

B<small>Y</small> the end of the year 1757 France stood at the zenith of her power, both at home and abroad. In America Britain's loss of Oswego in the previous year had been followed by the humiliating defeat at Fort William Henry in the summer of 1757, and the great expedition against Louisbourg had failed. On the continent of Europe, Britain and Prussia stood alone against the mighty coalition of France, Austria, Germany, Russia, and Sweden. The Duke of Cumberland had been forced to surrender his Hanoverian and Hessian army, supported by British subsidies, to the victorious allies of France that summer. At sea, in addition to the naval forces sent to America, Pitt had dispatched a great amphibious raiding force against the French base of Rochefort. Overcautious commanders, disregarding pleas by a brilliant young colonel named James Wolfe, balked at making the final assault, and the expedition, which had cost the British taxpayer a million pounds, sailed away, having achieved nothing. Despite last-minute victories by Frederick of Prussia late in the year, King George II was almost ready to ask for an armistice. Vast sums had been spent on the American campaign, on the navy and on subsidies to Frederick and his few little allied principalities, but nothing had come of it all.

Regardless of all these disappointments Pitt's courage did not fail him, and through increased taxes and loans he prepared to finance the campaign of 1758. That year British troops crossed the English Channel to serve on the Continent and a great land and sea operation was sent against St. Malo in Brittany. It consisted of 150 ships carrying in all 34,000 sailors and soldiers. The attempt failed, but it gave the French a scare, and made them conscious of the threat to their home waters. A later attempt at Cherbourg was a success, the British held the place for a week, burning forts, stores, and twenty-seven ships. Meanwhile in America a new attempt was to be made on Louisbourg, and a great army of British regulars and provincials was to assault the Champlain Valley, while another marched against Fort Duquesne. In view of Britain's European commitments, no one could accuse Pitt of stinting the efforts made on this side of the Atlantic. The tide had at last started to turn, Frederick was to hold his own this year on the battlefields of Europe, and in America, despite one terrible British defeat, New France at last was to be driven to the defensive.

For a quarter century after it was built in 1731, Fort St. Frederic at Crown Point, Pointe à la Chevalure, or Scalp Point, as the French called it, was the southern outpost of New France on the great Champlain-Hudson waterway. Throughout these years it was the headquarters post of the Champlain Valley frontier, the port of entry for travelers going from New York to Canada, and an important base from which the French Indians raided the British provinces. Despite all this it never knew a siege or a battle, nor heard a hostile shot save that of a musket of one of Robert Rogers' Rangers as he scouted the outskirts of the fort and figuratively thumbed his nose at the French.

In 1755, after Johnson's defeat of von Dieskau, Vaudreuil, the Canadian governor, had decided to advance his frontier to the south and to build a new fort at Ticonderoga, where the waters of Lake George empty into Lake Champlain. He sent his young relative, the Canadian engineer de Lotbinière, to build the fort, and work was started in the fall of 1755. All forts and posts built in Canada cost the King vast sums, many times what they could have been built for at home, and most of the excess went into the pockets of favored individuals.

In the case of the fort at Ticonderoga, Fort Carillon it was called, the principal recipient of this informal largesse appears to have been the engineer, de Lotbinière. By custom he held the franchise of the canteen, sole source of pleasure to lonely soldiers, and a never-ending fountain of great profit. Desandrouin, a regular French engineer officer, stated that the profits of the canteen alone amounted to 100,000 francs a year, certainly equivalent to $150,000 today. The engineer also hired from himself a herd of horses to haul sand to make the mortar, and they earned further very material profits at little expense to him, for they were fed and tended at the King's cost. De Lotbinière made a fortune out of the fort, yet it seems unlikely that he strayed beyond the bounds of the normal graft and perquisites of the period. In the final clean up of Bigot's gang after the Peace of 1763 he was not indicted along with the rest of that greedy crew.

De Lotbinière was a Canadian engineer of little training and no practical experience. French officers scornfully referred to him as "this Canadian Vauban." He proceeded to locate the fort in the wrong place, too far back from the narrows to control them, and eventually a redoubt, really a second little fort, had to be built on the tip of the point to make Fort Carillon effective. On the other hand the area between the fort and the point made an excellent camping place for any garrison in excess of what could be housed in the fort itself, and de Lotbinière may have had this in mind. Experienced officers who came from France with Montcalm were scornful of the Canadian engineer's fort, but they were probably unaware of frontier conditions and some of the problems that had to be met. Good or bad, the fort was to be one of the very great strategic points of North America. Over the next generation it was to be assailed five times, a record held by no other fort on this continent, and perhaps nowhere in the world. Three times it was to fall, and twice it was to be safely held, and all this within only a score of years.

Little was accomplished on the fort that first autumn and winter of 1755–56 beyond making a start and erecting shelter for the workmen, but by the following summer things were well under way. The

walls and bastions were first built of squared timbers, placed horizontally and backed with earth, a construction much like that of Fort
William Henry, but later the timbers were replaced by a masonry
facing. Some skilled civilian workers were employed, but much of the
labor was done by the soldiers, who drew extra pay for the work and
promptly spent it in the canteen to the further benefit of de Lotbinière's pocketbook. By the autumn of 1756 the fort was well along,
and thirty-six cannon had been mounted along its ramparts. Although
far from finished, it was well on the way to becoming a stout little
fort, particularly when its wilderness location was considered. Before
it could be attacked the British would have to solve a major problem
in logistics. It was quite small, intended to hold a permanent garrison
of only three or four hundred men. In wartime a winter garrison of
this size would be able to defend the fort against any sudden raid, and
when the approach of summer allowed a large expedition to move
against it, the French planned to shift additional troops down from
Canada by water.

The little garrison must have lived a rugged life in winter. Three
thousand cords of firewood were needed each season to keep the soldiers from freezing, and to cut this amount required one hundred
skilled woodchoppers working for thirty days, without counting the
labor of hauling the wood into the fort. No wonder the canteen
kept busy; after a day's stint of cutting and hauling, there was little
to do but drink or sleep, for gaming of any sort was stringently prohibited, for what reason it is impossible to say.

Soon Fort Carillon took the place of Fort St. Frederic and became
the headquarters of the Champlain frontier. It was there that Montcalm assembled his army for the expedition against Fort William
Henry, organizing his troops and making final plans, while his Indian
allies from the far west held picnics on the flats below the fort, and
feasted on boiled Englishmen, prisoners recently taken on Lake
George. It also was here that the marquis took his stand in the summer of 1758 and prepared to do his best, greatly outnumbered as he
was, against the onslaught of the British.

The British plans for the 1758 campaign were for Jeffrey Amherst to capture Louisbourg, while James Abercromby, the commander in chief in North America, seized Ticonderoga and advanced on Canada north down Lake Champlain. Brigadier John Forbes at the same time was to lead an attack on Fort Duquesne, left in peace since Braddock's unhappy expedition. Lord Loudoun, impressed by Bradstreet's conduct in the Oswego campaign, had promised to grant that officer's request for permission to attack Fort Frontenac, the vital French post at the outlet of Lake Ontario. This plan was later dropped by Abercromby and then reinstituted. Fort Carillon became the major objective on the mainland for 1758, and Abercromby was to lead the attack in person. Pitt, reinstated as British Prime Minister after a brief eclipse, unfortunately took it upon himself to prescribe many of the details which should have been left to Abercromby, whose hands thus became unjustly tied. He might have done better if granted more latitude, but this seems doubtful. The North American assignment probably was beyond his capabilities.

James Abercromby was a Scot in his early fifties who had seen a considerable amount of active service, and who had the reputation of being a sound, if uninspired, officer. He was made a major general in 1756 and sent to America to serve under Lord Loudoun from whom he inherited the command when the latter was dismissed by Pitt. Loudoun was a good man who deserved better than he got and whose plans for the attack on Canada were sound, but he became the scapegoat for the failure of the 1757 Louisbourg expedition and for the loss of Fort William Henry.

Loudoun had planned a winter attack on Ticonderoga which was daring and yet sound in concept. It might very well have succeeded but for Captain Robert Rogers' failure to produce the needed snowshoes, which forced abandonment of the attempt. Abercromby assumed command early in the spring of 1758. His health was not of the best, and he had grown somewhat old before his time, slow and unaggressive. He was, however, seconded by a most able assistant. George Augustus, Viscount Howe, a brilliant young man of thirty-four, was approved of both by high and low. Pitt esteemed him highly, and after his death the tight-fisted and unsentimental General Court of Massachusetts Bay thought so well of his memory that they voted the quite material sum of £250 of tax money to build a memorial to him in Westminster Abbey. He was one of the relatively few British regulars—Bradstreet was another—who could break down the barriers and meet provincial officers on a common and friendly level. Lord Howe as brigadier was second in command of the Ticonderoga attack, and it appears that in effect it was intended that he should be the actual combat commander. The two leaders complemented each other not too badly and together formed a high command quite suitable for the purpose at hand.

A great army of British regulars and colonial militia assembled along the upper Hudson and then moved up the river and on to the head of Lake George. It had been planned that the expedition should start early in May, and thus catch Fort Carillon with only its winter garrison. As was usual, however, unexpected delays took place, the militia was late in arriving, and it was not until the end of June that the army had assembled near the ruins of Fort William Henry. There were some 6300 regular troops and 5900 provincials from Massachusetts, Connecticut, New York, and New Jersey. These militiamen of course were mostly raw and untrained soldiers, though some of them had seen service in previous campaigns of the war.

Captain Alexander Monypenny was Abercromby's brigade major, and his sailcloth-covered orderly book lies in front of me as I write. It tells many of the details of preparations for the advance. Equipment was lightened. The officers dispensed with their sashes, and were limited to one portmanteau, blankets and a bearskin, the last useful either as a mattress or as an extra covering. They also were permitted to take a small tent. Instead of being allowed the usual varying number of rations, based upon rank, each officer was restricted to the same ration as the soldier. The colors of the regiments were left behind. All friendly Indians would have a red ribbon tied around the muzzle of their guns for identification. All in all the orderly book shows a very considerable amount of thought and planning, and a reasonable adaptation of standard European practice to forest fighting. Salt pork, flour, dried peas, rice, and butter were to nourish the British soldier, and it is interesting to note that the salt was to be knocked off the pork before it was weighed for issue. Spartan fare indeed! Gambling by soldiers was frowned on most severely; any man caught in the act was to be given three hundred lashes without bothering to hold a court-martial.

The little book prescribed the assignment to the troops of the eight hundred bateaux and the ninety whaleboats. The latter had been bought on Cape Cod and Nantucket the previous fall and sent up the Hudson, and then had been hauled by soldiers on low-wheeled trucks over the portage to Lake George. Various camp activities were ordered while the troops were awaiting word to launch their boats. Some regiments turned out to early-morning target practice, while those who had been issued rifles were told to familiarize themselves with the new weapon. Hitherto the first use of rifles in the British Army has always been said to have been in 1800, except for Patrick Ferguson's private issue of his breech-loader to his own company in the American Revolution. Here in 1758, however, we find the rifle an article of issue, on a small scale to be sure, only ten per regiment, but an official issue to British regulars. The expedition which moved against Fort Duquesne that same summer also received a few. Some open-minded British officer—and he must have been one with powerful friends in the War Office—had evidently been much impressed with the American rifle as used along the Pennsylvania frontier, and had taken one home. A considerable number were made in England, following the American design exactly, and they now appeared in the hands of some of the troops in the campaign of 1758.

Lake George discharged its waters over two hundred feet of falls and rapids in the years before dams and power plants turned them into drab utility. Where they entered Lake Champlain nature had created the high and rocky peninsula the Indians called Ticonderoga. Its point reaches to within a quarter-mile of the Vermont shore, and

high above the lake the guns of Fort Carillon decreed that none might
pass without permission of the French King. The portage road from
Lake George descended to almost the foot of the falls where the
French had built a sawmill. Here boats and canoes were launched
into Lake Champlain. The road then crossed the outlet on a wooden
bridge, climbed the farther slope, and continued for about another
two miles along the backbone of the peninsula out to Fort Carillon.

Montcalm's problem was where to make his fight. He had only
about 3500 men, far too few to meet the British in the open field,
yet nearly ten times what the little fort could hold. His decision was to
take his stand on the Heights of Carillon, the highest part of the
ridge, and about half a mile back from the fort. Here the ridge of the

[Lord Howe Killed]

SAWMILL

FRENCH CAMP

FRENCH CAMP

FRENCH CAMP

[the Landing Place]

ROAD

RAFT WITH CANNON

[the Log Wall]

LAKE CHAMPLAIN

LAKE GEORGE

Capt. Monypenny's Map of
ABERCROMBY'S DEFEAT
1758

Copy of the map he sent home with his report
of the battle and of the death of Lord Howe

WOOD CREEK   Ticonderoga

peninsula is only a quarter-mile wide. Its southwest slope falls steeply
into the lake, while the opposite and equally steep northeasterly side
runs out into a flat plain almost a third of a mile wide before it reaches
the shore of the lake. Across this narrow ridge, from one side to the
other, sweating Frenchmen, officers as well as men, hacked down the
virgin timber, and set up a wall of great logs, placed horizontally,
two and three deep, and pierced with loopholes for musketry. Some
of the logs were three feet and more in diameter, remnants of the
primeval forest. The top of the wall was crowned with sandbags to a
total height of from six to seven feet, so high that only the top of

the Frenchmen's hats, and the flags with their golden fleurs-de-lis could be seen above it. The ground plan of the wall formed a great U, its sides crowning the steep slopes on either side of the ridge, and extending well to the rear. In front of the wall all trees and bushes were cleared away for a distance of about one hundred yards and an abatis built of the tree tops, which were piled in an almost impassable hedge, the ends of their sharpened branches pointing toward the attacker. It was the predecessor of the barbed-wire entanglement of modern wars, and equally effective.

This great wall, raised in less than two days by the exertions of perhaps three thousand men, was practically impregnable to an attacker lacking artillery, but a few cannon could have knocked much of it down in short order. The line of the wall zigzagged across the peninsula in order to furnish salients from which the attackers could be enfiladed. It was hurriedly built, too low in places, and in others exposed to enemy fire from the flank, but, considering the time and the manpower available, its construction was a mighty feat. Montcalm placed one battalion in Fort Carillon as a reserve and to man its guns, while the rest of his force, except for small detachments sent out to harass and delay the enemy, lined the wooden wall with their muskets. They did not, however, have any cannon on the Heights of Carillon.

Abercromby embarked his army on July 5 and proceeded down Lake George, a great flotilla of almost nine hundred boats spread in ordered columns across the narrow lake. The British rowed to the foot of the lake, making a short halt during the night and reaching the outlet of Lake George on the morning of the sixth. The small French outpost at that point withdrew without offering any resistance, and the expedition landed on the west side in heavy woods, although the portage road to Lake Champlain lay on the opposite shore. The advance party moved downstream through the virgin forest, not quite sure just where it was going. After advancing for a mile or so the British floundered into contact with a French detachment which also had gone astray.

There was a brief interchange of shots, and most of the French were killed or captured, but a heavy price was paid for this petty victory. Lord Howe, pushing forward at the head of the detachment, where a senior officer had no right to be in such a situation, fell dead almost at the first shot. Everything collapsed into confusion, some of the troops continued to advance, while others returned to the landing place. Firing broke out toward late afternoon, but there was no enemy, it was merely British firing at other elements of their own forces.

In short all was chaos, and night fell upon a scared and disorganized army. Had the French been able to turn a pack of Indians loose upon them in the woods that evening there might have been a fearful slaughter, but Montcalm had less than a score of redskins in his little army. Daylight restored courage, and all the troops were drawn back to the landing place, moved over to the eastern shore, and the expedition advanced down the portage road without meeting any opposition, even at the sawmill where the crossing of the little river offered the French an excellent chance to fight a delaying action. All the advance elements of Montcalm's forces fell back upon their main defenses on the Heights of Carillon, followed by light elements of the British who approached the log wall but remained at a discreet distance from it. Abercromby's main army camped that night on the open ground north of the little river, perhaps a mile and a half from the French defenses.

Up to this point matters had not gone too badly. The British had achieved a major logistical success in bringing so great an army up to the immediate vicinity of their objective, the losses had been small, save for that of Lord Howe, and their enemy was penned up on a peninsula with the lake at his back. Here was opportunity for annihilation of the French, given a proper leader. Such, however, was now lacking, and incompetent command proceeded to bring disaster upon the British.

Lieutenant Colonel Eyre led one of Abercromby's regiments, and he was a most competent engineer officer. Montressor, the senior engineer, was ill, and, instead of sending Eyre to reconnoiter the position and suggest plans for the attack—one of the duties of an engineer officer in those days—the British general, perhaps because of a coolness then apparently existing between the two, bypassed that excellent officer and sent a junior engineer lieutenant instead. This young officer proved his incompetence by reporting that the defenses were weak and could be taken by a frontal infantry attack. Later in the day he was to pay for his poor judgment with his life.

Abercromby had left most of his artillery train on their barges, although nearly forty-eight hours had elapsed, but a few cannon had been advanced to a point within perhaps half a mile of the French defenses. Less than an hour could have had them pounding away at the log wall, and they could have promptly knocked down parts of it. But Abercromby, misled by his engineer's lack of skill, scorned to use his guns and ordered a frontal attack by his infantry. Had he taken the trouble to look at the French defenses himself, he might have chosen another course of action, but there is no evidence whatsoever to show that he at any time went within a mile of the log wall, and considerable reason to believe that he remained in the vicinity of the sawmill throughout the day. His sole leadership throughout the entire action seems to have been merely the ordering of another attack as soon as he learned of the failure of the previous assault.

Montcalm manned his great log wall with seven battalions of French regulars, La Reine, Béarn, Guyenne, Royal Roussillon, 1st Berry, Languedoc, and La Sarre, troops that he knew and in whom he had confidence. On the flat plain on his right he placed his small force of Canadian regulars, soldiers of La Marine Regiment, and his militiamen, expecting little of them, but hoping that they and the guns of Carillon would cover that flank. On his left the slope fell sharply to the water and there was room only for a handful of French volunteers on the narrow strand. The 2nd Berry was held in reserve in the fort along with a small body of gunners to man the cannon on the ramparts. Some three thousand men armed with muskets stood behind the great wooden wall and through its loopholes they could fire almost without risk upon anyone who dared to cross the open ground in their front. Another five hundred guarded the flanks, but their defenses were less secure, and they were less apt to be assailed. Provided that the French had sufficient powder and ball, and that the British failed to use their artillery, the position could be held indefinitely against charging infantry, however well led.

Governor Vaudreuil had planned to send an expedition in the early summer of 1758 up the St. Lawrence and on by way of Oswego to the Mohawk Valley, partly to overawe the Iroquois, but also to do as much damage as possible to the English settlements in that region. Late in June, Brigadier Lévis had led a party of four hundred regulars, four hundred troops of La Marine, and eight hundred Canadian militia off on that mission, regardless of Montcalm's warnings of an English move down the Champlain waterway. At last Vaudreuil appreciated the British threat and recalled the expedition, too late to get most of the troops back. By marching night and day, however, Lévis managed to get the four hundred regulars to Ticonderoga the evening before the battle, and this reinforcement was a very material help to Montcalm.

The French actually were in a most precarious condition, their backs to the lake, only five days provisions on hand, and a mighty army hemming them in. Of all the possible courses open to Abercromby he picked the one least likely to succeed. The correct solution is always easy by hindsight, but even at that time, a little thought would have brought the British commander to the realization that an immediate infantry attack was not the best course of action to take. He believed that reinforcements, perhaps six thousand in number, were on the way. Even so, had he merely advanced to the lake shore a little north of the fort and put some artillery in position, he would have secured command of the artery by which the reinforcements must come, and he would at the same time have cut the troops on the peninsula off from their supply base to the north. Starvation would soon have forced their surrender. His other alternative was to bring up artillery and blast the wooden wall to bits. Either of these plans, or even both at once, were perfectly practical to a force as large as his, and the fort would have fallen in a few days almost without bloodshed. Instead the British leader ordered execution of the worst possible plan, a frontal infantry attack, unsupported by any artillery, against a very strong defensive position. Abercromby must have lost his wits that day. His only possible excuse was fear of an immediate arrival of heavy reinforcements, and hence a belief in the need for speedy action.

Sir William Johnson, His Majesty's Superintendent of Indian Affairs, had promised to bring a considerable body of Iroquois to assist Abercromby as guides and scouts. At that particular time, however, the Five Nations were torn by internal dissensions into pro-French and pro-British groups, and it was with great difficulty that Johnson managed to persuade any Indians to come on the expedition. He at last got some volunteers together at Fort Johnson on the Mohawk River, but, despite his efforts to prevent it, they secured rum from the Dutch traders of Schenectady and proceeded to get completely drunk, as only Indians could. Sir William wrote that "liquor was as plenty among them as ditch water." This carouse further delayed the departure of Johnson's force. They finally joined Abercromby at Ticonderoga on the morning of the battle, some four hundred in number, too late to serve their most useful purpose as scouts during the advance from the landing place, when their presence might well have saved the life of Lord Howe. With Howe alive the chances are excellent that the fort would have fallen, and the whole course of the last of the French wars materially changed. Sir William led his Indians, presumably at Abercromby's order, to the slopes of Mount Defiance, and during the day they delivered a random long-range fire against the extreme left of the French lines. Their total bag, as reported by Montcalm, was one officer wounded. Sir William gained little glory in this year of 1758, but he was to more than make up for it in the campaign of the following year.

Early in the battle the British attempted to send barges armed with cannon down the river flowing out of Lake George, and thus get around the French left flank. The cannon of the fort took them under fire, sank two, and drove the rest away.

The initial British attack was made in the worst possible way, an uncoordinated attack by several regiments in long lines three deep. The only hope of a successful assault on so strong a position as this would have been the carefully coordinated simultaneous advance of several columns with narrow fronts and great depth. The slaughter would have been great, but the log wall might have been carried at one place at least. Instead each regiment attacked in a long thin line as soon as it was ready, regardless of the movements of its neighbor. The forces on the right moved forward before the center brigade was formed, and the assault had proceeded for some time before all the troops concerned were up to the line upon which they were supposed to form for the attack. The men at once got snarled in the abatis, some could neither advance nor retreat and merely awaited slaughter, while the Highlanders tried to hack their way through with their broadswords. Eventually a few soldiers would break through the sharpened tree tops, dash toward the wall, shrouded in the smoke of musketry, and fall dead or wounded. The hot July sun had rapidly dried out the leaves and small branches of the felled trees in the abatis which caught fire at several places. Brave Frenchmen dashed out from behind the wall carrying pails of water brought up from the lake and put the fires out before they became serious.

Almost three quarters of the Regiment of Berry were young recruits, and their first battle was more than their morale could endure. At one time in the conflict their courage left them and they fled from behind the log wall in utter confusion. Before the British could grasp the initiative, the reserve companies of grenadiers rushed up and plugged the gap, just in time to save the day.

The battle started somewhat after noon and lasted over six hours. The British attacked with the greatest of bravery at various places along the French lines, but never gained their objective. Time and again they tried, as the sun sank lower in the west, throwing their lives away uselessly, but it was all in vain. Perhaps the most gallant assault of all—and all were most gallant—was that of the 42nd Highlanders, the Black Watch, on the right of the French defenses.

Then it was that Duncan Campbell received his death wound and met the fate he had dreamed of many years before. Campbell was the Laird of Castle Inverawe in the western Highlands. Late one night in the 1740s a fugitive knocked at his door and begged asylum, saying that he had killed a man and was pursued. Campbell swore on his dirk to shelter him and hid him in a secret place. Soon the pursuers arrived, and told the laird that it was his own cousin that had been killed. That night and for other nights the murdered cousin came to Campbell in his dreams and begged revenge, but the laird had sworn on his dirk. Finally the ghost appeared for the last time and bade him farewell until they should at last meet at Ticonderoga, a name that meant nothing to Campbell. Later he became a major of the Black Watch and went with it to the wars in North America. Then to his horror, he learned that he was to take part in the attack on Ticonderoga, and the night before the battle the ghost again appeared. Such is the legend of Inverawe, immortalized in a poem by Robert Louis Stevenson.

The assault by the Black Watch was the last major effort of the British. Over half of that regiment were lost that day, 499 men in all. When this last attack was made the Canadian militia on the flats were ordered forward to assail the Scots on the flank, but, undependable as militia usually turned out to be, they failed to advance. Two of their officers charged forward alone, unsupported, and one fell wounded. Earlier in the day the French had been forced to fire on a body of their own militia that was running away to the boats. One of the group was wounded and the fugitives returned to their lines, where some hid under their abatis while others cowered behind stumps. The militia earned no glory in this battle, though Montcalm later wrote "nevertheless . . . I have considered it for the good of the service to praise them." It was the French regulars and the stout log wall that saved New France on that bloody day.

At last, just as the sun was dropping behind the Adirondacks, the

British gave up and retreated back as they had come. Soon the retreat became suspiciously like a flight, so hurriedly did the withdrawal take place. The army re-embarked and headed back up the lake, abandoning many provisions, baggage, and burned boats to the exultant French.

Despite his heavy losses Abercromby still vastly outnumbered the French, and he still had all his artillery to use. A renewal of the attack, after cannon had smashed down the wall, would almost certainly have succeeded, but Abercromby was not one of those who could salvage victory out of initial defeat. His losses were very great, 1610 killed, wounded and missing, almost all from the 6367 regular troops, while the French lost 377 out of their total of about 4000 in their defense of the log wall. From the point of view of numbers engaged and losses sustained this was by far the greatest battle that had yet been fought on American soil. Only the Battle of Long Island in the Revolution was to exceed it until the mighty conflicts of our Civil War set new records in death and suffering.

It is hard to account for Abercromby's actions on this unfortunate day. Although no military genius, Abercromby had the reputation of being a sound and experienced officer. A senior British officer, when he learned of the battle, expressed sorrow for the defeated general, and wrote that he could not understand how it had happened, it was not at all what he would have expected of Abercromby. There is, it would seem, one quite possible solution. A month before the battle, Abercromby was laid up for several days with a violent stomach disorder, and later, two weeks before the battle, he was struck again. Did the general perhaps suffer from some chronic stomach ill that hit him again on the day of battle and rendered him incapable of effective thought or action?

A few days after the battle Montcalm was reinforced by two thousand Canadians and six hundred Indians, but they came too late and succeeded only in consuming precious rations. The British for their part reoccupied their old camp at the head of Lake George and devoted the remainder of the summer to doing nothing, except for firing a *feu de joie* when they learned that Amherst had captured Louisbourg. A most inglorious summer for the British forces on the American soil, but two less-known leaders, both far exceeding Abercromby in competence, were to retrieve the reputation of their country and to deal vital blows to the cause of New France later in that summer of 1758.

Montcalm caused a great wooden cross to be erected at the center of the lines that his troops defended, and it was blessed by Abbé Piquet. Today a replica of that cross towers above the entrance road to restored Fort Carillon, flanked on either side by posts bearing the arms of France and two commemorative inscriptions written by Bougainville.

Chapter XVII

CONVENTIONAL WAR AT LOUISBOURG

LOUISBOURG was returned to the French under the terms of the treaty of Aix-la-Chapelle, and they at once set about repairing and strengthening the place. Soon its garrison was nearly as large as those of all the other Canadian cities and forts combined. The civilian population by the time of the start of the Seven Years' War was around four thousand, and the place had become an important fishing center, as well as a clearinghouse for trade of all sorts, much of which was illicit. Louisbourg was one of the great cities of North America and it had become its greatest fortress. Lord Loudoun's attempt on Cape Breton in 1757, which had failed through causes beyond his control, had alerted the French to their danger and had expedited their strengthening of the place. Supplies and reinforcements were sent from France early in 1758, and, although much of the former had failed to arrive, Louisbourg was, all things considered, in excellent condition to meet an attack. That one was coming seemed certain, for the British apparently made no attempt at keeping their intentions secret.

The 1758 assault was to be a vastly different affair from that of thirteen years before. Then an undisciplined army of Yankees, led by officers without military experience, attacked a strong fortress, defended both by nature and by works of man, but inadequately garrisoned by troops of mediocre quality commanded by officers who had never been to war. Now a European army, led by capable and experienced men, marched against a strengthened citadel adequately garrisoned by competent troops and supported by a fleet. The second siege of Louisbourg was a straightforward European operation that happened to be waged on the soil of North America, but conceded nothing to those special conditions of this continent which in most cases limited the action that could be taken.

The British had no colonial troops, with the exception of some rangers all were trained regulars. Their army had a total strength of more than eleven thousand. The quality of the French troops was high, many of them were regulars from France, and skilled officers from regiments disbanded in Europe had come overseas to leaven the companies of La Marine. Earthworks commanding all possible landing places had been prepared in expectation of the 1757 attack which never came. The Louisbourg garrison consisted of six battalions of regulars, two of foreign volunteers, and twenty-four companies of La Marine plus two artillery companies. Moreover there were the three thousand sailors of the fleet upon which to draw, as well as the able-bodied men of the civilian population. And finally the governor, the Chevalier Drucour, was a good and capable man. Louisbourg was in condition to make an excellent defense.

During the winter of 1757–58 the British had held a squadron of eight warships at Halifax, to the vast disgust of the officers who had hoped to enjoy a period of leave at home, and by early April they were patrolling around Louisbourg and attempting to enforce a blockade. But storms and fogs interfered, with the result that a number of French warships made port safely, although almost all the ships carrying stores fell prey to the British Navy. There was little secrecy about Pitt's intentions this year, but disasters in home waters prevented the French from reinforcing Louisbourg and affording it the necessary naval support. A powerful French fleet had been assembled in the Mediterranean early in 1758, but part of it was put to flight by Admiral Osborne, and the remainder was blockaded in a Spanish port. Poetic justice was rendered in this action. Captain Gardiner had been flag captain to Admiral Byng in 1756, and in this action he commanded a 64-gun ship. With it he dared attack the 80-gun

French warship which had borne Admiral de la Galissonière to victory over Byng. In a desperate ship-to-ship encounter Gardiner overcame the great French vessel, but, sad to say, the British naval officer was killed during the action. Another small fleet sailed from Brest and succeeded in getting some of its ships into Louisbourg through the partial blockade maintained by the British fleet. But the result of the various British naval successes was that Louisbourg lacked supplies and reinforcements when they were most needed, and French warships in North American waters were too few to be of avail against the British squadrons of Admirals Hardy and Boscawen. The British need fear no interference with their expedition by sea nor any risk to their lines of supply.

Colonel Jeffrey Amherst was a relatively young officer, specially skilled in staff operations, capable and dependable, but hitherto not distinguished. He was of the slow-and-sure type, obedient, sound, and efficient. Pitt selected him while serving in Germany as the commander of the new attempt on Louisbourg, and Amherst did not reach Nova Scotia until the end of May, when he met the great fleet of warships and transports just as they were starting for Cape Breton. Although he commanded the expedition, he remains a somewhat shadowy figure in the background, and the leader most evident at the front was a strange and unusual personality who was to achieve his fame and meet his death in North America, Brigadier General James Wolfe. He was only thirty-one years old, but had served in the British Army from the age of fifteen and was a dedicated and extraordinarily capable officer. Wolfe studied his profession zealously, a proceeding indulged in by but few British officers in those days, and he had made his regiment a model one, perhaps the best in the entire army. He was tall and thin, somewhat unprepossessing in appearance, and his health was poor. Wolfe was one of three brigadiers selected to serve under Amherst, the others being Lawrence, the governor of Nova Scotia, and one Edward Whitmore, who appears to have done nothing at Louisbourg to give him a place in history. Pitt, knowing that Amherst would be late in reaching America, had instructed the brigadiers and the senior admiral, Boscawan, to make tentative plans for the assault, and to start the troops toward Cape Breton without waiting for the arrival of the new commander.

A great armada of 157 warships and transports brought the expedition to Cape Breton on the second of June. The next day or two were devoted to reconnaissance, and then heavy seas, followed by fogs and driving rain, postponed any attempt at landing. At last on the eighth of June the swell subsided, the weather cleared, and the barges and longboats put off from the fleet and headed for the beaches. The real assault was to be delivered by Wolfe's division at the same point where the New Englanders had dashed ashore thirteen years before, while the other brigadiers were to hold their forces in reserve, although feinting attacks at other points.

The French defenders were about one half regulars, the remainder soldiers of La Marine, in all they totaled a little over three thousand men. The sailors from the fleet were almost as many again, but they were to prove of little help. The officers of the Colony troops, the companies of La Marine, were divided into three groups, each heartily detesting the others. For years many of the posts at Louisbourg had been perquisites which were retained by certain families and passed on to their children. Officers of this class had constituted the commissioned ranks in 1745, but since then two other sources had been drawn on, Canadian officers who perhaps had served in Indian raids but with no other experience, and regular officers of the French service whose regiments had been disbanded during the peace. An exiled Jacobite officer who was stationed at Louisbourg for some years wrote that these three groups were constantly bickering and quarreling with one another, and that may well be, but they met the final test of battle and put up a splendid defense. There were also, of course, the French officers serving in the regular battalions, who presumably were immune to these dissensions.

All possible landing places had been organized for defense, and, as soon as it was seen that the British attempt was to be made, two thousand Frenchmen moved to their prepared positions. At dawn, supported by cannon fire from half a dozen frigates, Wolfe's men headed for the rocky shore and at once came under heavy fire of artillery and musketry, so heavy that Wolfe signaled cancellation of the attack.

Just at this moment one of the boats carrying men of Major Scott's light infantry gained the shelter of a little rocky point, and, protected from the enemy's fire, got ashore. A little redoubt covered this particular spot. It had been occupied by about thirty Frenchmen in 1757, but for some strange reason was now undefended. Another boat at once followed. It was smashed to bits against the rocks, but Major Scott and a few others managed to reach dry land. The next moment, accompanied by only ten men, he was attacked by over sixty Frenchmen. Half of his men were killed, and he took three bullets through his clothes, but held on as more British splashed ashore and came to his aid. Soon the backbone of the local defense was broken and the French fled, while more cheering British poured ashore and gained a firm and lasting foothold.

Now bad weather stepped in again, and the troops on shore were isolated for a couple of days from their supplies and reinforcements. This was the time for the French to counterattack and drive the invaders back into the sea, but nothing was attempted, and the chance to save Louisbourg was lost. The weather improved and sailors from the British fleet carried guns, provisions, and other supplies ashore, while the soldiers established their camp and built defenses to protect it. Some prefabricated blockhouses had been brought along, and these were soon put in position on the perimeter of the area.

The siege in a general way was initiated and carried on much as it had been thirteen years before, but these were disciplined troops, and there was none of the wandering, looting, and horseplay such as the New England farm boys had indulged in during the previous affair. Nor were men harnessed together to haul the guns through the miry swamps. Instead military engineers directed the building of roads, while the artillery and ammunition were being brought ashore. This last was not done as expeditiously as it had been in 1745, for stores were still being landed almost a month after the initial attack. Everything proceeded with caution and deliberation just as though some fortified port in Europe were being invested. One prompt offensive action was taken nevertheless, for Wolfe was at once sent to occupy Light House Point and within little more than a week after the landing he had cannon emplaced there and firing on the French battery on the island at the harbor entrance. Just after the landing the French had abandoned the Grand Battery, as they had done in 1745, but this time they did their best to demolish it. Within less than a week the French citadel was surrounded on all sides by land and cut off from the sea by a reasonably effective blockade.

A siege such as this was necessarily a rather slow and dragged-out undertaking, and it was particularly so in a climate such as existed at Louisbourg, where fog often prevented any artillery fire by either side. This same fog, however, was a help to the British as it screened their actions and allowed them to continue their works unhindered. Sailors from the fleet were used to help build the necessary roads over which the artillery was to be moved forward by ox teams. In places exposed to the fire of the French embankments were built along the road to give protection to those passing. One must not think of the artillery fire as being constant even on clear days, it was sporadic, sometimes a period of heavy firing and then a night or two with nothing to be heard at all save a musket shot as some nervous sentinel fired at an imaginary foe. Slowly and steadily the besiegers moved their batteries forward, and the nearer they got to the city the more damage they did to its walls.

A factor not present in the earlier siege was the French fleet bottled up within the harbor, five ships of the line and seven frigates, carrying in all 544 guns and crews amounting to some three thousand men. This naval force would have furnished a powerful reinforcement for the French had it been effectively used. There was, unfortunately, much disagreement and discord between the two services and from the very start almost all the captains wished to flee and save their ships, rather than to remain and try to save Louisbourg. They were proba-

bly right, for warships cooped up in a landlocked harbor are of little
or no use to defend a fortress, and are excellent and inflammable
targets for bombs and incendiary shells. At sea these ships might have
made themselves a considerable nuisance to the British fleet, even if
they had not dared meet it in battle.

The army naturally felt that the naval officers were a group of
cowards and the navy did almost nothing to disabuse this idea. After
the siege was well under way the big warships were moved close up
to the wharves of the city, and their stores and most of their crews put
ashore. A few of the latter were added to the gun squads manning
the walls, but most of them set up tents out of the way of the British
fire and sat out the siege in idleness. Those of the skeleton crews who
remained on shipboard were soon to undergo the new and unpleasant
experience of being a target for explosive shells, and they were not
going to enjoy it at all.

There was one most honorable exception. The Sieur de Vauquelin,
a former officer of the merchant service, commanded the frigate
Arethuse, and he put his ship at the extreme western end of the harbor,
almost alongside the city walls and added the fire of his guns to those
of the fortress. He had a crew of only fifty men, but he managed to
cause the British much annoyance during the three weeks he held
this position. Eventually the British guns damaged his ship and he
was forced to withdraw from his exposed location. Then the shot holes
were patched, and Vauquelin was sent off to France with dispatches
reporting the state of the siege. The prevailing wind and the fog fortunately allowed him to evade the British fleet.

Various little amenities were observed during the progress of the
siege. Governor Drucour sent a letter to Amherst asking the fate of
some officers captured by the English and later sent them servants and
spare clothing. Amherst replied and presented Madame Drucour with
some pineapples. She in turn sent him fresh butter and champagne,
fifty bottles of it, one journalist reported. Drucour sent a request to
Amherst for a place to put his wounded where they would be safe
from the artillery fire. The British commander suggested that they

should be sent either to the now silenced Island Battery or put on one of the warships which would be neutralized and moved to the east end of the harbor. Drucour refused both these possibilities. While the flag of truce had gone to the British camp to carry the governor's letter a pleasant little incident occurred. An English lady, accompanied by three redcoated officers, strolled over to the French lines where a certain Captain Joubert was in command. Conversation with the Frenchman brought out the surprising fact that the two were cousins, somewhat distant it is true. History fails to tell us who she was or how she had managed to accompany the expedition. The lady —and she appears to have been such rather than a camp follower— asked permission to enter the French lines to pick greens for a salad. This was granted, and the war stood still while she culled her dandelions and cress.

Now that the Grand Battery had been abandoned and the Island Battery put out of action, the harbor was open to the entrance of the British. The governor accordingly sank three warships and three merchant vessels in the harbor's mouth, but unfortunately the job was botched and the passage, although made difficult, was not blocked. Now only the five great warships remained. The army and the navy continued to bicker. At last some of the ships' guns and their crews had been added to those of the fort, but the navy seems never to have had any enthusiasm for the defense of Louisbourg. Toward the latter part of July a lucky British shell burst in the magazine of one warship and the resulting conflagration spread until only two of the fleet survived. The loss of their ships apparently greatly relieved the minds of their commanders, who exhibited outward signs of regret but actually, according to the perhaps biased report of an army officer, were happy that their problem had been solved for them by the enemy. Then to complete the destruction of the fleet, the British four days later attacked the last two ships of the line in small boats, captured them from their skeleton crews, towed one off as a prize and burned the other which was too firmly aground to be moved. Each ship had a crew of about one hundred men on board, all asleep below decks, and no watch was kept, or it was ineffective.

Meanwhile the besiegers' artillery had been advanced nearer and nearer to the walls of the city, which were gradually being reduced to rubble. The French guns replied valiantly, Madame Drucour appeared on the battlements daily to encourage the men, and she herself helped to fire the cannon. The harbor was now defenseless and soon British ships could be worked in past the sunken hulks to take the citadel under fire from within. The French had made only one sortie, others which had been planned never got started due to one cause or another. Their one attempt penetrated into the advanced British trenches, but was soon repulsed. Captain William Amherst, the commander's brother and aide-de-camp, wrote in his journal that the French who made the sortie had been well primed with brandy before they started. They came on shouting "Kill! Kill!"

Louisbourg was now in sad shape, the warships gone, the army garrison reduced to two thirds of its initial strength, and the walls breached sufficiently for storming parties to fight their way in. Drucour had long realized that he could hope for no relieving force, and that once the British had succeeded in making a landing the fate of the city was certain. All that he could hope to do was to prolong the resistance to the best of his ability in the hope that by the time he at last had to give up it would be too late in the season for the enemy to move up the St. Lawrence against Quebec. He made a gallant defense and secured the desired delay.

On the twenty-sixth of July the French asked for terms, but were offered only unconditional surrender. This Drucour refused as too humiliating and he determined to continue the fight come what might, hoping for more favorable terms. His opposite number on the civil side, the Commissaire Ordinnateur Prevost, persuaded him to change his mind and surrender by citing the fate the civil population would suffer if a final assault were made. Visions of reprisals for last year's massacre at Fort William Henry haunted the minds of the French.

The army had made a spirited and courageous defense against

heavy odds and deserved great praise. The navy, on the other hand, had, with one or two exceptions, acted in a contemptible manner, and had done little to aid the cause of the French. Two years later the admiral, the Marquis des Gouttes, was to pay a heavy price for the actions of his command. News was received from France that he had been broken, degraded from the ranks of the nobility and sent to jail for a score of years, a penalty almost as severe as that suffered by the unhappy Byng and certainly more shameful.

Now that the great fortress was once again in British hands Pitt decided to take no more chances and ordered it leveled to the ground. Today little remains of what was once one of the great cities of North America save for a few earthen mounds, great blocks of masonry too solid to be readily destroyed, the outline of its streets and the foundations of some of its buildings.

All the other French settlements in the region were uprooted, one task force clearing the St. John River of Acadians who had moved in there, while Wolfe had the invidious task of destroying the little fishing villages of Gaspé and burning the fishermen's boats and nets. Canada was now defenseless from the east and only the difficult waters of the St. Lawrence stood guard between Quebec and a British fleet. But the season was too late and the attempt had to wait for another year.

Chapter XVIII

BRADSTREET NO DAWDLER

CAPTAIN John Bradstreet had been put in charge of moving much-needed supplies to Oswego in the unhappy summer of 1756, and his bateau men had worked wonders considering all the difficulties which had to be overcome. It was almost certainly at that time that Bradstreet was seized with the idea of destroying Fort Frontenac. Governor Shirley shortly thereafter authorized him to attack or to annoy the French at that place, if he should find it possible, but the rush to strengthen Oswego's forts and the subsequent advance of Montcalm prevented anything of this nature being done.

After the fall of the British post Bradstreet served as aide-de-camp to Lord Loudoun and secured the latter's approval of an expedition against the fort. Late in 1757 he was promoted to lieutenant colonel, although he seems to have acted as such prior to this time, and made Deputy Quartermaster General. He was building bateaux at Schenectady when Abercromby recalled him for service in the abortive Ticonderoga expedition. Bradstreet, with the enthusiastic support of Lord Howe, at last secured Abercromby's reluctant approval to a Frontenac expedition if and when Fort Carillon was captured. After the failure at Ticonderoga and the retreat of the British Army to the head of Lake George, he again pressed his claims, and a council of war in mid-July granted his request, at the same time ordering construction of a fort at the headwaters of the Mohawk, where the portage to Wood Creek and Lake Oneida began. This was to be called Fort Stanwix, and today it is the site of Rome, New York. It was intended to replace Oswego as the guardian of the Mohawk Valley from the west.

Bradstreet was no dawdler, and his little army started to move the day after the council of war was held, while advance parties were pushed ahead to occupy "The Great Carrying Place," where Fort Stanwix was to be built. All had arrived there by the tenth of August. The next day Brigadier Stanwix assigned some twenty-seven hundred soldiers and nearly three hundred bateau men to Bradstreet, while the rest of the force was put to work on the new fort. One difficulty arose. Bradstreet was only a lieutenant colonel, and so was outranked by the colonels of the colonial regiments, who did not feel that they could serve under him. The matter was adjusted quietly and apparently without any unpleasantness or rancor by drafting large detachments from the regiments and leaving their colonels and a few others behind.

Indian scouts were hard to find, and, despite the efforts of Red Head, an Onondaga chieftain who, disgusted with the French, had attached himself to Bradstreet and the British, only two score could be persuaded to go. Red Head gave much valuable information about conditions at Frontenac, but the others proved of little use.

On the twelfth of August the expedition set off, and no one but their leader knew their destination. Here at last appear the two vital military principles of promptness and secrecy, fulfilled for almost the first time in North America. The expedition certainly started under happy auspices, and a really competent commander, plus good luck and good weather, was to lead it to success, tactically in perhaps a rather small way, but with immense results in the much more important field of strategy. And again it was logistics that decided the affair, not the actual fighting which was minor and almost bloodless. Once the siege artillery had arrived at Frontenac, the fate of the French fortress was sealed, and only the immediate arrival of a large relieving force or incredibly poor luck or bad judgment on the part of the British could have changed it. This little expedition—for it was very small compared to Abercromby's of the month before—was an almost perfect example of what a qualified commander could do when the routes decreed by the geography of North America were exploited to their full.

From "The Great Carrying Place" the expedition portaged to Wood Creek, where a number of roughly built dams allowed bateaux to be passed downstream through a series of what were really crude locks. Each of the 123 bateaux carried about eighteen men and fourteen barrels of supplies, and there were also 95 whaleboats, now a long way from their home waters south of Cape Cod. Wood Creek offered other difficulties beyond that of low water, for many trees had fallen across the channel and had to be cut and hauled to one side, hard and unpleasant work in the sultry August weather. Moreover the water of the creek was always badly polluted by the discharge of swamps and by decayed vegetation, so much so that knowing traders carried a keg or two of fresh water for use until they reached Lake Oneida. So there was some sickness among the men, but Bradstreet had managed to provide an ample supply of rum, and this was dealt out with a liberal hand. The head of the lake was reached after five days of portaging and channel clearing. The party had covered only fifteen miles, but these were by far the hardest of the trip. The next day alone the expedition reeled off thirty-eight miles before making camp on the banks of the Oswego River, six miles downstream from the outlet of Lake Oneida, where a group of friendly Indians were catching great quantities of eels and drying them for their winter use. These fishermen reported that a small party of savages from Abbé Piquet's mission had left the day before, apparently without having gotten wind of the British expedition. They were wrong, nevertheless, for Bradstreet had sent a small party ahead to reconnoiter Oswego, and these scouts had left two of their number and their boat on a little island in the river, while they explored ahead on foot. The men on the island foolishly built a bonfire and promptly lost their scalps, while the Indians found papers in the boat that showed that the British had something under way.

The bateaux and whaleboats slipped easily down the river until

they reached the falls, about twelve miles upstream from Lake Ontario. Here there was a drop of a dozen or so feet, followed by nearly
a mile of rapids. They did not bother to unload the boats, but manhandled them across the short portage, the same one over which
Frontenac, the builder of the fort they sought, had been carried by his
shouting Indians two generations before. The crew of each boat was
reduced to three or four, who undertook to run the rapids. In most
cases this was successfully accomplished, in a wild ride of a mile in
about three minutes, which meant a speed of nearly twenty miles an
hour. A few boats met disaster, including one loaded with a cannon
and a mortar, which were soon recovered. The last dozen miles to
Oswego were made in an hour and a half, and the entire river and
lake trip of seventy miles was completed in nine days.

They found the walls of the old stone trading post still standing,
but there were no signs at all of the defensive works that Montcalm
had destroyed two years before. Abbé Piquet's great cross still pro-
claimed the French victory, but Red Head's Indians at once cut it
down and burned it.

Before noon on the following day the little army had pushed out
into Lake Ontario, notorious for its rough waters, but this day nature
was kind and there was a dead calm, although on the morrow the
party was held up on shore for half a day until the waves subsided.
The little flotilla hugged the south shore of the lake so that land could
be reached promptly if the water became too rough. In the course of
the afternoon enemy Indians were encountered, and on the following
day, the twelfth since the start, while some fifteen miles from Frontenac, they heard warning guns being fired from the French fort.
Winds held Bradstreet and his men up most of that day, and only
by late afternoon could they proceed. Next morning, despite continued
rough water, they reached the vicinity of the fort, but were unable to
land.

Fort Frontenac, as has been said before, was a point of immense
importance, the supply depot for all the French West, and the naval
base of Lake Ontario, yet it was almost beneath contempt as a fort.

It was commanded by high ground in the near vicinity, and its walls, although of stone set in mortar, were so thin that artillery could easily breach them. Its garrison was 110 men, of whom only fifty were soldiers, the rest storekeepers, artisans, and voyageurs. A proper complement would have been at least six hundred soldiers. The fort was square, about one hundred yards on a side with bastions at each corner, and, although its general form was much like that of Fort William Henry and Fort Carillon, it was nowhere nearly so strong. In fact it really was merely the equivalent of a stockaded post, except that its surrounding walls would not rot away in the course of a few years. The gun platforms were of wood, and the embrasures in the walls were too narrow to allow effective fire to be delivered.

A French regular officer reported that when a gun was fired, the whole fort shook. There was ample artillery, some sixty cannon and sixteen mortars, and much of this ordnance had been captured at Braddock's defeat or at Oswego. The garrison, however, was too small to serve the guns. The fort enjoyed one advantage in that its surroundings were largely rocky ledge, and the attackers could not well make the normal siege approach by digging trenches, but instead would have to build a covered way above ground with fascines (bundles of twigs and sticks) and gabions (hollow cylinders of wickerwork which were put in position and then filled with earth).

The Ontario naval force was tied up at the wharves, and it was a powerful one; its largest vessel, *La Marquise de Vaudreuil,* normally carried a crew of eighty-one men, sixteen carriage guns, and eight swivels, the last small cannon pivoted in iron mounts which fitted into holes in the bulwarks, like modern oar locks. There were also two somewhat smaller craft of twelve and nine guns and two big bateaux armed with cannon. One of these vessels, probably *La Marquise de Vaudreuil,* had been captured from the British at Oswego. Had this little fleet been at sea and alert, it could have blown Bradstreet's armada of little bateaux to bits, but several of the French ships were out of commission and all were short-handed, further evidence of New France's lack of funds, of manpower, and of foresight. Canada's command of the Great Lakes existed only in theory, for an inactive fleet which allowed itself to be caught unawares in port by a few score little rowboats was actually only a liability. The power to control Lake Ontario, and hence all the far west, which the French had possessed since the destruction of Oswego and its little British fleet, was thus utterly neglected and thrown away, another example of the failure of both nations at this period to appreciate and to exploit the opportunities of sea power when applied to inland waters.

It was on the thirteenth day after leaving "The Great Carrying Place" that the British reached Fort Frontenac. An attempt was at once made to board the two largest French vessels which lay at anchor, but it failed. The wind continued, and the army was unable to land until the end of the afternoon. The artillery was worked ashore, four brass 12-pounders and four eight-inch howitzers, but Bradstreet had only seventy rounds per gun, far too little for a normal siege. Moreover, since the French would almost certainly be reinforced once their plight was known, the British might be driven to raising the siege. Speed thus was essential, and Bradstreet proceeded to apply it to his assault, but he also added the elements of deceit and surprise.

The fate of the fort, barring an act of God, was already sealed, simply because Bradstreet had got his siege guns to his objective. The success of the expedition might be thought to result from the actions of the next few days or even hours, but these actually would be incidental in importance to the great logistical feat Bradstreet had accomplished in bringing his cannon through difficult country with both celerity and secrecy, and thus catching the French unawares. Their complacency existed not only at Frontenac, but also at Quebec where Vaudreuil believed that the British would not venture out onto Lake Ontario for fear of the French fleet.

There was a little hill something less than half a mile from the fort, and, as soon as the artillery was ashore, the British put a gun or two behind it and opened fire on the enemy in order to occupy their attention while further preparations were under way. A year or two earlier the French had built an earthen breastwork about two hundred and fifty yards away from the fort, but their force was much too small to man it. As soon as it was dark Bradstreet with some noise and ostentation moved a few guns to the shelter of this earth-work and proceeded to cut embrasures through its top. Meanwhile on the other side of the fortress a working party of five hundred started to build another battery only a hundred and fifty yards from the target. They made so much noise, however, in dragging their material through the low brush and bushes that they were soon discovered, and fire was opened on them in the dark. Only one man was wounded. The French, of course, had been firing on and off all day at any targets that the British presented, but their shots did almost no harm at all. Late in the night the moon came up, and by its light the de-fenders continued their fire, now and then wounding a man.

By daylight both British batteries were in action against the walls of Frontenac. Soon the two little warships slipped their cables and tried to escape, but a few cannon balls from Bradstreet's men caused their crews to abandon them after running them into shallow water. The walls of one of the bastions were breached by the British can-non, and the French quickly bowed to the inevitable and raised the red flag of surrender, red because, their national colors being white, they could not use that more customary color for a flag of truce or of surrender. The losses on both sides were almost negligible, for the French had only two killed, while of the attackers only a few suffered minor wounds.

Now was the time for the Indians—English ones this time—to get into the act, and they proceeded to perform exactly as would be ex-pected. "Immediately after the surrender of the fort, our Indians [who had all, except five or six] kept at a mile's distance during the attack, came running from the woods where they had been conceal'd; like ravenous beasts, full of expectations, of satiating their blood-thirsty fury on the captives; but were stopp'd by Col. Bradstreet [but they] . . . entreated him to close his eyes, and turn his back upon them, agreeable to the practice of the French, but he . . . positively denied them . . . [and] . . . told them . . . to enrich themselves by plunder. . . . The search for valuable goods, became then their entire pursuit."

Governor Vaudreuil ordered out a relief force of militia as soon as he heard that Frontenac was threatened, but it did not arrive until long after the British had departed. Later, when he learned that the post had fallen, he ordered the construction of new vessels on the lake and planned to rebuild the fort the following spring. Actually the location was a poor one, since bateaux could slip into the St. Lawrence without passing near the fort. Montcalm believed that the new post should be built farther eastward on the shore of the river, but the days of New France were almost over and the post was never replaced.

The Canadian governor in his report to the home government as usual exaggerated and distorted the facts, writing that his relieving force scared the British away, that they went off in great confusion, and that "most of them abandoned their clothes and even their muskets." There is no question that the withdrawal was rapid, but it was made only after the British had destroyed all that they did not wish to take away with them. Speed was the watchword of this most beautifully executed raid. Throughout the entire operation Bradstreet drove his men so hard that by the time of their return to "The Great Carrying Place" many were nearly worn out.

Members of the fort's garrison, before they were released on parole to make their way down the St. Lawrence to Montreal, told Bradstreet that a force of four thousand Canadians and a thousand Indians was coming from Montreal by way of Frontenac and Oswego to raid the Mohawk Valley. The British commander retaliated by replying that a big English expedition was heading north by land to attack La Presentation, Abbé Piquet's mission fort, knowing that this would be reported to the abbé and that the French expedition would be held there. Both forces, of course, were entirely fictitious.

This Bradstreet was really a broth of a boy. Unfortunately he knew it, and was far from modest. But he got things done, an ability too many leaders of colonial days failed to possess, and one can forgive him his vanity and self-assertion. After the Frontenac expedition he drops out of our story, but he continued in service and died in New York, a major general, just before our Revolution started.

The spoils of Frontenac and its warehouses were immense, seventy-six pieces of ordnance, some ten thousand barrels of provisions—said somewhat optimistically to be sufficient for twenty thousand men for six months—a great quantity of skins and furs, and 800,000 livres' worth of Indian trade goods, perhaps $2,000,000 by today's values. Most of this had to be destroyed, because it was too bulky to carry away. The two larger vessels were dragged back into deep water and loaded with part of the plunder, while the torch was applied to all else, shipping, barracks, sheds, and provisions, in a mighty holocaust. The stone walls of the fort, however, seem to have been left standing, mostly undamaged, since large quantities of gunpowder and much time would have been required to level them. On August 29, the seventeenth day, the departure was made for Oswego, and "The Great Carrying Place" was reached without incident after twenty-four days of absence. At the head of Wood Creek, at stockaded Fort Bull, a day or so before the return to the now rapidly rising walls of Fort Stanwix, a halt was made and the plunder divided among the men. It consisted mostly of clothing and furs, and there was enough so that every man received two or three skins, a shirt, a coat or blanket, and perhaps a wool cap.

The Frontenac expedition was a model enterprise. It was conducted with speed, secrecy, and a clear idea of its purpose. As a military operation it was minor, as a logistical undertaking it was outstanding, but strategically its results were immense, for it cut the French lifeline to the west and was the crack which foretold the fall of New France. Vaudreuil hoped to continue to supply Niagara by convoys of bateaux which would hug the north shore of Lake Ontario and carry field-pieces which could hurriedly be landed and put in action should the convoy be attacked by British vessels. By one expedient or another Fort Niagara was to be held by the French for another year, but its time had almost run out.

Bradstreet perhaps can be charged with missing two opportunities. Had he known it, he could have gone on to Niagara and taken it even more easily than he had Frontenac, for its garrison at that moment was only about forty strong. The British leader naturally did not know this, and his mission was the destruction of Fort Frontenac by a speedy raid to be followed by a rapid withdrawal. Moreover his raid had been so fast and strenuous that his force would have required rest, recuperation, and resupply before undertaking further action. The supply problem could have been met through the provisions captured from the French, but time was required for the other needs, and Bradstreet had to give thought to the possible arrival of the great French war party of which he had been warned by the Frontenac garrison. Probably he felt that he had done enough for the present, and that the loss of Frontenac would so weaken Niagara that it could be left alone until the following year.

The other opportunity Bradstreet lost was that of seizing the naval command of Lake Ontario, assured him by the two little war vessels, the only ones remaining on the lake, that he took to Oswego and then burned. Had they been retained in commission by the British they would have practically cut off all French communication with the west and certainly would have greatly reduced, if not entirely eliminated, all flow of supplies. Abercromby realized this and ordered Bradstreet to keep the ships cruising on the lake as long as possible, but the boats had been destroyed before the order was received. It is problematical, of course, whether the little warships could have survived the winter, as they had no place to seek shelter, either from the ice of the lake, which froze miles out from shore, or from the torch of raiding parties of French and Indians. Probably the solution would have been to unrig and sink them in shallow water, raising and re-equipping them the following spring, as had been done by the British on Lake George.

The news of the fall of Frontenac gave pleasure to one man in Canada, Bigot, the intendant. Army quartermasters in our own times have always covertly welcomed fire in a storehouse or barrack, as it allowed them to clear the records of all the little unexplained shortages that had accumulated since the last accounting. In the same way Bigot now had a perfect opportunity to square all the thefts and peculations that had taken place at the western posts, and he took full advantage of it. Paris for some time had been casting more than suspicious glances at his accounts and had sternly warned him that he must reform his ways drastically.

Bradstreet's model expedition was but one of the bright spots that brought the year 1758—ushered in by Abercromby's appalling blunder —to a happier close, one which to the critical observer foretold the coming fall of New France. Louisbourg had fallen, this time to British regulars, and Brigadier General John Forbes had started the second attempt against Fort Duquesne, third of the objectives decreed by Pitt for the campaign of that year.

Chapter XIX

REVENGE FOR BRADDOCK

Fort Duquesne at the Forks of the Ohio had been left in peace since Braddock's sad affair, and it continued to be the base and the supply depot for the Indian raiding parties that harried the Pennsylvania and Virginia frontiers. Pitt's plans for 1758 called for a major effort against Louisbourg, an invasion of Canada down the Champlain Valley, and lastly an offensive action on the southern frontier. This meant an attempt on Fort Duquesne. Command of this last operation was given to Brigadier General John Forbes, who had served as a senior staff officer under Lord Loudoun before his promotion. He was an excellent officer, of long experience, particularly in matters concerning supply, and he possessed other attributes most desirable in a commander. Forbes was sound, resourceful, well trained and strong minded, with a high sense of duty, but he was a sick man, who was to wear out his body in this summer's campaign. His second in command, and his firm friend, was another officer of great worth, a Swiss, Lieutenant Colonel Henry Bouquet of the Royal American Regiment, the 6oth, the only regular British regiment in which a foreigner could hold a commission. Raised in America, this regiment was recruited largely from Pennsylvanians of German ancestry, and many of its officers were Swiss or German by birth.

Braddock's Duquesne expedition had been planned as a dash to the fort, carrying along all the supplies and provisions. Had it succeeded the British would have been left sitting at the end of a long and most tenuous supply line with a major problem to be faced in maintaining that position. Had they decided to destroy Duquesne and withdraw back east of the mountains, the threat would have remained because a new fort could have quickly been re-established by forces from the other nearby French posts of Venango, Le Boeuf, and Presqu' Isle. Forbes chose an entirely different plan of campaign, one of which he had learned from study of a recent French book on the military art. This was to advance slowly, establishing a series of fortified supply posts as the expedition advanced, each near enough to the other to be able to reinforce its neighbor if there were need. Using a series of such bases an expedition could leapfrog forward, fall back if necessary, even wait out a winter and start ahead again in the following spring. Essential supplies would thus be distributed along the line of advance and could be pushed forward as needed. And finally the relative nearness of these fortified posts to each other would allow the road to be maintained and patrolled with ease. Forbes' advance was to be slow, steady, and sure, quite the opposite of the disastrous one of 1755.

At once a major problem arose. Along what route should the expedition move? The obvious and superficial answer of course was to follow Braddock's old road. There it was; all that would be needed would be to clear away bushes and make minor repairs to parts of the road and the bridges. A major drawback to this route, however, was that it started from an area where supplies were hard to get, and horses and teams were in scant supply. An advance from Pennsylvania directly west would have its start from a well-populated area with ample food supplies, as well as horses and wagons. An entire new road would have to be built, and it would have to be pushed across the Alleghenies, a most serious matter, but it would avoid the major river crossings necessitated by the Virginia route.

In addition to the logistical and strategical considerations there was also a serious political problem to be considered and solved. Once Duquesne had fallen, the route of the army would presumably become the trade route to the Ohio country. Naturally both Virginia and Pennsylvania wished the road to start in its dominion. Sir John St. Clair, who had served as supply officer to Braddock, held the same position under Forbes, and he initially favored the direct route through Pennsylvania, later shifting to the Virginia road. Forbes, however, despite very considerable pressure, remained firm for building a new and direct route over the Pennsylvania mountains. Virginia fought hard for its road. Colonel Byrd offered the services of sixty Indian scouts, but only if Braddock's road was to be followed. Forbes wrote Bouquet: "My good friend Byrd is either made the cat's foot off himself, or he little knows me, if he imagines that sixty scoundrels are to direct me in my measures." George Washington's violent opposition to the plan approached the point of insubordination and seriously damaged the British general's confidence in the Virginian. One cannot but feel that the future President may, perhaps unconsciously, have allowed economic considerations to outweigh the military in his mind at this time. His actions certainly destroyed some of his value to the expedition, and he remained deeply pessimistic as to its success.

Forbes believed in adapting his methods to meet North American conditions. He realized that the bayonet was of little use in woods fighting and appreciated the tactics of the rangers. He wrote to Bouquet that numbers of the British should be equipped like the savages, and said, "I was resolved upon getting some of the best people in every corps to go out a scouting in that stile . . . and I must confess in this country, wee must comply and learn the art of war from enemy Indians or anything else who have seen the country and warr carried on in it." Not very grammatical, perhaps, but a clear indication of an open mind. Forbes also ordered the manufacture of a quantity of skyrockets to be used for signaling "in those hellish woods."

The expedition included a large part of the 77th Highlanders, some companies of the Royal Americans and provincial troops from Virginia, Pennsylvania, North Carolina, and Maryland. The provincials were deficient both in equipment and training, their muskets were mostly unserviceable and they did not even have kettles in which to cook their rations. Considerable effort was made to attract and to hold the services of friendly Indians, but largely without success. A slow methodical advance such as this was to be was not at all to the taste of the red man. Moreover the campaign dragged on into the late fall, when the Indian wanted to be hunting his winter's meat.

Attempts were made to detach the Indians of the Ohio country from the French interest. Many Delawares and some Shawnees had moved west from the Susquehanna waters and had established themselves in the Ohio headwaters, a little north and west of Fort Duquesne. Christian Frederick Post, a devoted Moravian missionary who had labored for fifteen years among the Indians and knew the Delawares intimately, undertook the perilous task of carrying a message of peace from the Pennsylvania governor to the Indians living within the French zone of influence. He ran grave danger both from hostile Indians and from the French garrisons in the region. French officers learned of his presence and tried to bribe the Indians to give him up, but Post was protected both by his position as a bearer of belts, and by the faith and trust that he had built up among the Indians over the many years of his missionary labors. He delivered his message, made a short stay in the region as he exhorted Indians at various villages to make peace, and managed to return east in safety.

Bouquet directed that all friendly Indians should wear yellow headbands and yellow armbands with streamers, and he sent a quantity of cloth of this color to the Ohio Indians, telling them to wear such identification if they wished to come eastward with peaceful intent.

During October of this year a great Indian conference was held at Easton in the presence of the Pennsylvania governor and his council. A major result of the meeting was the promise made to the Indians that the lands beyond the Appalachians should remain Indian and that all white settlement should be held east of the mountains. A message of peace to the Ohio Indians was also drafted, and Post again ventured to carry it westward, this time accompanied part of the way by two Pennsylvania officers and a handful of soldiers.

The little party slipped by Duquesne a few miles to its north. The night when they made their camp nearest to the French fort, Post wrote in his journal, "The wolves made a terrible music this night." When Post finally arrived at the Indian town of Kushkushkee, about twenty-five miles northwest of Duquesne, he found himself surrounded by a crowd of bloodthirsty Indians who had just returned from an unsuccessful attack on a British post, and his life was in great danger. He delivered his message and argued for peace, while French officers from the fort in turn pleaded their cause and attempted to make Post's Indian hosts deliver him into their hands. The missionary's arguments, strengthened considerably by the news of the arrival of the British within a very few miles of Fort Duquesne, swung the balance against the French. Post in that year of 1758 served the British Empire well, and his actions were a major cause of the large-scale defection of the Ohio Indians from the French interest that fall and winter. Late in the year, after the British had occupied the site of Fort Duquesne with only a small garrison, the French planned to move against it from Venango, but the Kushkushkee Indians forbade the move, saying that they would stop the French if it were attempted.

During the summer the road had been pushed forward, from Shippensburg to Chamber's Fort on the Conococheague, to Fort Loudoun a dozen miles farther west, to Bedford, then called Raystown, and on to the highest of the ridges. St. Clair, an odd and difficult character, was driving the road forward to the best of his not inconsiderable ability. From the foot of the Allegheny Ridge, the highest point of all that must be crossed, he wrote back to Bouquet: "The work to be done on this road is immense & if I have not two hundred men more, I do not know when it will be finished. The work I have to do is all digging, pick axes, crows & shovels is what is most wanted. Likewise more whiskey."

This new road was not being built through entirely virgin country, for an old trading path ran along its entire route from Bedford, the last settlement, all the way to the Forks of the Ohio. It was, however, only a trail for pack horses and so of scant value to the expedition with cannon and heavy wagons. Forbes conceived the idea of brushing out narrow auxiliary roads parallel to and on either side of the new road at a distance of one hundred yards. Scouting parties could easily move along these and make sure that there was no ambush that might endanger troops advancing along the main road.

Lieutenant Colonel Adam Stephen, a capable young officer, was in command of Washington's 1st Virginia Regiment while the latter was acting as temporary brigadier of the Virginia troops. Stephen was assigned a road-building mission from the Allegheny Ridge to the top of Laurel Hill. Part of this route went through dense woods and swamps, so unpleasant a region that it was known as "The Shades of Death." Then the road climbed the rocky slopes of the Laurel Ridge. The young lieutenant colonel wrote back to Bouquet in cheerful and flippant mood: "There is nothing would have a greater effect upon these rocks, than the essence of fat beef gradually mixt with a puncheon of rum, this would add weight to every stroke given them . . . The salt pork [we have eaten] has very near dry'd up . . . [the] spring, at this encampment." Stephen was a good and efficient officer, but he ran into trouble with the irascible Sir John St. Clair, who put him under arrest. The knight was obviously in the wrong but would not admit it, and the affair was quietly dropped and the provincial officer restored to duty. The risk of a clash between regular and provincial always lay near the surface, but most of the senior officers had enough common sense not to allow any open break to occur.

As early as mid-August several groups of British scouts had viewed the French fort at close range. A party led by a Lieutenant Chew of the Virginians, and including five Indians, had to stop and hide in a thicket a mile or so from the fort while the Indians made magic and repainted their faces. Then they moved nearer, but stopped again while magic amulets were tied around the necks of all the party in order to ward off enemy bullets. After stripping to breechclouts and moccasins they went on with their mission. Chew thought that he saw about three hundred French—actually there were a great many more—and reported that "The [French] Indians kept a continual hooping and hallowing." The magic of the amulets must have been powerful for all the party returned safely, though Lieutenant Chew met his death before the campaign ended.

There is no need to follow Forbes' little army at length. A tough, courageous, and woefully ill general, assisted by a highly competent and loyal second in command, drove his men slowly westward, building roads through woods, over swamps and up precipices, and establishing fortified supply bases at Bedford and on Loyalhanna Creek, where Fort Ligonier became the jumping-off place for the final move against Duquesne.

The road over Laurel Hill was probably the hardest of all to build, but it was at last accomplished and by the first week in September work was commenced on Fort Ligonier. Shortly thereafter Bouquet sent Major James Grant of the 77th with a party composed of Highlanders, Royal Americans, and provincials forward to reconnoiter the French fort and if possible to wipe out some of the Indians camped around it. It was said that Indians never put out sentinels at night, and that they should be easily surprised at that time. Grant grossly mishandled the business, splitting his men up into three detachments, each of which was engaged separately by the French and their Indian allies and badly cut up. The Highlanders suffered by far the worse casualties, while some of the provincials ran away without firing a shot. Grant was surrounded and forced to surrender, and over a third of his force failed to return to Ligonier. Forbes, who was by now so unwell that he had to be carried in a litter slung between two horses, showed his irritation in a rather pained letter to Bouquet, the only bit of the surviving correspondence which expresses anything other than confidence and friendship. In mid-October the French retaliated and attacked the Loyalhanna camp with a force of about one thousand, a small part of which was composed of Indians. The attack was easily repulsed by the British.

A thoroughly ill and worn-out commander arrived at last at Ligonier on November 2, and shortly held a council of war, the opinion of which was that the expedition could go no farther that year. This was almost at once followed by a French raid on the horse herd grazing a few miles away from the fort, certainly a cause of annoyance to put it mildly. A prisoner, captured just after the raid, reported that most of the French Indians had gone home, as well as many of the French, some of whom were militia from the Illinois country and Louisiana. He claimed that the fort's garrison was now quite weak. Forbes at once decided to move forward over the last forty miles and attack Duquesne. During the night of November 24, while the troops were encamped near the scene of Braddock's defeat, they heard a great explosion as the French blew up their fort and abandoned the Forks of the Ohio. A day later the British reached the place to find only ruins. The approach to the fort was lined on either side by a long row of posts each bearing on its top the head of a Highlander and below it was lashed his kilt. An English boy, escaped from the fort shortly before its destruction, said that five of the captured Highlanders had been burned at the stake on the parade ground of the fort, and others had been tomahawked.

The real cause of the fall of Duquesne was Bradstreet's destruction of the supplies at Frontenac. Although at times the French fort was both partly garrisoned and partly supplied with provisions from the settlements to the west and the south, it was dependent upon Frontenac for its Indian trade goods and its military supplies. Had Forbes not marched against it, Fort Duquesne could have held out into the following year as did Forts Venango, Le Boeuf, and Presqu' Isle, but its power to serve as a base for Indian raids was gone, and it could have been left harmlessly alone to die a gradual death as the vital loss of Frontenac made itself increasingly felt. Thus it might be possible to say that Forbes' expedition was unnecessary since it was aimed at the fingertip of an arm which was soon to be cut off at Frontenac, although this of course did not happen until the Pennsylvania attack was well on its way. The expedition achieved a useful purpose in maintaining pressure along the French southern front and in encouraging the defection of many of the Indians from the French. It is sad to have to note that Forbes, worn out by his exhausting toil, died shortly after his return to Philadelphia, a tired old soldier of forty-nine.

Thus the year 1758 ended with another victory. There had been a major disaster at Ticonderoga, but Louisbourg had fallen, the French lifeline to the west had been cut at Frontenac, and now Duquesne would no longer spew out bloodthirsty savages to harry the borders of the middle colonies. Not only was New France at last on the defensive, but she was pulling back her frontiers. Except for a western trading post or two and the one remaining strategic point of Niagara, Canada now stretched only from the lower St. Lawrence to Abbé Piquet's mission post sixty miles east from Lake Ontario, and south to the head of Lake George. Three routes of travel and hence of attack penetrated to her heartland, by sea and up the St. Lawrence, down that great river from the Great Lakes, and north down the Champlain Valley. Before another year had passed the enemy would be moving to the attack along all these approaches. The British had developed methods and means for campaigning in the wilderness, able leaders had appeared, and Pitt would see that men and supplies were available. New France had been driven into a corner and was ripe for the knockout blow, but it still would be two more years before the fleurs-de-lis were replaced by the Union Jack of Great Britain.

Chapter XX

NEW FRANCE TOTTERS

T HE year 1759 was to deal harshly with New France. Britain's naval supremacy had reduced the flow of supplies from the mother country to a mere trickle, Louisbourg had been lost, Duquesne abandoned, and it was evident to the rulers of Canada that even the resulting new frontiers could not be held. Pitt had determined to subdue the country, and ample means to accomplish this objective were made available to the commanders in America. The Prime Minister's instructions to Amherst for the 1759 campaign were to move north down the Champlain Valley against Fort Carillon and Crown Point and on toward Canada, while Wolfe moved up the St. Lawrence and assailed Quebec. Amherst also was to ensure the safety of Fort Pitt at the Forks of the Ohio, and to re-establish the post at Oswego. Brigadier Stanwix was assigned by Amherst to the Fort Pitt mission, while a force under Brigadier Prideaux was sent to Oswego. Pitt had given the commander permission to undertake an additional operation should he feel it wise, and accordingly Prideaux was directed to move against Niagara, once he had made Oswego safe.

Amherst himself was to lead the Champlain Valley attack. He had a force of some eight thousand men, about half British regulars, the rest colonials from New England and New Jersey. In late June he moved north to the head of Lake George, where he began another fort to replace the ruined William Henry. The general was never a man to move in a hurry, and it was not until after mid-July that he started against the French fort at Ticonderoga. The careful Amherst had taken pains to learn all that he could about the French fort. As early as mid-March, an engineer officer of the regulars, a Lieutenant Brehm, was sent to examine Fort Carillon. Escorted by Rogers and a large body of Rangers, Mohawks, and British regulars, Brehm prowled by moonlight around the snow-covered lines where Montcalm had made his stand the summer before, finding them much strengthened, and with cannon now in place. Then he went over to the eastern shore of the lake and climbed the hill which the French called "Diamond Mount" because of the rock crystals found there. Years later, during the Revolution, the Americans would build a second fort there and call it Mount Independence. Brehm examined Carillon at length and wrote a detailed report of its defenses for Amherst. Some prisoners were taken, and they said that the fort had a garrison of about four hundred soldiers, one hundred workmen, and something like one hundred Indians. Provisions were short, the daily ration was a pound and a half of bread and a quarter-pound of salt pork, and that was all except for a considerable amount of venison brought in by the Indians. Scurvy raged. Forty men had already died, and another sixty-five were in the hospital. Meanwhile the British, forty miles south at Fort Edward on the Hudson, were keeping hale and hearty on a ration which that winter included onions, cabbages, potatoes, and turnips.

Monypenny was now a major, and his little orderly book, which had survived Abercromby's defeat, continued in use during the early summer. This year the regimental colors were to be carried, reversing the procedure of the year before, and the equipment of the soldiers was lightened. Only the grenadiers took swords, although the two Highland regiments could, if their commanders wished. Officers left their sashes behind and carried light muskets. Gage's light infantry, the new attempt to solve the ranger problem, were ordered to brown the barrels of their carbines, and their jackets might be made quite plain, "the less seen in the woods the better." One of the regular regiments, the Royals, had been equipped with captured French muskets at Louisbourg in 1758, and they now exchanged them for the regulation Brown Bess. Finally Amherst decreed that no women at all should accompany the troops.

The French knew that they could no longer hold Fort Carillon, their resources were too strained, and they were being attacked on too many fronts. Brigadier Bourlamaque, the second senior officer after Montcalm, was in command at Ticonderoga with orders to hold that position only until a British expedition arrived in force. He was then to execute a delaying action as he withdrew to his final defensive position at the Isle-aux-Noix at the outlet of Lake Champlain. Accordingly no resistance was offered to the advance of the British or to the landing of their army at the foot of Lake George. A force of about four hundred men was left inside Fort Carillon, but the old lines built for the 1758 battle and subsequently strengthened were not occupied. Amherst landed his forces on August 22 and rather leisurely brought his artillery up toward the fort. The British took shelter in the old French lines and with a little pick and shovel work made themselves excellent protection from the lively cannon and mortar fire of the fort, which continued for four days and kept the attackers pinned down until they could get their own heavy guns into action. The French threw a considerable number of 13-inch mortar shells, terrifying missiles in theory but hardly as dangerous as they sound, for being made of cast iron and loaded with black powder, they burst into relatively few pieces, much different from the lethal shower of fragments the modern high intensity shell produces. The mortar shell usually buried itself partly in the ground before the fuse exploded it, and the burst was somewhat cushioned and forced upward. These shells were, however, most effective against the interior of forts. Actually the British suffered few casualties, although Colonel Townshend, Amherst's close personal friend, was cut down by a cannon ball.

The British at last got their heavy guns into position, but before they were ready to fire the French abandoned Carillon and headed north. Discipline apparently broke down, and the brandy barrels were broached. The attackers captured many drunken Frenchmen as the rest of the garrison took to its boats. Captain Hebecourt, the commander, had left a lighted fuse in the powder magazine, and Amherst, who had been told of this by a French deserter, offered a reward of a hundred guineas to anyone who would enter the fort and put out the fuse. He had no takers. An hour before midnight the powder went off in a great explosion and the barracks caught fire. A courageous sergeant of the light infantry braved the flames, and brought away the French flag which had been left flying, but the fire continued, despite British efforts to put out the flames, and did not burn itself out for nearly a week.

Amherst's losses were light, sixteen killed and fifty-one wounded, vastly different from Abercromby's tremendous casualties of the year before. Conditions, of course, were very different. Amherst made a slow and cautious investment, bringing up his artillery in the traditional manner, while the small French garrison attempted only to delay the fall of the fort. In this they succeeded to a greater extent than could have been expected, for the British were delayed almost two weeks by the siege and the subsequent preparations for the advance on Crown Point. Before he was ready to move against Fort St. Frederic, Amherst learned that it had been blown up and abandoned, as the French retreated northward to the foot of Lake Champlain.

The commander in chief decided to repair Fort Carillon, which he renamed Fort Ticonderoga. The stone walls of the barracks remained. The rest of the fort, except for the bastion which had contained the powder magazine and over it a stable containing half a hundred unfortunate horses, suffered relatively little damage. In his journal Amherst wrote that he would "repair the fort upon the same plan as the enemy had built it which will . . . give no room for the engineers to exercise their genius."

On August 4 the army reached Crown Point to find that Fort St. Frederic was only partly destroyed. On this same day Amherst learned of the fall of Niagara to the forces of Brigadier Prideaux, who unfortunately had been accidentally killed through the carelessness of one of his own gunners. Sir William Johnson had taken over the command, but Amherst at once sent Brigadier Gage to replace the Indian commissioner. Instead of at once pushing on after the retreating French, as a Wolfe or a Bradstreet would have done, the commander in chief started making plans for a new fort at Crown Point, building roads, and brewing spruce beer. Not until the following year would the British reach the foot of Lake Champlain.

Amherst believed in being safe and sure, certainly a better policy than that pursued by Abercromby in 1758, but hardly correct when the enemy was on the run. His journal says: "No likelihood of the enemy's coming but I can't be too sure." There was, however, a real excuse for his caution and failure to advance northward at once. The British must necessarily proceed by water, and the French at that time had command of the lake through their three little lateen-rigged chebecs and a schooner, whose cannon could blow the British bateaux to bits. So Amherst set to work building a fort and constructing a little navy, and the army remained at Crown Point until mid-October. There was nothing to oppose its advance toward Montreal except four puny warships and Brigadier Bourlamaque's 2900 men on Isle-aux-Noix at the outlet of Lake Champlain. The officer in command of the little fleet was Joshua Loring, a Massachusetts man who, after service as a privateer officer during King George's War, had been made a captain in the Royal Navy. His son of the same name was to achieve notoriety during the Revolution as the British commissary in charge of rebel prisoners.

The British general perhaps was overcautious that summer of 1759, but the presence of the little French warships was sufficient to justify his action. Amherst, however, is open to criticism for not pushing the construction of his fleet to the utmost, and for wasting time on another fort. The building of this new fort at Crown Point seems quite unnecessary by hindsight, since Fort Ticonderoga was also being repaired. There was no need for two forts so near together on the same waterway. Of course the work on new Fort Amherst kept the men busy and out of mischief while the fleet was being built and until Captain Loring could chase away the little French chebecs. The new fort cost the British Crown vast sums, was never really completed, and, after the last French war was over, had the wooden facing of its walls burned when a washwoman heating her water let the fire get out of control. Today its great earthen ramparts and the walls of its stone barracks still stand, partly preserved but not restored, while its neighbor to the south at Ticonderoga, its walls and barracks rebuilt on their surviving foundations by the late Stephen Pell, remains the best existing example of a colonial fort.

The soldiers, both regulars and provincials, were put to work on the new fort, while ship carpenters got out timbers and plank for the British warships. A French deserter in mid-August gave Amherst details as to the armament and crews of the chebecs and the schooner, and the latter decided that his intended fleet was not powerful enough. Accordingly he ordered construction of a radeau capable of carrying six 24-pounder cannon. This was a great scow-shaped craft eighty-four feet long by twenty feet wide, decked over and with bulwarks. It had two masts but never sailed well except before the wind. It was more a movable floating battery than a warship, but its fire power was much greater than anything the French could bring against it. It was learned that the French were building a large sloop at Isle-aux-Noix, so early in September a small party of volunteers set off, loaded with incendiary materials, to attempt to burn the vessel. They almost did it, but made too much noise and were discovered while attaching the combustibles. Amherst had told them to wait until the early morning hours, but they were impatient and climbed on the boat before the French had all gone to sleep. It was a courageous venture that deserved better luck.

In mid-September Major Robert Rogers set off from Crown Point on his greatest raid. He had more than two hundred picked men, and his objective was the destruction of the Indian village of St. Francis near the St. Lawrence forty-five miles downstream from Montreal. The raiders went by whaleboat to the end of Lake Champlain, moving only by night and successfully evading the French vessels. Then they hid their boats, which the French shortly discovered, thus receiving warning that something was on foot, and marched overland through very difficult country to the Indian village. In a sudden dawn attack they surprised the place, killed some two hundred Indians, and burned everything, including the chapel, and, as Amherst informed Pitt, the mission priest as well. This last Rogers did not mention in the report he wrote about the raid, but his reticence is understandable. The French and their Indians poured out after the Rangers like a hive of angry hornets, and the English retreated to the east and south, vigorously pursued. Many were caught and promptly dispatched, while only about a third of the force managed to return by way of Lake Memphramagog and the Connecticut River. It was said that some treasures from the chapel, particularly a silver statue of the Madonna, were carried away and lost in the wilderness, and even today there is talk that they may still be found.

Amherst's army at last took to its bateaux and headed north on September 11, guarded by the great radeau, and preceded by the brig and the sloop, both of which soon got far ahead of the flotilla. Suddenly the French fleet appeared between the army and its advance warships. The situation became tense. The bateaux huddled together near shore, covered by the heavy guns of the radeau, and the French vessels disappeared to the north. The wind blew hard, and Amherst landed his men for safety and to boil their pots and stretch their legs. Loring, realizing that he was too far ahead, had begun working back to the south when he discovered the French fleet, which fled at his approach and took shelter in a little bay. During the night two of the chebecs were sunk by their crews and the third run ashore, while the schooner apparently escaped to safety at Isle-aux-Noix. Amherst now had control of the great waterway and could advance against the French defenses at the outlet of the lake. Just at this moment, however, he learned of Wolfe's victory at Quebec, and believing that Lévis's army would now fall back on Montreal, he decided that a further advance was unwise. Accordingly he returned to Crown Point, and continued work on the fort. Further operations against the French were over for the year. By mid-winter the colonial regiments were sent home and the regulars started off for their winter quarters. Amherst moved back to Albany and, after tarrying there for a few days, climaxed his year's activities by walking all the way to New York, a distance of 160 miles in a week.

The 1759 campaign in the Champlain Valley again highlights the vital importance of water transport. Lack of naval superiority had stalled Amherst's advance until developments on the St. Lawrence made impracticable any further operations in the lake region. Amherst certainly should have foreseen and anticipated his naval requirements more effectively than he did, and could have concentrated on building warships and let the new fort wait. Then the long summer months would not have been wasted in comparative idleness at Crown Point. Even so it seems probable that, cautious as the British commander was by nature, and relatively strong as were the French defenses on Isle-aux-Noix, the army probably could not have advanced this year beyond the northern end of the lake.

Amherst's achievements in this theater of operations, although falling short of expectations, and due more to French weakness and lack of supplies than to British energy, were very considerable. The French forts which had long guarded the critical approach to New France had at last fallen, and a British army in command of Lake Champlain stood on the threshold of the country. Meanwhile two other British successes had further narrowed the frontiers of Canada, and, barring French victories in Europe and a peace unfavorable to England, had assured the downfall of the unhappy land.

After the fall of Canada labor continued on the great fort at Crown Point, which was to cost some £3,000,000 yet never to serve a useful purpose in war. Late in 1760 the commanding officer was the excellent Colonel Haviland, who apparently believed in a tight discipline and, accordingly, did not enjoy the love of the colonials serving under him. Captain Samuel Jenks of the Massachusetts troops wrote in his diary: "I heard that Col. Haverland, going round the fort, fell down & broke his leg. Poor man! I am sorry it was his leg."

The fall of Frontenac in 1758 had left the vital French post at Niagara in a precarious condition, short of men and supplies, with its supply line through Lake Ontario open to attack by the English should they keep a naval force on the lake. Bradstreet, however, had burned all the vessels and abandoned both Frontenac and Oswego, and supplies from the St. Lawrence could still be forwarded to Niagara.

In the spring of 1759 the extremely capable Chevalier Pouchot, captain in the regular regiment of Béarn and knight in His Most Christian Majesty's military order of St. Louis, was sent to command at Niagara. He had served there previously from the fall of 1755 until 1757, strengthening and improving the fort and learning the ways of the Indian. Niagara, however, was an important trading post, a place where a man of less integrity than Pouchot could make his fortune, and the governor sent a Canadian officer to exploit the opportunities of the post. Pouchot returned east, greatly to the regret of the Indians, who appreciated the fair treatment he had given them.

The French had built a great stone house at Niagara back in 1727. Ostensibly, in order to placate the Iroquois who feared the building of a fort at this important place, it purported to be only a house for the fur trade. Actually, however, it was very stoutly built and was a most effective fort, more so than the usual stockaded post. A palisade had been built around it in a four-sided square with bastions at the corners, and in this condition the fort remained until Pouchot, in 1755, began a great earthen wall and a ditch across the point of land projecting into Lake Ontario on the eastern side of the Niagara River, on the tip of which stood the stone house. The other two sides of the triangular fort were formed by steep bluffs rising from the river on one side, the lake on the other, and crowned by low ramparts. A fort of very considerable strength would result, but the chevalier had not finished the work before he was summoned eastward to other duties.

Governor Vaudreuil received warnings of growing discontent among the Five Nations, and, realizing the danger threatening Niagara and the Indian's friendly feelings toward Pouchot, decided in March, 1758, to send the Béarn captain back again to the strategic post. But

he only gave him half the force he needed to garrison the fort, 149
regulars. Pouchot was a realist, as was Montcalm. Both knew what
lay ahead for Canada, and, when the captain said good-by to his commander, he remarked that they would next see each other in England
as prisoners.

Pouchot's little force, supplemented by an equal number of Canadians, proceeded on foot up the frozen St. Lawrence, which was just
beginning to break up. Early in April they reached a place, some
eight miles upstream from Abbé Piquet's mission of La Presentation,
where the two new ships, ordered by Vaudreuil to be built immediately after the fall of Frontenac, were almost ready to launch. Each
carried ten 12-pound cannon, quite a powerful armament, particularly
on an inland lake. The party tarried here three weeks until the little
warships, *L'Iroquoise* and *L'Outaouaise,* were launched, rigged, and
equipped, and then sailed on to Niagara. Pouchot at once relieved the
fort's Canadian commander, who eventually was to be lodged in the
Bastille for his peculations, found guilty, and then released with an
admonition. No work had been done on the defenses of Niagara since
the chevalier's departure, a year and a half previously, but he at once
resumed construction. Toward mid-May French agents among the
Iroquois sent word that the English were stirring, and that the Five
Nations would be on their side this year. Sir William Johnson had
recently held a big Indian conference on the Mohawk at Canojoharie,
and the Iroquois had largely succumbed to his blandishments. At
about this same time Pouchot learned that a great expedition, led by
Wolfe, was sailing against Quebec.

That spring the Indian trade was exceptionally active at Niagara,
and much fur was received at the fort, perhaps five times the normal
take. While it was evident that the Five Nations were in a ferment,
there was no definite word of an attack on Niagara and all seemed
peaceful. In June Pouchot sent Indians to scout to the eastward, and
late that same month a party returned from Oswego, Britain's sole
approach to Lake Ontario, reporting no English at that place. Just to
make sure they had paddled up the Oswego River for a few miles.

Had they gone but a mile or two farther they would have met the British preparing to portage by the falls. So Pouchot remained in ignorance. Then, on July 6, *L'Iroquoise* sailed into Niagara, reporting no English at Oswego. Actually Colonel Haldimand was there with twelve hundred men, while the main British force had landed two days before about three miles east of Niagara. The French vessel had followed the north shore, the British the south. Thus Pouchot's intelligence service had failed him completely, and the enemy had arrived without warning. He at once sent word to the commander of Fort Venango on the Ohio headwaters to come to his aid with all the French and Indians he could scrape together. The garrison of Niagara consisted of 486 men, only 149 of whom were regulars.

Brigadier Prideaux had made a prompt movement up the Mohawk and on to Oswego, where he was joined by Sir William Johnson with a party of Indians that ultimately amounted to some nine hundred. Leaving Lieutenant Colonel Frederick Haldimand with a thousand men to secure Oswego, he took about two thousand regulars, a few New York provincials and Johnson's Indians on to Niagara, landing in a little swampy cove around a bend in the bluffs, just out of sight of the fort. The fact that not a single one of the Five Nations came to warn of the British advance indicates the degree of their defection from the French this year of 1759. Prideaux unloaded his artillery and supplies, and, moving forward to within half a mile of the defenses, started the approaches of his siege works. He also had boats hauled across the base of the little peninsula to the Niagara River and used them to put artillery on the west bank of the river, thus placing fire on the fort from two different directions. The siege proceeded with the usual digging of zigzag trenches and battery positions, but it was several days before the cannon opened fire. The French plied their guns with vigor against the attackers but could do little harm to the men advancing with shovels, fascines, and gabions.

The Iroquois with the British apparently acted largely as spectators. Others of their nation who were inside the fort with the French opened negotiations with the British contingent of their tribe under a flag of truce, suggesting that all the Indians should remain neutral during the siege. Johnson's Indians in turn sent deputies into the fort to talk to Pouchot, telling him that they did not know how they had become involved in this war and were ashamed of their actions. During these discussions the French ceased their fire, but the attackers kept right on digging. The next day conferences continued between the two groups of savages. The emissaries from the fort talked in Johnson's presence to the British adherents, who promised to drop out of the fight and to move their camp back out of the zone of action.

The British had been using some Indians as guards to cover the working parties at night, but several had been killed by the fire of the French, greatly discouraging the Indians who went to war to scalp and to plunder, not to get killed themselves. They stopped guarding the trenches at night, the Iroquois inside the fort were allowed to leave and cross the river, and the contest was continued by white men alone. The Indians watched from a safe distance until they could determine the winning side.

Shortly after dark, a week after the siege had been started, Brigadier Prideaux was walking along the trenches when a gunner, not noticing the general, touched off a coehorn. This was a small four and a half inch mortar named after its Dutch inventor, the Baron Menno van Coehoorn, second only in fame to the Marquis de Vauban as a military engineer of the seventeenth century. The shell hit the commander in the back of the head. Sir William Johnson, although technically only a civil commissioner in charge of Indian allies, took over command on the strength of an old colonel's commission he still retained. He at once sent word to Haldimand to come to Niagara, then canceled the order, but the regular lieutenant colonel came west as fast as he could to take over the command that was rightfully his as senior officer. Haldimand, however, did not reach Niagara until after the fall of the fort, and he had enough sense and good judgment not to contest the command with Sir William. Amherst, as soon as he learned of Prideaux's death, sent Brigadier Gage to take charge, and his subsequent arrival settled the question. Later Amherst complimented Haldimand on his unselfish waiving of the contest for command, a contest which would not have been for the good of the service.

Johnson was now in full command of an army committed to a siege operation, something about which he knew little or nothing, and, although he did not yet know it, a relieving force of considerable strength was advancing on his rear. Throughout the remainder of the operation he showed good common sense and excellent judgment, and proved that, although an amateur, he had qualified as an able commander. This was all the more marked because the expedition lacked competent engineers, and at this period it was largely the engineer officer that directed the operations of a siege, acting as a specially qualified staff officer upon whom the commander leaned heavily for technical advice.

The British pushed their trenches forward, establishing their batteries nearer and nearer to the fort, and the earthworks gradually crumbled. The guns across the Niagara River fired red-hot shot, as did some in the batteries in front of the fort, and fires were started, though they did little damage. The French kept up an active artillery fire, but, running out of wads for the cannon, had to tear up the straw mattresses of the soldiers and use them. At one time a spent British cannon ball came down Pouchot's chimney and rolled harmlessly under the bed on which he had just lain down. Luckily for him it was not a mortar shell. Even a spent cannon ball could do real damage, as many a soldier sadly learned when with his foot he tried to stop a ball bumping and rolling along the ground, and was fortunate if he got off with only a broken ankle. Pouchot found his Canadians of little or no help; they refused to expose themselves in order to return the fire of the English, and, if placed in position at an embrasure, slumped down into shelter as soon as the officer left and went to sleep. Soon most of the French muskets were no longer usable, despite desperate efforts to repair them. Apparently the French also followed the British practice of sending their obsolete and worn-out firearms to America.

Two weeks after the start of the siege a few Indians entered the fort under a flag of truce and reported that the commander of the Venango fort was near at hand, and that belts from the western Indians had been given to Johnson's Iroquois, who had promised to continue neutral. The belts had been given in the presence of the English commander, and it must have disturbed his equanimity to see how little he could now depend on his formerly faithful Iroquois. The relieving force consisted of about six hundred French, half of them soldiers and militia from the far Illinois country, and a thousand Indians, mostly from the west. Their leaders had received a note from Pouchot outlining the disposition of the besiegers' troops, but the French advanced overconfidently and without proper reconnaissance. At the last minute their Indian allies quit them, unwilling to engage in battle with the Five Nations, who also decided to continue their neutrality and await the results of the battle. Why risk a bet when you only have to wait a bit for a sure thing?

The British had thrown together hurried defenses of tree trunks, and behind them they awaited the attack of the relieving force. They held their fire until the enemy were close, and then overwhelmed the attackers with a few well-placed volleys. The attack collapsed into rout. Now the fence-sitting Iroquois became brave and dashed off to pursue the retreating foe, seeking the scalps and plunder of an enemy defeated by others than themselves. The chase lasted for miles with many killed, and practically all the French officers were either killed or became captives of the British. Pouchot had watched part of this action from the ramparts of the fort. When he saw so large a party of British moving off to intercept the relief, he believed that the trenches must now be but lightly guarded. He dispatched a party of a hundred and fifty volunteers to make a sortie, but hardly had they started when the forward trenches erupted a horde of sweating Englishmen, naked to the waist, and the French wisely fell back into the fort.

Pouchot believed that the musket fire he had heard resulted from a skirmish, not a battle, and he did not appreciate the extent of the disaster until Johnson sent an officer under a flag of truce to inform

him of what had happened and to give him a list of the officers captured. The chevalier could not believe it possible, and was convinced
only after one of his own officers had been taken to see the captives.
That was the end, Pouchot realized, especially since many of his men,
particularly the Germans of La Marine, were on the verge of mutiny.
He asked for terms, and relatively generous ones were granted. Both
commanders had visions of what had happened at Fort William
Henry, and Johnson took great precautions against any possible trouble, attempting, although unsuccessfully, to exclude all Indians from
the fort. He allowed the French to retain their arms and ammunition
until they actually embarked on the boats that were to start them on
the long trip east to New York. It was quite impossible to stop the
plundering of private effects by the Indians and, one regrets to say,
even by British officers, but no Frenchman was hurt in any way,
despite attempts of bloodthirsty Iroquois to gain scalps and glory from
someone else's victory. The French lost 109 killed and wounded
out of their little garrison, but the losses of the force that attempted
to relieve the fort were never determined. They probably amounted
to several hundred. The British casualties evidently were quite minor
except for the deaths of Prideaux and another senior officer.

Shortly after the expedition had left Oswego on its way to Niagara
a body of French under the Chevalier Pierre La Corne and of Indians
from Abbé Piquet's mission attempted to seize that place and cut
Prideaux off from his base. Lieutenant Colonel Haldimand had not
yet had time to set up any defenses, except for a barricade of pork
and flour barrels, behind which he stationed his men, and fought off
the attack. Some of the Canadians soon lost courage and started to
run back to their boats, bowling Abbé Piquet head over heels as they
fled. He reached up and managed to hang on to one of the fugitives,
crying: "Save your chaplain!" This was a very different attitude
than the one he had had but a short time before, when he had given
absolution to all and admonished them to give no quarter. Haldimand's men held to their defenses while the French and Indians
gathered in a wood out of gunshot. The next day, after a little further

banging away with their muskets, La Corne's men headed back for La Presentation.

Except for the two little warships, there were no French left between Detroit and the St. Lawrence. Amherst had directed Brigadier Gage, sent west by the commander when he learned of Prideaux's death, to build a fort at Oswego, and then to proceed down the river and capture the fort at Abbé Piquet's La Presentation. The first of these tasks, Gage undertook at once, but the second mission was more difficult. He would have to move by water in bateaux, and the two French warships were at large, ready—or perhaps in view of their earlier performance one had better say at least able—to blow the British boats to bits. Moreover La Presentation was not many miles west of Montreal, from which point reinforcements could quickly be sent to aid the considerable force already in the near vicinity of the mission. Gage made no move in that direction, and was criticized by both Amherst and Pitt for not making the attempt, but he was probably correct in his decision, and could not have taken the place with the forces then at his command. Johnson had strongly advised Gage to make the attempt on Abbé Piquet's mission, saying that its capture would detach all the Oswegatchie Indians of that place from the French interest, but he could not convince the general. So the year 1759 ended with the French driven from the Ohio and Niagara, the British again firmly established at Oswego, and the westernmost French post at Abbé Piquet's missionary fort.

Chapter XXI

THE PLAINS OF ABRAHAM

The city of Quebec stands on the tip of a high peninsula extending out into the St. Lawrence from its northern shore. To the north and west it is guarded by the St. Charles River, while the high bluffs of the great river secure its eastern and southern flank. The plateau upon which the city stands extends southwestward for several miles along the St. Lawrence until it drops down into the valley of the Cap Rouge. In 1759 the city crowded the heights of the peninsula and a part overflowed down onto the low land at its base. The fortifications, mostly low walls covering the approach to the city from the plateau on its southwest, were of little value, built of masonry bonded with mortar which could be scratched out with one's fingernail.

The real strength of the place was due to nature, not to man. The steep bluffs, averaging nearly two hundred feet in height west of the city, also extended eastward from the St. Charles to the hamlet of Beauport and the Montmorency River, which at its mouth cascaded into the St. Lawrence over falls of two hundred and fifty feet in height, but only a dozen yards in width. The Montmorency was fordable directly at its mouth at a low tide, as well as at one other point a couple of miles upstream, but it constituted a formidable barrier to any attack by land from the east. Batteries at both the upper and the lower levels of Quebec commanded the passage by the city, where the narrowness of the river bed caused swift currents to flow. Then the river flowed northeastward into a wide basin, surrounded by mud flats at low tide, quite wide along the northerly shore, where the land between the Montmorency and Beauport rose abruptly into bluffs similar to but not so high as those upriver from the city. From Beauport to the St. Charles the bluffs lay farther back from the river's edge, with a plain of considerable width between. Montcalm had covered all the northern shore with defensive works, redoubts along the water's edge at several points, and trenches and batteries on top of the higher ground, manned by an army of twelve thousand men, regulars, Canadian troops, militia, and Indians.

The French had long believed that Quebec enjoyed another most important defense, the St. Lawrence, the navigation of which was felt to be of such difficulty that an enemy fleet could never reach the city. Remembering Walker's disaster in 1711, they perhaps had forgotten that Phips brought his fleet to Quebec in 1690 with little trouble. But Admiral Charles Saunders sailed his great fleet of warships and transports up the St. Lawrence in June of 1759 without any difficulty at all. He had twenty-two warships and 119 transports and supply vessels, a vast armada. The British seized some French pilots for the final passage by the Isle d'Orléans, but some of the ship captains boldly guided their own vessels and made the trip without difficulty. And so the French late in June saw what they had hoped never to see, a great enemy fleet in the river below their capital city.

General James Wolfe brought with him an army of nearly nine thousand men, and there were also many sailors in the fleet, some of whom could be made available for duty ashore. The army landed on the Isle d'Orléans on June 27 and set up its tents. The following night the soldiers were treated to a magnificent if somewhat terrifying sight, that of French fire ships drifting down on the British fleet, blazing throughout and with cannon and grenades exploding right and left. Fortunately for the British, these fire ships, whose life was relatively short—probably less than an hour at their peak effectiveness —were ignited by their crews, either in panic or through poor judgment, much too soon. Some drifted ashore, while others were towed aside by British tars. Shortly after they sent down the fire ships the French attempted to set some of the British fleet adrift by fouling a great raft composed of top masts and yards with their anchor cables. This did no harm at all and was welcomed by the British who were in need of spare spars.

Admiral Saunders now put guard boats out at night to intercept any further rafts and tow them out of the way. The French then designed a floating booby trap, a small square raftlike box loaded with explosives, which came downriver with the current. A midshipman brought his boat alongside and jumped on board the raft, which at once exploded and tossed the boy up into the air. He came down into the river unhurt but his boat was damaged and some of his crew were injured.

Before the entire British fleet had arrived the French made an attempt on one of the warships in what is perhaps the earliest use of a submarine in warfare. Three sailors had proposed the construction of a submersible boat and were allowed to go ahead with its construction. Details are vague, but the craft was about nine feet long, pointed at one end, and divided into three compartments, the middle one of which could be flooded in order to submerge until just awash. The other two divisions held the explosive and the crew. Presumably one man had his head and shoulders inside each of these compartments and propelled the contrivance by swimming, since the size seems too small to allow the men to be inside. The crew succeeded in reaching a warship, attaching their craft to it and swimming away in safety, but the slow match had got wet and went out.

On the night of June 29 British forces crossed the river to the south bank, and, after a slight skirmish the next morning, occupied Pointe Levi, where further slight resistance was met from an enemy force of perhaps six hundred men. Construction of batteries was at once undertaken, both at Pointe Levi and on the western tip of the Isle d'Orléans. Soon cannon were also in position directly opposite the city, and by July 12 they were delivering an effective fire. A group of Quebec citizens, watching construction of the batteries and fearful of the destruction soon to rain down upon them, asked permission of Vaudreuil to make a sortie, and this was granted. Some fifteen hundred citizens, habitants, a few regulars, some Indians, and pupils from the seminary crossed the river from near Sillery, but shortly after they had climbed the steep southern shore they became nervous and confused. Finally in the excitement the seminarians fired on their own people, thinking them British, and all were seized with panic and made for home at top speed.

British scouting parties explored the surrounding countryside in all directions. One, led by Major George Scott, who now commanded six companies of rangers, met a number of hostile Indians, and the leader thought it best to avoid contact and to return. Wolfe, then evidently in one of his more difficult moments, was quite short with the major when he reported and criticized him for the action. Scott flared up, had the temerity to talk back to his commander, and got away with it. The major was apparently the son of a close friend of Wolfe's mother, and this would perhaps explain such unusual conduct in a junior officer. Scott was a most excellent officer and Wolfe realized it. We met him before in Acadia at Chignecto and again at Louisbourg. After the fall of Quebec he was promoted to lieutenant colonel, married a Boston girl and went to the West Indies as governor of one of the islands captured from the French. There he died while still quite young, and the British Empire lost a useful servant.

A hospital and storehouses were built on the Isle d'Orléans, but on July 9 most of the troops remaining there were moved north across the river on to the plateau just east of the Montmorency, where a well-defended camp was established. Here Wolfe made his headquarters in a little stone house. The camp was within artillery and even extreme musket range of the French on the west side of the Montmorency, but Montcalm took no action against the British camp, feeling that if he did they would merely move somewhere else, and that they were quite harmless where they were.

Wolfe's artillery rained shot and shell on the city, and the destruction soon became great. The cathedral caught fire, and many private houses were burned as well. During the night of July 18 two warships and five smaller craft sailed up the river by Quebec as harmless cannon shot were hurled after them. The French now for the first time had to worry about their communications with Montreal, and this was to become a source of increasing concern as additional ships passed up the St. Lawrence and continued on well up the river. The French had floating batteries with which they at times attempted to harass the British, but with little if any success. Late in July they turned loose their most formidable fire raft, a great string of schooners, fire rafts and shallops, all chained together into a flaming line six hundred feet long. The British sailors rowed out, grappled ahold and towed the fearful thing safely away from their shipping. One sailor is recorded as saying to his mate: "Dam-me, Jack, did'st thee ever take hell in tow before?" The next day Wolfe is said to have sent word to the French that, if any more such attempts were made, he would see that fire rafts were laid alongside of the two transports on which he had put all his prisoners.

The British now had been in front of Quebec for more than a month, and no progress had been made beyond the destruction of many buildings in the city and much ravaging of the countryside. Wolfe had hoped that the French would come out of their works and attack him, but Montcalm was wise and waited. The French defenses were strong, and time was passing, with the fierce Canadian winter in the offing.

A number of great landing craft had been prepared by the British, in many ways forerunners of those developed during the Second World War. They were big rafts, capable of holding three hundred men, supported by empty casks and barrels lashed beneath the deck. Three sides had railings, while the fourth carried a hinged landing ramp, which, until dropped for the rush ashore, formed a shield against enemy fire. But it was discovered that they were too cumbersome to handle, and they never saw action. The British also had flatboats, each of which could carry seventy or more soldiers, as well as a crew of perhaps a dozen sailors. These boats were carried on shipboard to Quebec in a knocked-down condition and then were quickly assembled by means of brass bolts and nuts. They moved swiftly under oars and drew from eighteen to twenty-two inches of water when loaded. These craft were found most useful.

Wolfe seems to have been confused and despondent at this time, and did not know what to do, but finally, perhaps in desperation, he decided on an attack on the French positions just west of the Montmorency. Apparently he still hoped that he could entice the French out of their defenses, and thought that by seizing a redoubt on the edge of the mud flats he would force the enemy to come down off

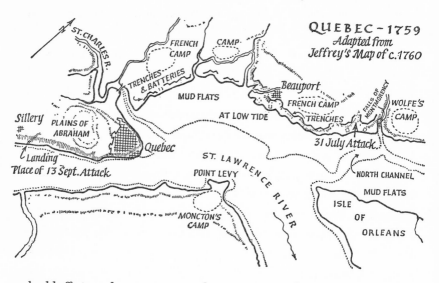

the bluffs in order to recapture the strong point, bringing on a general engagement. One body of troops was to be rowed ashore against the most easterly of the French redoubts, while a second forded the Montmorency below the falls at low water. Late in the afternoon of July 31 the attempt was made, supported by naval gunfire, by troops who had been sitting packed into flatboats for half a day while waiting to attack. At last the Grenadiers and some of the Royal Americans plunged into the shoal water up to their waists, formed up and charged ashore on to what one survivor called "the ouzy beach." They easily captured the redoubt with its two cannon, but at once came under heavy fire from the French on the top of the bluff. Instead of waiting for the troops fording the outlet of the Montmorency, and

another body coming from the south shore at Pointe Levi, they dashed
up the steep bluff in a search for glory. They did not make it. Clawing
their way up the steep hillside they suffered a destructive musket fire
and received heavy casualties. Then a sudden violent thunderstorm
burst, wetting the priming of their muskets and turning the slope of
the bluff into mud upon which they could secure no footing. They
fell back, while many of the dead and wounded rolled downhill to
the flats below, where the Indians promptly came after their scalps,
as the defeated British withdrew. Half a thousand men were lost in
this abortive attack, and nothing was gained.

Wolfe was the same driving, demanding, vain, and secretive man
that he had been at the second siege of Louisbourg the year before,
but now to this were added the loneliness and responsibility of command and serious ill health. Always a proud, reserved, and dedicated
man, with little or no sense of humor, and now weighted down with
the burden of command, he was a most difficult man with whom to
work. He had three excellent subordinates, Brigadiers Robert Monckton, George Townshend, and James Murray, all sons of peers, and
thus above Wolfe socially despite his major-general father. Wolfe's
relations with these men—although two were friends he had himself
chosen for the position—can best be described as strained. He never
really consulted with them or in any way took them into his confidence, although they were all able officers of considerable experience.
The Honorable George Townshend was perhaps the most interesting
of the three, a cynical and sarcastic man of the world with less military service than the other two but with excellent political connections.
He was a clever if somewhat caustic cartoonist, yet probably the most
characteristic of all the pictures of Wolfe came from his pen, a hasty
watercolor sketch apparently made just before the general's death.
Townshend drew some extremely amusing cartoons of his commander,
which were circulated with loud laughter in the headquarters mess,
but caused Wolfe, who could not see a joke, particularly when aimed
at himself, to become red in the face and hint at demanding satisfac-
tion when the siege was over, if both still lived. Others of Townshend's

sketches made at this period, while only rough drawings, show the northeastern Indian of the mid 1700s as he really appeared, and are the only representations of the red man drawn by a competent artist that were produced until many years later.

While the armies glared at each other across the Montmorency and the St. Lawrence, and the British artillery pounded away at the city, with the French cannon doing little damage in return, partisan warfare with all its accompanying cruelties flared up around the outlying regions. French Indians scalped Englishmen who wandered too far afield, and rangers and light infantry retaliated. Wolfe permitted scalping only of Indians or of Canadians disguised as Indians, but many of the latter were killed, usually because, although civilians, they had acted, or were suspected to have acted, as guerrillas, and to have fired on the British. After the defeat of July 31 Wolfe stepped up the ravaging of the countryside by his rangers and light infantry. He was strict in forbidding the doing of harm to women or to churches. The militia captain of St. Paul, fifty-five miles below Quebec on the north shore of the great river, deserted from the French and reported that Governor Vaudreuil had ordered him, "if he should make two or more British officers prisoners, to reserve one only for intelligence, and scalp the others; all sailors and private soldiers were to have no quarter granted them." His story may or may not have been true, but it circulated through the army, and did nothing to make easier the fate of Canadian civilians.

In early August, Wolfe sent Brigadier Murray with twelve hundred men up the river to co-operate with the naval force already there, to do what mischief he could to the French and perhaps even to make contact with Amherst, who, it was hoped, would by now have captured Ticonderoga and Crown Point and be working his way down the Richelieu. The commander in chief, of course, was still cooling his heels at Crown Point, while building his little warships, and no help would be had from him this year, beyond the threat of his advance which did hold a considerable French force at Isle-aux-Noix, instead of marching to the aid of Quebec. Murray found that he was opposed by a mobile force under the able Bougainville, and he confined most of his activities to the south shore, laying waste the surrounding regions. Then in mid-August by means of a diversionary movement of boats he succeeded in deceiving Bougainville and landed unopposed at Deschambault, forty miles upstream from Quebec, where he destroyed a depot of military supplies before the French arrived in sufficient force to cause his departure.

Wolfe's mission was to capture Quebec, but he was completely at a loss and did not know which way to turn, as he admitted in a letter to Pitt written on September 2. He even considered giving up all attempts on the city that year and falling downstream sixty miles to Isle-aux-Coudres, where pilots for the difficult passage upstream by the Isle d'Orléans were usually taken on shipboard. There he would build a fort and leave a strong garrison until the following year, when another attempt might be made against the capital of New France. Wolfe had recently been laid up for some time by a serious fever which added to his despondency.

In apparent desperation—for this was the first time he had sought their counsel—he asked his three brigadiers for suggestions, at the same time offering his own proposed plans of action, which called for a further attack on the Beauport area, or for a move up the Montmorency River and an attempt to cross it. The brigadiers vetoed the general's schemes, and instead advocated a landing in force upriver above Quebec. The naval ships allowed the army free use of the great St. Lawrence as a highway, while the French were tied to wretched roads. A landing anywhere upstream would gravely threaten the French supply line to Montreal, and seemed the most likely way of forcing Montcalm to come out from his defenses and fight. It is true that Bougainville was covering this area with his mobile force, but a successful landing had already been made at Deschambault, and a second one could certainly be made at some point upstream, and a major part of the army put on the north shore somewhere between Quebec and Montreal.

Wolfe finally accepted this plan, and, as soon as he was once again on his feet, although still far from well, he reconnoitered the river above the city. Eventually he made the decision to land at the Anse de Foulon, two miles above the city, and to try to get his men up the face of the cliff by a narrow path which existed there. Just how he learned of the existence of this path is not known. The French had endeavored to block it and to conceal it with bushes some time in August, so it could hardly have been visible to Wolfe's telescope. There is some reason to believe that as early as mid-July the general had considered an assault at this point, but was dissuaded by Admiral Saunders, who believed that the tide and current would make a landing too difficult.

Wolfe made his plans for the attack without further consulting the brigadiers. At the last moment the three wrote him a joint letter, saying that they were not clear as to his plans and would like more details of just what was proposed. The commander returned a very cool note which said in effect that they knew all that was necessary for subordinates to know. The brigadiers were all heartily in favor of an upstream landing, but they believed one at the Anse de Foulon would entail unnecessary risk, and that a point farther from Quebec, such as Deschambault, would be safer and achieve the same result. At this moment Governor Vaudreuil for once was wiser than Montcalm for he believed that the British would try to land above the city, while the French general was sure that they would again attempt Beauport. Wolfe gave Montcalm further cause for this belief, since he had the navy make various demonstrations at that point during the night before the landing. The commander of one of the ships participating was Captain James Cook. Thus at Quebec on opposing sides were the two men who later were to achieve fame as explorers of the South Seas, Bougainville and Cook.

Meanwhile a large part of the British army had been carried upriver on transports and warships, which, moving up- and downriver with the tide, kept Bougainville's force marching back and forth until they were well-nigh exhausted, and at last had to drop down to catch their breath at Cap Rouge, about eight miles above Quebec. Well before dawn on September 13 the first British troops were landed at the Anse de Foulon—thereafter to be named Wolfe's Cove—and the advance elements started to climb the rugged cliff. Vergor, who had cravenly surrendered Fort Beauséjour in Acadia a few years before, commanded the force guarding the cliff above the landing place. He expected no trouble and let most of his men off to work in their fields and sleep at home that night, so not only was he taken by surprise, he was overwhelmed as well. Vergor put up no defense at all, and there was little musket fire which might have given warning to the French in the city.

The remainder of the story is too well known to relate in detail. The British poured up the path, about four thousand men in all, silenced the nearby battery of Samos, and hauled up a cannon or two with great effort. The little force formed up on the Plains of Abraham, a plateau just west of the walls of Quebec. So few they were that they could form a front line of only two ranks, each man was separated by three feet from his mate on either side, and there were gaps of about forty yards between each of the seven battalions, certainly "a thin red line." The front line, which alone took part in the battle, amounted to nearly 3300 men, and in addition there were reserves and rear-area guards at the Anse de Foulon totaling perhaps another 1200 men.

The French were caught completely by surprise, at first thinking the movement was merely a diversion. After considerable delay word of the British landing was sent to Bougainville, but he was miles away and could not be expected to arrive with his men before the latter part of the forenoon. His force of nearly three thousand men would have been of great help, particularly as they would have come up in rear of the British. For some unexplained reason Montcalm chose not to wait for this material reinforcement, and instead moved his force of about three thousand regulars and fifteen hundred militia and Indians out from the city and formed them up facing the British. He easily could have brought up more men from the Beauport camp but failed to do so. It would seem that the French general was not at his best that morning. The British appeared to him to be starting to entrench on the plateau and that may have been the reason for his overhasty action. A little less precipitancy would have allowed him to assemble a force materially larger than that of Wolfe. Montcalm ordered his men to attack at once. They advanced against the thin ranks of the British, opening fire at 130 yards, a range much too great to be effective. The long line of redcoats waited silently while the French continued forward, letting drive another ragged volley or two. Finally when the enemy was within forty yards, the Brown Besses hurled their ounce balls into the faces of Montcalm's men, and the British charged forward with the bayonet. The French broke and fled for the city gates, and only the effective fire delivered by a party of Canadian militia sheltered in a patch of woods slowed up the British enough to let most of the Frenchmen escape. Wolfe, charging in the front line—where no general had a right to be at all—was mortally wounded, and Montcalm met the same fate as he was leaving the field. The British casualties were 664, against about 1400 for the French.

Lieutenant John Knox of the 43rd Regiment, whom we met earlier in Acadia, was present at this battle, and he reported that never before, either in battle or at musketry practice, had he ever seen such effective fire as that delivered by the center of the British line where he was posted. He also noted that he saw French officers, the memory of Fort William Henry hanging heavily on their consciences, beg, hat in hand, for quarter, repeatedly declaring that they had not been at Lake George in 1757.

One eminent modern historian believes that the superiority of the British musket and of the British musketry was largely responsible for the victory. Brigadier George Townshend, writing many years after the battle, said that he remembered that it was so, but this is too simple an answer. Undoubtedly the British put down a more effective fire, but there was little to choose between the firelocks of the two countries. Actually in some ways the French arm was better; it certainly was a more rugged weapon, since its barrel was held in place by stout metal bands, while the Brown Bess was only pinned together. Of course the French muskets may all have been discards from Europe, yet so may have been those of the British. It seems most probable that gun for gun those of the regular troops of the two nations were on a par, but the British fire discipline was undoubtedly much the better. The mere fact that the French let fly their initial volley at an excessive range, while the British held theirs until the ideal moment, speaks for itself. It was discipline, not weapons, that won this battle. This was the first North American battle fought on a formal European basis on the open field. The French regulars were somewhat less in number than the British, and their militia was of dubious assistance, at least until they delivered their fire which covered the retreat, but the two forces were not too unequal in size, particularly when one considers that only the British front line was engaged. The majority of the British regulars were fresh from home, well-disciplined troops trained for formal warfare, while the French regulars had long been in Canada and lacked replacements. There can be little doubt but that at this battle the quality and training of the French soldier was materially less than that of his opponent.

Wolfe was dead and Monckton was badly wounded, so Townshend, the next senior officer, took command, moved the victorious troops back on to the Plains of Abraham, and began defensive works. By late morning Bougainville arrived in the near vicinity with two thousand of his men, but the battle was over, and it was obvious that nothing more could be done for the moment. He moved his force back westward to Lorette, about nine miles from Quebec. Here Governor Vaudreuil arrived the next day, accompanied by the defeated army, which had abandoned its tents, supplies, and provisions, all of which were left at the Beauport camp to the mercy of plundering Indians and hungry habitants. The retreat was a most hurried and shameful one. A senior French officer wrote home to the War Minister: "No rout was ever more complete than that of our army. Posterity will hardly believe it." A few days later Lévis, who had inherited the command, came east from Montreal. By this time the troops beleaguered in Quebec had surrendered under generous terms, and the new commander realized that nothing could be done for some time to come. Accordingly the French were distributed into winter quarters, and posts were established to guard against further sudden invasion by the British. Five days after the battle the city had surrendered and the British had occupied it. More than two generations had passed since Phips's unsuccessful attempt on Quebec, but at last the capital of New France had fallen.

History has, I think, been overkind to Wolfe. Undoubtedly his was the command, his the victory, and he gave his life in the battle, but quite unnecessarily and in defiance of normal military procedure and of common sense. The victory would have been impossible without the British Navy and the splendid co-operation given Wolfe by Admiral Saunders, who within a few years was to be knighted by King George III and become First Lord of the Admiralty. It was the three brigadier generals who had succeeded in persuading Wolfe to abandon a second attack on Beauport and to turn his eyes upstream. The final choice of the Anse de Foulon was his, the subordinates wished a safer landing farther west, but without their advice and counsel Wolfe might well have suffered a second bloody defeat at the bluffs of Beauport. James Wolfe deserved well of England and ably earned his place as a military hero, but one must not forget that the great achievement made at Quebec by Wolfe's command was rendered possible only by the able assistance given him by his subordinate officers, his soldiers, and the British Navy.

Chapter XXII

THE LAST CAMPAIGN

J OHN KNOX, still a lieutenant—he was not to be made a captain until all the fighting was over—found that life in Quebec during the winter of 1759–60 was hard. Once the garrison had occupied the city and the remainder of the army had sailed for home, the troops set to work to make the place defensible and livable. Great damage had been done to the private dwellings of the city, and the streets of the lower town were almost impassable from the debris of ruined houses. The soldiers were quartered wherever any shelter remained, some in the Intendant's Palace, some in the convent of the Ursulines, where the good nuns, either shocked by the hairy legs of the Highlanders or knowing with pity the kind of winter that was ahead, knitted them long woolen stockings. Others of the troops had to take over ruined buildings, put some sort of a roof on them and made them snug against the nip in the air the fall winds already were bringing.

Many French wounded from the recent battle were hospitalized in the city, but there were no funds available for their support. A French commissary came to Quebec under a flag of truce to see to their welfare, and the British commander lent him funds to take care of his men. Lending money to the enemy in wartime is an act that seems surprising to the modern mind, but the spirit of chivalry then still existed, but hand in hand with utter savagery as well.

Some of the citizens of Quebec had left the city, but others stayed on, and pleasant relations between the French and their conquerors existed from the very first. Brigadier Monckton went south to New York to recover from his wound, and Townshend returned to England. This left Murray in command of the garrison and governor of the city and its surroundings. His rule was fair and just, and did much to promote happy relations and good will. A British soldier who thought that he could rob the French with impunity soon learned to the contrary as the hangman's noose suddenly choked off his life. French habitants moving around the city after dark and before curfew were required at all times to carry lighted lanterns. Some of the people in surrounding parishes retained their hostility, but with minor exceptions the only threats to the garrison came from the cold of winter and from disease. Only a few days after the fall of the city, redcoats could be seen helping Canadians harvest their crops and sharing their rations with them, even to giving them part of their rum.

Knox had one amusing experience. He had been sent to the General Hospital for duty as commander of the guard maintained there. One day the Mother Superior invited him to an English breakfast, which turned out to consist of inch-thick slices of bread smothered with butter and a silver coffeepot which the good lady stated contained a full half-pint of tea leaves, thoroughly boiled for an hour or so. The discreet lieutenant told the nun that he was sorry she had gone to such trouble for he never had cared for tea, and he made his English breakfast on bread and milk.

There was much to do to the city to make it safe against the counterattack which Lévis was expected to make at almost any time before the onset of winter. The walls required much work, lacking as they did both a banquette—the raised platform on which soldiers stood to fire their muskets—and embrasures for the cannon, still to be dragged into position. Everyone was kept busy, and nearly a thousand of the garrison were constantly employed on guard duties alone. Woodcutting parties were assigned to the vitally important job of getting in the vast quantities of firewood that would be needed.

The uniform regulations of that day made no provision for clothing suitable for a climate such as that of Canada, and various expedients were undertaken, especially so once the snow and northern winds had come. Spare blankets captured from the French were issued to be cut up and made into mittens, stockings, and leggings, and it soon was found that moccasins and two pairs of stockings were much warmer than the issue shoe. Appearance was forgotten and anything that would keep off the cold was put to use. Knox speaks of soldiers "in rough fur wrought garb of the frozen Laplander," and says: "I have frequently been accosted by my acquaintances, whom, though their voices were familiar to me, I could not discover . . . who they were." Sleet storms sometimes made foot travel well-nigh impossible until ice creepers had been hammered out by the blacksmiths and issued to all. Before this was done Knox on one particularly icy day had to march a guard from the upper town to the lower down the very steep road. He soon found that there was just one way to do it, and each soldier held his firelock up in the air, solemnly sat himself down and coasted merrily along downhill on his bottom. Fortunately, this particular guard was not composed of Highlanders.

Cutting and hauling wood, and protecting these working parties from lurking Indians, kept most of the healthy men of the garrison more than busy when they were not on guard duty. The woods were miles away and the sledges had to be dragged by the men, so few were the horses and oxen. The rations of course were the usual salt food, and the dreaded scurvy soon made its appearance, although the habitants of the region were only too glad to exchange fresh food for salt. Sickness among the troops was great, and most of it seems to have been scurvy. In the course of the winter of 1759–60 and early spring nearly seven hundred British corpses were stacked away in snowdrifts, waiting until the ground thawed out enough to allow burial. Toward the end of April, 1760, twenty-three hundred men out of a total initial force of seventy-three hundred were on the sick list. Allowing for the dead this meant that an entire one third of the forces defending Quebec were out of action, a terribly high proportion. It was found that an infusion made by boiling the tips of the "hemlock-spruce" was a most effective remedy for the scurvy. The sick were made to drink great quantities of it, and also to rub it on their skins, while the healthy had to mix it with their rum. It was not the same spruce as that used for brewing spruce beer, but some other unidentified variety, perhaps juniper.

In the course of the winter the funds in the military chest became sadly depleted, and Murray hit on the novel idea of borrowing money from individuals in his army. He offered a rate of five per cent, and raised £8000, of which a quarter came from the thrifty noncoms and privates of the Scottish Highlanders.

In February, 1760, the French sent a force to occupy Pointe Levi, but the British promptly drove them out and then successfully resisted a counterattack. The defenses of Quebec by now had been considerably strengthened, and a number of detached blockhouses had been built well in advance of the walls. Thus the city was as well prepared as possible to resist the attack expected in the early spring. Notice that it at last was on the way came on April 27, when an exhausted French gunner sergeant was rescued from an ice cake floating by the city. His bateau had overturned, and he had managed to struggle, frozen and half-drowned, on to the broken ice. The next day Lévis' army appeared at Sillery, while Vauquelin's little fleet anchored at Wolfe's Cove.

Lévis had sent word of his plight to France late in the fall. Aid had been promised and was dispatched, but the vigilant British Navy saw to it that it never reached the St. Lawrence. The French had hoped to make a winter assault on Quebec, but it did not get under way, due primarily to a shortage of provisions suitable for use in the field. The grist mills were all frozen and could not grind meal for the expedition until the spring thaw released their water wheels from the ice. Early in the late Canadian spring Lévis started down the banks of the St. Lawrence with an army of thirty-nine hundred regulars and three thousand militia, a force much greater than that of the British. At about the same time Bougainville went south to hold Isle-aux-Noix, and Pouchot, captured at Niagara but now exchanged, took command of the new fort under construction on an islet a little downstream from Abbé Piquet's mission at La Presentation. The plan was to hold the southern and western gateways to New France while Lévis ejected the British from the eastern frontier.

In all Lévis had at his command about 6700 regulars. He allocated approximately 2800 of them to Bougainville and Pouchot, and, adding some three thousand militiamen to the remainder, he set off from Montreal on April 20, marching along the north shore of the St. Lawrence, while his two frigates and a few smaller vessels carried the supplies and the artillery. By the twenty-seventh of April the French were approaching the outskirts of Quebec. The British outposts withdrew before them. Lévis had with him the chief engineer for Canada, Captain Pontleroy, an outstanding officer of French regulars, who had been active with Montcalm at the battle of Carillon in 1758. Whether Pontleroy had a delicate digestion or just liked milk is something that history does not record, but wherever he went in New France his cow went with him, and he studiously avoided going on any trip where the cow could not accompany him. Indians must have been surprised and amused to see a bateau gliding along some Canadian river with the animal standing amidships, placidly chewing her cud.

As the first faint signs of spring appeared Murray had advanced his outposts. In mid-April he sent troops to occupy Cap Rouge, seven miles or so above Quebec, but no sooner had they arrived than the ice went out of the river and, on April 27, Lévis' army appeared. At this time Brigadier Murray had just under 2300 men on the sick list, and could produce a force of only 3866, many of them still too sick to be effective, to oppose Lévis' 6900 Frenchmen.

The defenses of Quebec on the land side were still far from good, but much work had been done on them since the previous fall. Murray decided to march out and take a stand on the Plains of Abraham. It is hard to tell what led him to this decision. He had a very considerable force of artillery at hand, and possibly this was what made him decide upon this course, aided, perhaps, by memories of the way the French had fled before a volley or two of British musketry a few months before at this very same place. He marched his little army out on to the plateau, carrying their entrenching tools and planning to dig defensive works and await the assault of the French, who now were gathered in the Sillery woods. Lévis advanced a portion of his army forward to start forming a line of battle, but they came under such heavy fire from the British artillery that their commander ordered them to fall back. Murray, believing the French to be retreating, changed his plans and ordered the British to advance. This meant leaving the higher ground of the Plains of Abraham and moving downhill into swampy ground and deep drifts of still unmelted snow. Then the British general discovered that the main forces of the French were still in the woods, and he suddenly was faced by the advance of a force much larger than his and from higher ground.

The British artillery had at first delivered a highly effective fire, but the movement down onto the lower terrain mired the guns in the swampy ground, in places knee-deep in mud, and stalled them in snowbanks. The British held their own for an hour or so, while the French gradually forced back their flanks. Greatly outnumbered and partly outflanked, the British were in danger of being cut off from the city, and Murray ordered a retreat. All the bogged-down cannon were lost. The French had suffered considerable punishment and did not exert much pressure against the withdrawing British, who at last regained the city after having lost nearly a third of their army in this unfortunate affair. The losses of the French were somewhat less, a little over eight hundred casualties in all. The Indians who had accompanied Lévis' army had watched the battle from the edge of the woods, and, as soon as the British had quit the field of battle, descended upon the dead and wounded with their scalping knives, not even sparing some of the French who lay there.

A young Irishman, Henry Hamilton, who had served at Louisbourg and Quebec with the 15th Regiment, survived the winter, and now he was again in the midst of battle, soaking wet, exhausted, hungry and deserted by his fleeing soldiers. Years later, when governor of Detroit, he would gain notoriety as the "Hair Buyer," being accused, probably unjustly, of offering a bounty for scalps of American rebels. Later he would be acting governor of Canada for a year and then governor of Jamaica, but at this moment he was still a lieutenant, and two French regulars were aiming their firelocks at him. He wisely surrendered and was led to the adjutant of the Berry Regiment who told him that the Indians were out of hand and that the only way to save his life was for him to exchange coats. After a little hesitation Hamilton put on the white coat tendered him, and then ordered his guards in excellent French: *"Allons, mes enfants, marchez."* They enjoyed the joke and marched him safely to the rear. Throughout his captivity he received excellent treatment, and soon he was exchanged.

Murray now prepared to face a siege, and await the hoped-for arrival of warships and reinforcements. Lévis was far from well equipped to undertake a siege, but he started his works and prepared to bring up his few guns. It was not until May 11, almost two weeks after the battle, that his batteries started firing. Two days before, on May 9, both armies were wild with excitement to see a warship sail by Pointe Levi into the basin below Quebec. Everyone knew that the fate of the city would be determined by the nationality of the first fleet to appear, and for a few moments there was doubt as to which country the frigate belonged. All telescopes were pointed at the ship. Then British colors climbed to her mast and she started saluting Quebec. Lévis, of course, was greatly worried, but this was only a single ship, not sufficient in itself to turn the tide. A French fleet might well be just downstream, so the siege continued, despite the great and constantly growing scarcity of food for the French army. Then, on May 16, three more British warships hove in sight. Lévis bowed to the inevitable and hastily raised the siege, leaving behind tents, tools, scaling ladders, and cannon.

The newly arrived warships sailed upstream and engaged the little French squadron that had accompanied Lévis, taking or destroying all its vessels. The French commodore was Vauquelin, the officer who had done such good work with his little frigate at Louisbourg two years before. Excellent officer that he was, the taint of previous merchant service nevertheless clung to him, and the snobbish officers of the Royal Navy would never accept him as one of their own kind. All the more so, perhaps, because he had fought valiantly at Louisbourg, while the officers who were of the noblesse had shirked. After the destruction of the French ships the British fleet came downstream and accelerated Lévis' departure with well-directed gunfire which enfiladed his trenches.

The unsuccessful attempt on Quebec left the British holding all their gains of the previous year. The garrison of Quebec, once it had caught its breath and reorganized, could now turn to the offensive. The men, however, had suffered sadly and would need rest and reinforcements. Murray had started in the fall of 1759 with a force 7300 strong, but when relief finally reached him in the following spring he had only 2517 fit for duty, while the hospitals held 2553 sick and wounded. History has given scant credit to Murray for his defense of Quebec that winter and spring against both disease and the enemy.

All that really remained of New France in that spring of 1760 was Montreal and a few surrounding miles. Fort Lévis ninety miles to the west, Isle-aux-Noix thirty miles to the south, and Jacques Cartier one hundred and twenty miles down the St. Lawrence—these were now the frontiers of Canada. The main drive of the British was to be against Montreal from the west, led by Amherst himself, while Brigadier Haviland was to drive north from Lake Champlain by Isle-aux-Noix and down the Richelieu, and Murray move west up the St. Lawrence with what he could salvage of the Quebec garrison and a fleet. These three forces were to converge on Montreal, starting from widely separated points, and Amherst planned that all should arrive in front of that city at the same time—most wishful thinking in those days of difficult travel and dubious communication. Nevertheless all three forces actually met almost exactly as planned.

By far the largest force accompanied the commanding general from Oswego and down the St. Lawrence, some ten thousand men in all, and they got off to a late start in early August. Brigadier Murray left Quebec on July 14 with an army of twenty-five hundred men, four warships, and many smaller vessels, while Haviland was directed to set off from Crown Point with three thousand men on August 10, and was only a day late in starting. The Quebec contingent worked its way slowly up the river against the current without major incident. Occasionally Frenchmen touched off long-range musket shots that did no harm. Now and then one of the larger ships went aground on muddy shoals, but was hauled off without damage. The trip was pleasant, scenic, and leisurely; stops were made from time to time, on occasions to skirmish with enemy detachments, but more often to trade for vegetables, eggs, and poultry. Inhabitants of parishes along the river made their submissions, took an oath and gave up their arms. Three Rivers was passed, where the garrison of some two thousand watched the expedition pass by out of range of their cannon. By August 12 the mouth of the Richelieu was reached, thus threatening the rear of Bougainville's forces at Isle-aux-Noix.

On August 14 Haviland's force reached the foot of Lake Champlain and proceeded to invest the fort built on the little island in the Richelieu River that was defended by Bougainville's men. The British pushed cannon along the river bank to take the island fort from its rear, as well as to fire on the few remaining vessels of New France's Champlain squadron. The French did what they could to hold off the attackers. They had luck with one 18-pounder cannon, a ball from which in a single shot took eight legs off six Britishers. Bougainville, threatened in his rear by Murray's advance, soon bowed to the inevitable, abandoned the fort and withdrew toward Montreal. Thus both the southern and eastern defenses of Canada had collapsed, while a great army was coming from the west.

It was not until the tenth of August that Amherst's expedition got under way from Oswego in its bateaux, whaleboats, and five row galleys, the last apparently being fairly large open barges, each of which carried a heavy brass 12-pounder, or in one case a howitzer, in its bow. There were also two warships built by Captain Loring in

1759, the snows *Mohawk* and *Onondaga,* the latter being solemnly christened with that name with much ceremony in the presence of Sir William Johnson's Indians. These snows were really brigs, with an additional mast placed just in rear of the mizzen mast. This extra mast carried the fore and aft spanker and made handling the sails a little easier. Both ships were somewhat larger than the two remaining French vessels, were well armed, carried crews of ninety or one hundred men, and had Indians painted on their sails. The French brig *L'Outaouaise*—or *The Ottawa Maid*—was of 160 tons burden, probably about seventy-five feet long on the deck, a fair-sized little ship, while the schooner *L'Iroquoise* was somewhat smaller. Vessels of such a tonnage, while quite small for warships, would have been considered as fair-sized merchant vessels at that time. Lévis, after the fall of Canada, returned across the Atlantic to France in a two-hundred-ton ship.

Sir William Johnson managed to produce quite a contingent of Indians in this year of 1760. The Five Nations and even many of the tribes hitherto allied to the French were beginning to read the writing on the wall. Soon Indians living along the St. Lawrence would start to leave the French and seek peace with the British. More than thirteen hundred Iroquois had answered Johnson's call and assembled at Oswego, but many were women and children, out for fun and free food. Some seven hundred warriors actually accompanied Amherst. The waterborne army moved north down the lake and on down the St. Lawrence without difficulty, reaching the site of Abbé Piquet's mission on August 17. The mission Indians had left the place during the previous winter, and in July the stockaded fort and the surrounding huts and bark houses were destroyed by the French, lest they be of use to the invaders.

An old acquaintance now leaves our stage. Abbé Piquet had given up his mission in May of that year, and, fearing capture by the British, had made his way west to Michilimackinac and then down the Mississippi to New Orleans and home to France. He had served New France well, leading his flock to war against the British upon many an occasion. He had first come to Canada in 1733 during the long period of peace following the end of Queen Anne's War. When King George's War got under way in 1744 he had his first taste of wilderness campaigning when he accompanied Marin on the Saratoga raid which produced thirty scalps and sixty prisoners. After the relatively short war had ended, the abbé established his mission of La Presentation and gathered a considerable number of Indians to whom he and his clerical assistant gave military training. Throughout the last French war the abbé and his followers seldom missed a campaign. He was a zealous and dedicated man, but with a cheerful and happy disposition. His Church, proud of him and what he did, wrote: "He frequently found himself in the vanguard when the king's troops were ordered to attack the enemy." Had there been campaign ribbons in those days, his might have read: Saratoga, 1745; Oswego, 1756; Fort William Henry, 1757; German Flats, 1757; Fort Carillon, 1758; Oswego, 1759. While today we believe that much of what Abbé Piquet did was wrong, we must remember that he sincerely believed otherwise, that enemies of his country were enemies of his Church, and that he was doing what the Lord wished. He was a true servant of his Church and of his King.

The engineer officer Desandrouins—many years later as Rochambeau's chief engineer he was to be present at the siege of Yorktown and Cornwallis' surrender—had been given the mission of building Fort Lévis. The site was a tiny islet in the St. Lawrence a little downstream from La Presentation, and it was almost all solid rock. In the spring of 1760 Captain Pouchot was sent to replace Desandrouins and to command the new post, which was built almost entirely of timber. It had thirty-seven cannon, but only sixteen of these were large enough to be of real use. The garrison consisted of about three hundred and fifty soldiers of La Marine and of the militia, but many of the latter soon deserted, leaving but a few more than three hundred to hold the place against Amherst's attack.

Pouchot left some interesting memoirs of his service in Canada. He recorded that in mid-June of this year Fort Lévis was visited by a vast horde of moths, a plague which lasted for two weeks. They were of all colors, gray, spotted, yellow, and white, and they got into the food, burned themselves in the candles so that it was practically impossible to write, and made a tremendous nuisance of themselves. After a rainfall dead moths littered the ramparts to a depth of two finger's breadth, and the fish in the nearby waters gorged themselves so that they became deliciously fat, especially the eels. Dead moths had to be swept out of the fort like snow, and the stench of their decay was most unpleasant. This visitation was succeeded by a plague of white gnats, which fortunately did not bite, and there must also have been plenty of mosquitoes. The islet was covered with thousands of little frogs, and huge and delicious mushrooms abounded in the vicinity. With fish, frogs' legs, their small size balanced by their quantity, and mushrooms to supplement the pork and peas of the regular ration, the officers' mess at Fort Lévis must have fared well that spring.

One of the two French warships ran aground on a shoal and was considerably damaged. She was worked back to the fort for repairs, but does not appear to have again been in action. The remaining vessel, *L'Outaouaise*, was attacked on August 17 by several of the British row galleys and captured. Amherst then landed his troops on both banks of the St. Lawrence and proceeded to besiege Fort Lévis. He had ten thousand men, the fort three hundred, and he could without any risk have bypassed the place and continued on his way, or at most have left a small force behind to contain Pouchot. Murray had sailed boldly by Three Rivers, which was held by a much larger garrison, but Amherst was always cautious and took no risks that he could avoid. Thus three hundred Frenchmen were able to hold up the advance of an army of ten thousand for two whole weeks. Amherst proudly boasted after Montreal had fallen that never had three armies, operating in the wilderness and widely separated, made so perfectly timed a junction. Had he been a little more aggressive and pushed on by Fort Lévis, as Pouchot had feared he might, he would have beaten the other two armies to the objective by almost two weeks.

The British got some of their cannon ashore and started their batteries, while their little navy pounded away at the fort, and in return suffered considerable damage. The shore batteries fired red-hot shot, a grave threat to a fort built largely of timber, and Pouchot registered a protest, claiming this was against the rules of warfare, although it is hard to see why. One British vessel ran aground near the fort and had to be temporarily abandoned. Finally the handful of Frenchmen gave up and the way to Montreal lay open. A large portion of Johnson's Indians, utterly disgusted that they were prevented from butchering and scalping the garrison, quit and left for home, while some of the others discovered the graves of the slain French, dug them up and scalped the corpses. Amherst took five days after the surrender for the repair of his ships and for establishing a garrison in the captured fort.

The army finally got under way again, moving down the St. Lawrence without trouble. On September 1st the boats ran the Long Sault where Cornwall, Ontario, stands today, with the loss of four men, but came to grief on the lower rapids. Amherst noted that the Long Sault rapids were "frightful in appearance but not dangerous." He probably became overconfident and careless when the flotilla approached the Buisson, the Trou, and the Cascades, the last falls before the calm waters of Lake St. Louis and the island of Montreal were reached. There misfortune caught up with the expedition, and thirty-seven bateaux, seventeen whaleboats, and a row galley were lost, while the bodies of eighty-four drowned soldiers were hauled ashore and given hasty burial. The next day was devoted to getting the rest of the army by the rapids, this time with more care and no further losses, and on the following morning, September 6, the first of the troops were landed on the island of Montreal. They marched to within sight of the city and encamped.

Governor Vaudreuil could see the tents of Murray's force to the eastward, and south across the river his gaze met the arrival of the first of Haviland's men. So, on September 7, Colonel Bougainville came to Amherst under a flag of truce to request an armistice.

Vaudreuil believed that a courier was on the way with news of a peace being signed, but the British general refused and demanded surrender of Canada.

Surrounded on all sides by three armies and vastly outnumbered, there was nothing else for the French to do, and on September 8 a capitulation for the surrender of the entire colony was executed. The clauses affecting the civilian population were generous, but, with memories of Fort William Henry and other Indian atrocities still rankling in his mind, Amherst decreed harsh terms for the army, complete surrender accompanied by inability to serve again during the remainder of the war. This was particularly hard on the officers as it would reduce them to a half-pay basis. Vaudreuil protested vigorously, but his emissary, the Chevalier de la Pause of the Guyenne Regiment, was abruptly silenced by the British general, and told the reason for this harshness. Amherst wished "to manifest to all the world, by this capitulation, his detestation . . . [of] the infamous part the troops of France had acted in exciting the savages to perpetrate . . . unheard of barbarities . . . [and of] other open treacheries, as well as flagrant breaches of faith." This really was quite unfair, because in so far as can be learned the French regular troops were always most proper in their conduct, and the irregularities had all been the result of action or lack of action on the part of the soldiers of La Marine or of the militia. Yet the regulars, all that remained to Lévis after the wholesale desertions of the last few weeks, were the ones to be punished. The French could do nothing but accept Amherst's conditions. The surrender was marred by one unworthy act, for the French burned their flags after the capitulation, and then stated on their word of honor that they had possessed no flags during this campaign. The two British regimental flags lost at Oswego in 1756 were recovered, but that was all.

The fall of Montreal ended the fight for Canada, but, regardless of the outcome in America, the final fate of the country remained to be determined on the battlefields of Germany, in India, in the West Indies, and on the high seas. The nation that at last won this long and exhausting war would decree the terms of peace and the final disposition of the spoils. Lévis' army was sent home to France and the fighting was over in Canada save for one brief flare up. In June 1762 the French undertook an expedition to Newfoundland, and seized St. John's without difficulty. Amherst, still commander in North America, promptly sent his brother with a force of regulars and colonial troops to eject the intruders. The French, deserted by their warships, were captured with little bloodshed. This was the last action fought between the two countries in North America, and it marked the end of some seventy years of bloody warfare. Louisiana, of which the Illinois country was a part, constituted a separate colony, and was not included in the Montreal surrender. In 1762 under a secret treaty this colony was transferred to Spain by the French, but all its eastern portion would be awarded to Britain under the terms of the final peace.

The war dragged on in Europe with both sides approaching exhaustion, while the British Navy continued to seize the overseas possessions of the French, and at the same time to maintain an effective blockade in European waters. The French Navy was driven from the seas and the commerce of that country well-nigh ruined. Lack of men, food, and military supplies was the real reason for the final fall of Canada, and this resulted from two major causes. The long continental war had reduced France to dire economic straits, and little, either of men or of money, could be spared for the much less important North American theater. The few supplies and reinforcements which could be allocated to New France had to run the gauntlet of the British Navy, and, as the war dragged on, the supply ships which reached the St. Lawrence in safety became ever fewer. Analysis of the final causes of the defeat of the French in the New World will show that the British Navy, supported by the British taxpayer, deserves at least as much and probably more credit for the final victory than do all the generals and their armies that fought the land campaigns on the frontiers of the opposing colonies.

In the spring of 1762 an armistice was at last agreed upon, and the Peace of Paris was finally signed in 1763. Of all her former North American possessions France was allowed to retain only the two little island fishing stations of St. Pierre and Miquelon. Elsewhere throughout all of the great continent the fleurs-de-lis of France gave way to the Union Jack of Great Britain, and Canada became absorbed into the growing British Empire. Yet today, two centuries later, the second-largest French-speaking city in the entire world stands on the banks of the St. Lawrence.

INDEX

DATE DUE

OCT 10 7

OC 31 77

SE 29 '81

OC 13 81

FE 8 83

OCT 9 88